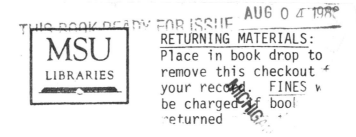
M

DISTRIBUTION OF DISTANCES IN PREGEOGRAPHICAL SPACE

To Sannie,
Friso and Nicoline.

Distribution of Distances in Pregeographical Space

HANS KUIPER
Assistant Professor in Spatial Economics, Erasmus University, Rotterdam

Gower

Published by
Gower Publishing Company Limited
Gower House
Croft Road
Aldershot
Hants GU11 3HR
England

Gower Publishing Company
Old Post Road
Brookfield
Vermont 05036
U.S.A.

British Library Cataloguing in Publication Data

Kuiper, J.H.
  Distribution of distances in pregeographical space.——(Studies in spatial
  analysis)
  1. Geography——Mathematics 2. Spatial
  analysis (Statistics)
  I. Title II. Series
  910'.01'8   G70.23

Library of Congress Cataloging-in-Publication Data

Kuiper, J. H.
  Distribution of distances in pregeographical space.

  Bibliography: p.
  1. Regional economics--Mathematical models.
2. Space in economics--Mathematical models.
3. Distance geometry. I. Title.
HT391.3.K85 1986   910   86-7673

ISBN 0 566   05214 8

Printed and bound in Great Britain by
Paradigm Print, Gateshead, Tyne and Wear

Contents

		page
Preface		1
Foreword		3
1.	Introduction	5
1.1.	General comments	5
1.2.	The distance distribution and the road-area distribution	7
1.3.	The contact distribution	7
2.	Theoretical concepts	10
2.1.	Introduction	10
2.2.	Theoretical concepts	10
2.2.1.	Distances	10
2.3.	Measuring distributions of distances	14
2.3.1.	Measuring the distance density function	16
2.3.2.	Measuring the road-area density function	19
2.3.3.	Measuring the contact distribution	20
2.4.	Some examples	22
3.	Distance distributions	32
3.1.	The distance distribution in a square	32
3.1.1.	$p=1$	32
3.1.2.	$p=2$	41
3.1.3.	$p=\infty$	46
3.2.	The distance distribution in a rectangle	49
3.2.1.	$p=1$	49
3.2.2.	$p=2$	55
3.2.3.	$p=\infty$	60
3.3.	The distance distribution in a circle	64
3.3.1.	$p=2$	64
4.	The road-area distribution	67
4.1.	The road-area density function in a square	67

4.1.1.	p=1	67
4.1.2.	p=2	73
4.1.3.	p=∞	76
4.2.	The road-area density function in a rectangle	77
4.2.1.	p=1	77
4.2.2.	p=2	81
4.2.3.	p=∞	81
5.	Contact distributions	83
5.1.	Points continuously distributed	83
5.1.1.	The square	84
5.1.1.1.	p=1	84
5.1.1.2.	p=2	86
5.1.1.3.	p=∞	86
5.1.2.	The rectangle	87
5.1.2.1.	p=1	87
5.1.2.2.	p=2	90
5.1.2.3.	p=∞	92
5.1.3.	The contact distribution in a circle	94
5.1.3.1.	p=0	94
5.2.	Points are distributed in a discrete way	96
5.2.1.	The square	99
5.2.1.1.	p=1	100
5.2.1.2.	p=∞	110
5.2.2.	The rectangle	115
5.2.2.1.	p=1	115
5.2.2.2.	p=∞	120
6.	Distributions of distances in some special cases	127
6.1.	The distance density function in two squares	127
6.1.1.	p=1	128
6.1.2.	p=2	137
6.1.3.	p=∞	152
6.2.	The contact distribution in two squares	155
6.2.1.	p=1	155
6.3.	Conclusions	170

7.	<u>Comparing calculated and observed distributions</u>	
	<u>of distances</u>	174
7.1.	Introduction	174
7.2.	Comparing observed and analytically calculated	
	contact distributions	175
7.3.	Shape analysis	180
7.4.	Network analysis	182
7.5.	Goodness of fit tests	186
7.5.1.	The chi-square test	186
7.5.2.	The Kolmogorov-Smirnov test	188
8.	<u>Results of comparison of calculated and observed</u>	
	<u>contact distributions</u>	191
8.1.	Introduction	191
8.2.	Road networks	191
8.3.	Shapes of countries	196
8.3.1.	A compactness index	199
8.4.	Observed contact frequency distributions; histo-	
	grams	201
8.5.	Results	206
8.5.1.	Introduction	206
8.5.2.	Statistical tests; results	206
8.5.3.	Discussion	209
8.5.4.	A graphical presentation	211
8.5.5.	The comparison of surfaces	225
8.5.6.	Discussion	233
9.	<u>Results of the shape analysis</u>	235
9.1.	Introduction	235
9.2.	The grid cell method	235
9.3.	Results	239
9.3.1.	A graphical presentation	239
9.3.2.	Discussion	251
9.3.3.	Statistical results	252
9.3.4.	Discussion	254
10.	<u>Network analysis</u>	259
10.1.	Introduction	259
10.2.	The estimation method	260

10.2.1.   The minimum distance method   261

10.2.2.   The minimum chi-square method   262

10.3.   The observations; a graphical presentation   263

10.4.   Test results   278

10.5.   Discussion   285

11.   General Conclusion   288

References   293

Preface

Metric topology is an essential ingredient to spatial economic analysis; combined with mathematical statistics it becomes an input to spatial econometrics.

Hans Kuiper has done some path-breaking work on the distribution of distances in pre-geographical space as defined by Beguin and Thisse; moreover, it deserved him the first European Ph.D. in Spatial Analysis, based on an agreement between the University of Dijon, the Université Catholique de Louvain and the Erasmus University at Rotterdam.

No easy reading, this book, but in line with the difficulty of the subject matter, the treatment of which required profound mathematical skills and inexhaustible patience.

Already announced in Formal Spatial Economic Analysis, the topic of this book has been given an extensive development, and the methodologies used, in both the theoretical and applied parts, are certainly worthwhile being introduced to.

Lectori salutem........

Jean H.P. Paelinck
Professor of Theoretical Spatial
Economics in the Erasmus University
at Rotterdam

1

Foreword

This book deals with theoretical issues and uses this theoretical background for applied research. It was written at the Spatial Economic Section, in particular the Theoretic Spatial Economy Group of the Erasmus University in Rotterdam, under the supervision of J.H.P. Paelinck to whom I am extremely grateful for his friendly and stimulating guidance. To work under Jean's patronage has always been without any doubt an in dispensable experience; I have been greatly benefitted from his helpful comments and suggestions.

The Theoretic Spatial Economy Group provided a pleasant and professional environment; in particular I want to acknowledge Jaap Prins, for his enthusiast and inspiring work and discussions; we had a very good cooperation during many months. Especially I want to recall his work on the computer and also the beautiful plots he produced, which will be a pleasant surprise for the reader of this book.

In spring 1984 I got the opportunity to work at SPUR, Université Catholique de Louvain, in Louvain-la-Neuve. I gratefully acknowledge the support of this university and especially prof. H. Zoller, who created the right intellectual and stimulating environment for me.

With respect to the technical realization of this book I would like to thank Caroline van der Laan for her excellent typing, and Joop van Dijk for the figures.

Finally, I am very grateful to my parents, represented by H.J. Kuiper and ir. L.P. van Oeveren for their patience and generous support.

Hans Kuiper

Rotterdam, November 1985

1 Introduction

1.1. General comments

Pregeographical space is defined as any set of at least two places endowed with a length-metric and an area measure (Beguin, Thisse, 1979). According to Beguin and Thisse "place" is an undefined term; it corresponds to an elementary spatial unit, i.e. to the spatial unit in which no distinction is made. Places can be characterised by their relative position; the relative position can be expressed by means of the dimension of length and a metric. Subsets of places are expected to have a spatial extension: there has to be a way to express their area; therefore the dimension of area and a measure is used. The unit of area is obtained by forming the product of the unit of length by itself.

Two types of place representations are used in spatial analysis: places are either defined as small parts or points of a surface; that is, (a) singletons have either a finite positive area-measure and the places are called dimensional or (b) singletons have a zero area measure and the places are said to be a-dimensional.

To find a distance distribution, one needs a set containing at least two places and a measure to calculate the distance between those places; collecting all possible distances inside the set, one finds a distance distribution.

This study deals with distances in pregeographical space, starting with analytically calculated distributions of distances in geometrical spaces, and ending with empirically observed distributions. When a distance distribution has to be analytically determined, the starting point is mostly a well-defined space, filled with points in a regular way, and a well-defined distance measure. Another way to derive a distribution is simply to count all distances between the points of a set (if necessary with the aid of a computer); in that case points can be represented by their co-ordinates but a well-defined distance measure is needed. When distributions of distances on maps are observed (with the help of the table of distances), one generally deals with a random shape and a random point pattern, and the distances are measured on road networks.

First we started to derive analytically a number of distributions of distances in well-defined geometrical spaces such as squares, rectangles and circles, using well-defined distance measures (such as Euclidean or Manhattan distances), and point patterns (chapters 3, 4, 5 and 6); relevant studies in the field are Thanh (1962), de Smith (1977), and Paelinck (1983).

In chapters 7, 8, 9 and 10 an attempt is made to bridge in several steps the gap between analytically determined distributions of distances and those observed on geographical maps. Distributions are compared, and hypotheses made about shapes, point patterns and distance measures. A practical tool to handle random shapes is the representation of space by a Boolean matrix; papers by Taylor (1971) and also Blair and Biss (1967) are relevant.

In chapter 8 observed distance distributions on maps between cities in a number of European countries are compared with analytically determined distance distributions in well defined areas with regular point patterns and well defined distance measures. In chapter 9 distance distributions calculated between points in a randomly shaped area (e.g. a country) that is represented by a boolean matrix, are compared with distance distributions derived in a well defined area using well defined distance measures and finally, in chapter 10 the observed distributions of distances between a random set of points (representing cities) on a map are compared with calculated distributions of distances between the same set of random points using a well-defined distance measure; the papers by Taylor (1971) and Love and Morris (1972, 1979) are relevant here.

Strategic questions to raise before determining a distance distribution are the following:
- How are the points distributed ?
- How is the shape of the area ?
- How are distances measured ?
Dependent on the answers to these questions, at least three types of distributions of distances can be defined:
1. A distance distribution
2. A road-area distribution
3. A contact distribution.

The diagram on page 9 shows the most significant characteristics of each type of distribution.

1.2. The distance distribution and the road-area distribution

Both distributions are derived in pregeographical spaces. The space in which the places are located is of well-known shape and dimensions, for example a rectangle or a circle (examples which will be extensively treated), or of random shape (Ten Raa, 1983). In order to calculate distances between places as a distance measure, the Minkowski distance measure for p = 1 (Manhattan) or p = 2 (Euclidean distances) can be used. Ten Raa has developed a general expression for a distance distribution using random shapes and a random value for the p-norm used. The distributions of distances are described by their density functions. The distance distribution shows the (relative) number of distances between places occurring in an area, arranged according to their distance value. The road-area density function shows the area covered by roads between places in that area, arranged by the values of the road distances.

1.3. The contact distribution

In geography one often deals with yet another distribution, which will be called contact distribution. In the literature, "distance distribution" is nearly always interpreted as "contact distribution" (Thanh, 1962; Taylor, 1972; Hammersley, 1950; De Smith, 1977; Bunge, 1966); a contact density function shows the number of contacts or visits between places arranged according to the distances separating those places. Here, places are defined as small points of the surface; they have a positive finite area-measure. As long as the borders of the area are of no restriction, the number of contacts starting in a point increases as the distance value increases.

Especially in geography one mostly observes contact distributions; often distances between cities in a region (which are space-consuming things on a map) are involved.

Similarly to calculating the distance and road-area density functions, one can start deriving a contact density function on a well defined area, for instance a square, a rectangle or a circle; a distance measure (p = 1 or p = 2) is also needed. Here too, starting from a random shape is possible (Ten Raa, 1983). Contact density functions may be determined analytically using well-defined shapes or by making a computer simply count all distances between the locations in a random shape (for example a country); one covers the shape with a grid containing a number of cells, cells getting the value 1 when falling within the shape, the value 0 otherwise. In that way a random shape can be represented by a boolean matrix; between all pairs of cells with value 1 the distances are measured by Manhattan or Euclidean distances (chapter 9).

The shape of the area is less important when only a sample of grid cells (as mentioned before) with value 1 is considered; one can think of a country with a number of cities in it, each city to be represented by a grid cell (value 1). The computer calculates frequencies based on the distances between cities, measured as Euclidean or Manhattan distances (chapter 10).

Finally, a contact frequency distribution inside a country or region can be found by examining a map containing a table of distances; these distances between the main cities of the country or region are mostly measured along road networks; for a number of West-European countries these contact frequency distributions have been plotted (chapter 8).

Distance distribution Road area distribution	Contact distribution	Comments
		analitically determined distribution - well defined shape - well defined distance measure - well defined point-distribution
		analitically determined distribution - random shape - general distance measure p - well defined point distribution
		analitically determined distribution - well defined shape - well defined distance measure e.q. p=1 or p=2 - well defined point distribution
		computer counted distribution - random shape - well defined distance measure e.q. p=1 or p=2 - well defined distribution
		computer counted distribution - random shape - well defined distance measure e.q. p=1 or p=2 - random point distribution
		observed distribution on a map - random shape - distance measured over random networks - random point distribution

2 Theoretical concepts

2.1. Introduction

In this chapter we will go into the different ways in which distance distributions, road-area distributions, and contact distributions are defined. To that end we shall start from Kuiper and Paelinck (1982), which gives the method of derivation and some distributions, keeping in mind that some of the definitions used in that paper have been changed. Before looking closer at the definition of the distributions (2.3) we need to describe some mathematical tools required (2.2), define the concept of distance (2.2.1 and 2.2.2), and explain how "measures" are defined (2.2.3). Some examples will conclude this chapter.

2.2. Theoretical concepts

2.2.1. Distances[1]

Let X be a non-empty set, of which elements will be called "points". A numerical function d is called a metric or distance function if for every a,b,c $\in$ X it satisfies the following axioms:
(1) $d(a,b) > 0$;
(2) $d(a,b) = 0 \iff a = b$;
(3) $d(a,b) = d(b,a)$;
(4) $d(a,b) < d(a,c) + d(c,b)$;
$d(a,b)$ is called the distance from a to b.

(1) states that distances between different points are always strictly positive; according to (2) the distance from a point to itself is zero. Axiom (3) states that the distance from a to b is the same as the distance from b to a; one may therefore speak of the "distance between a and b". Axiom (4) is called the triangle inequality.

Examples of metrics are:

-----

1. References are Lipschutz, 1965; Halmos, 1979.

- the function d defined by $d(a,b) = |a-b|$, where a and b are real numbers, is called a metric on the real line R^1; the function d defined by $d = \sqrt{(a_1 - b_1)^2 + (a_2 - b_2)^2}$, where $a = (a_1,a_2)$ and $b = (b_1,b_2)$ are points in the plane R^2, is a metric on R^2, or, in more general terms: let $(a_1,a_2) \in R^2$, then $\|a\| \triangleq \sqrt{\sum_{i=1}^{2} a_i^2}$ is called the norm or Euclidean norm of a. $\|a - b\|$, the distance between a and b, is a metric on R^2.

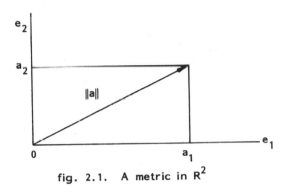

fig. 2.1. A metric in R^2

- Let X be a non-empty set and let d be a function defined by

$$d(a,b) = \begin{cases} 0 & \text{if } a = b \\ 1 & \text{if } a \neq b; \end{cases} \qquad (2.1)$$

then d is a metric on X.

- A general expression for distances in a metric space has been defined by Minkowski as:

$$d(a,b) = (\sum_{i=1}^{n} |x_{ia} - x_{ib}|^p)^{p^{-1}}, \quad p \geqslant 1. , \qquad (2.2)$$

If $p = 1$, one finds

$$d(a,b) = \sum_{i=1}^{n} |x_{ia} - x_{ib}|, \text{ the so called Manhattan or rectangular distance measure,} \qquad (2.3)$$

if p = 2,
$$d(a,b) = \sqrt{\sum_{i=1}^{n} (x_{ia} - x_{ib})^2} \text{ , the Euclidean distance measure, } \quad (2.4)$$

and if p = ∞,

$$d(a,b) = \max (|x_{1a} - x_{1b}|, |x_{2b} - x_{2a}|); \quad (2.5)$$

the distance between the points now being the dominating co-ordinate value. This is graphically illustrated (see Paelinck, 1983, p. 46) in fig. 2.2).

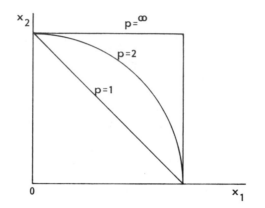

fig. 2.2.   Special cases of the Minkowski distance

When p < 1, the Minkowski distance does not always satisfy the triangle inequality. The limits for this distance function are:

$$\lim_{p \to \infty} d(a,b) = \max (|x_{1a} - x_{1b}|, |x_{2a} - x_{2b}|) \text{ and}$$

$$\lim_{p \to 0^+} d(a,b) = \infty$$

$$\lim_{p \to 0^-} d(a,b) = 0$$

$$\lim_{p \to -\infty} d(a,b) = \min(|x_{1a} - x_{1b}|, |x_{2a} - x_{2b}|) \text{ (Muller, 1982).}$$

Distance is a structuring element for the definition of space (Paelinck, 1983); it is a metric relation defined by the 4 axioms in 2.2.1, which is in principle dimensionless. The distance concept can be useful for the calculation of abstract economic distances between regions. Each region can be characterised by a vector, the elements of which represent a set of regional characteristics, for instance population, employment, income, and so forth. The interregional economic distance indicates the degree to which regions possess a similar structure: if there is a close correspondence between the economic structure of two regions, the defining variables in both regions will not show considerable differences, so that the economic distance between these regions will be relatively small (for more details and the way the economic distances are calculated, see Paelinck and Nijkamp 1975, pp. 177 ff).

Besides economic distances one can distinguish geographical distances; the length of routes between places can be used to measure geographical distances (Huriot, Thisse, 1984), a network distance being defined as the minimum length of a route from one place to another (see also Muller, 1982 and Falk, Abler, 1980). Length is a classical elementary dimension; it is, defined as a set, the set of all one-dimensional figures; the network distance can be measured by considering the path between two points a and b, represented by the curve f(x) (fig. 2.3), and summing all small pieces dℓ, where

dℓ is calculated via $d\ell = \sqrt{(dx)^2 + (df(x))^2}$ (2.6)

the sum ℓ thus being: $\ell = \int_a^b \sqrt{(f'(x)^2 + 1)}\, dx$ (2.7)

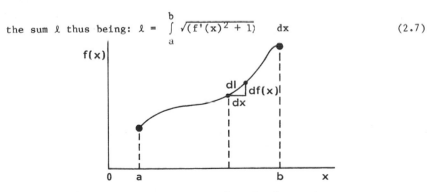

fig. 2.3.   Measuring the length of a path

2.3. Measuring distributions of distances

In chapter 1 three distributions of distances in a bounded space were defined:
1. the distance distribution;
2. the road-area distribution;
3. the contact distribution.

To find these distributions all distances between the points inside the defined area must be counted. Let us start from a set of points in two-dimensional space R^2, the space being continuously filled with points; between each pair of points a distance can be measured after a distance measure has been defined.

A density function is found by examining each point in the set separately; all distances related to each point are collected. Summing (or integrating) the results over all points yields the density function of distances. Integrating this density function, $f(\ell)$, over all distance-values yields a positive number, which does not equal 1; therefore the relative density function, $f^r(\ell)$, is defined such that
$$\int_\ell f^r(\ell) = 1.$$

The three distributions differ especially in the way the number of distances, reckoned from a point, are _measured_; therefore, we start by defining an area as a compact set in the real plane; take one random point in the set and define for each distribution how the distances related to that point are measured.

Distributions are analytically determined using three different distance measures, $p = 2$, $p = 1$, and $p = \infty$, so distances between points (q_1, q_2) and (x_1, x_2) are measured by:

$$d(q,x) = \sqrt{(q_1 - x_1)^2 + (q_2 - x_2)^2} \qquad \text{(a)}$$
$$d(q,x) = |q_1 - x_1| + |q_2 - x_2| \qquad \text{(b)}$$
$$\text{or } d = \max(|q_1 - x_1|, |q_2 - x_2|) \qquad \text{(c)}.$$

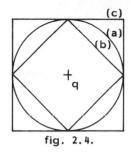

fig. 2.4.

Let A be the set of points for which a distance density function has to be calculated; let $q \in A$, where $A \subset R^2$, q being an interior point of A. To find the distance density function all distances in A have to be counted.

The absolute number of distances ℓ starting in q is determined by the number of points at distance ℓ from q; two sets of points have to be defined now:

$$S(q,\ell) \triangleq \{x \mid d(q,x) = \ell\} \qquad (2.8)$$

is the set of points x at distance ℓ from q; according to figure 2.4 those points are located on a circle (ℓ) if p = 2, on a square ($\ell\sqrt{2}$ x $\ell\sqrt{2}$) if p = 1 and in a square (2ℓ x 2ℓ) if p = ∞, and

$$S(q,\ell,A) \triangleq \{x \mid d(q,x) = \ell \wedge x \in A\} \qquad (2.9)$$

is the set of points x at distance ℓ from q and located in A, so

$$S(q,\ell,A) \begin{cases} = S(q,\ell) & \text{if all points at distance } \ell \text{ from q are situated} \\ & \text{in A} \\ \subset S(q,\ell) & \text{if the points at distance } \ell \text{ are partly situated} \\ & \text{in A} \\ = \{0\} & \text{if all points at distance } \ell \text{ are situated outside} \\ & \text{A} \end{cases}$$

So, in general the number of points in the sets is infinite; a measure for the absolute number of distances ℓ starting in q can be calculated by defining a measure for the number of points in $S(q,\ell)$ and $S(q,\ell,A)$.

-15-

This measure

$$
\mu\{S(q,\ell)\} = \begin{cases} 2\pi\ell & \text{if } p = 2, \\ 4\ell\sqrt{2} & \text{if } p = 1, \\ 8\ell & \text{if } p = \infty, \end{cases} \tag{2.10}
$$

so, is equal to the perimeter of the circle or square on which the points are located. If $S(q,\ell,A) \subset S(q,\ell)$ the measure for the number of points is equal to the fraction α of the circle or square located in A, so

$$
\mu\{S(q,\ell,A)\} = \alpha\mu\{S(q,\ell)\} \tag{2.11}
$$

2.3.1. Measuring the distance density function

The relative number of distances ℓ from q, $n_q(\ell)$, is defined by

$$
n_q(\ell) \triangleq \frac{\mu\{S(q,\ell,A)\}}{\mu\{S(q,\ell)\}} \tag{2.12}
$$

When $\mu\{S(q,\ell,A)\} = \mu\{S(q,\ell)\}$, this measure will have its maximum value: $n_q(\ell) = 1$ (all points at distance ℓ are located in A). We define $n_q(0) = 1$, because all points at distance 0 are located in A. $n_q(\ell) = 0$ if $\mu\{S(q,\ell,A)\} = 0$ (which means that all points at distance ℓ are located outside A).

The complete distance density function is found by considering for each point q in A all relevant distances ℓ and summing for each ℓ all relative numbers of distances (chapter 3).

Example 1. Let us consider Euclidean distances, and let A be an interval where the set of points $x \in A$, $x = (x_1, x_2)$, satisfy the inequalities;

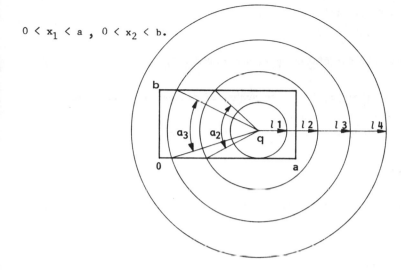

$0 < x_1 < a$, $0 < x_2 < b$.

fig. 2.5. Euclidean distances in a rectangle

The points at distance ℓ from q are situated on the circumference of a circle (ℓ); a measure for their number can be:

$$\mu\{S(q,\ell)\} = 2\pi\ell \qquad (2.13)$$

In figure 2.5 different values for ℓ are chosen, ℓ_1, ℓ_2, ℓ_3, ℓ_4; the circle with radius ℓ_1 is completely located within A, the rectangle, so $S(q,\ell) = S(q,\ell_1,A)$ and

$$n_q(\ell_1) = \frac{\mu\{S(q,\ell_1,A)\}}{\mu\{S(q,\ell)\}} = \frac{2\pi\ell_1}{2\pi\ell_1} = 1 \qquad (2.14)$$

The circle with radius ℓ_2 is partly located in A, so

$S(q,\ell_2,A) \subset S(q,\ell_2)$. $S(q,\ell_2,A)$ can be measured by

$\mu\{S(q,\ell_2,A)\} = \alpha_2\ell_2$, so the measure for the number of distances ℓ_2 becomes:

$$n_q(\ell_2) = \frac{\mu\{S(q,\ell_2,A)\}}{\mu\{S(q,\ell_3)\}} = \frac{\alpha_2 \ell_2}{2\pi \ell_2} = \frac{\alpha_2}{2\pi} \,. \qquad (2.15)$$

Obviously for distances ℓ_3 one finds:

$n_q(\ell_3) = \frac{\alpha_3}{2\pi}$; since $\alpha_3 < \alpha_2$ the number of distances is decreasing as ℓ is increasing.

Finally consider distance ℓ_4: $S(q,\ell_4) \cap A = \emptyset$, and therefore

$$\mu\{S(q,\ell_4,A)\} = 0, \text{ so } n_q(\ell_4) = 0. \qquad (2.16)$$

Example 2. Let us consider Manhattan distances in the same set A (fig. 2.6).

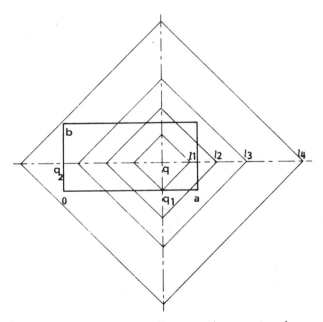

fig. 2.6. Manhattan distances in a rectangle

$$n_q(\ell_1) = 1$$

$$n_q(\ell_2) = \frac{q_2\sqrt{2} + (b-q_2)\sqrt{2} + (b-q_2)\sqrt{2} - (q_1+\ell_2-a)\sqrt{2} + q_2\sqrt{2} - (q_1+\ell_2-a)\sqrt{2}}{4\ell_2\sqrt{2}}$$

$$= \frac{a+b-q_1-\ell_2}{2\ell_2} ; \tag{2.18}$$

$$n_q(\ell_3) = \frac{b\sqrt{2}}{4\ell_3\sqrt{2}} = \frac{b}{4\ell_3} \tag{2.19}$$

$$n_q(\ell_4) = 0. \tag{2.20}$$

2.3.2. Measuring the road-area density function

Consider once again a random point q in R^2, the real two-dimensional space and Manhattan distances ℓ. Let $S*(q,\ell) = \{x; d(q,x) < \ell\}$; $S*(q,\ell)$ contains all points within a distance ℓ from q. The whole set can be covered with roads of distance ℓ starting in q. We want to define a measure for the number of roads; as before, this measure will keep its maximum value as long as there are no restrictions on the set in which q is located ($q \in A$, where $A \subset R^2$). Now define $S*(q,\ell,A) \subseteq (S*(q,\ell) \cap A)$ so that it is a set of points located inside the square $S*(q,\ell)$ and A.

A measure for the fraction of A that is covered with roads is defined as

$$nr_q(\ell) \triangleq \frac{\mu\{S*(q,\ell,A)\}}{\mu\{S*(q,\ell)\}} \tag{2.21}$$

Example 3. The interval A is considered with Euclidean distances (fig. 2.5).

$\mu\{S*(q,\ell)\} = \pi\ell^2$ (the area of the circle); a measure for the road area of distance ℓ_1 is:

$$nr_q(\ell_1) = \frac{\mu\{S*(q,\ell_1,A)\}}{\mu\{S*(q,\ell_1)\}} = 1 \tag{2.22}$$

$$nr_q(\ell_2) = \frac{\mu\{S*(q,\ell_2,A)\}}{\mu\{S*(q,\ell_2)\}} = \frac{\alpha_2 \ell_2^2}{2\pi\ell_2^2} = \frac{\alpha_2}{2\pi} \qquad (2.23)$$

$$nr_q(\ell_3) = \frac{\mu\{S*(q,\ell_3,A)\}}{\mu\{S*(q,\ell_3)\}} = \frac{\alpha_3 \ell_3^2}{2\pi\ell_3^2} = \frac{\alpha_3}{2\pi} \qquad (2.24)$$

$$nr_q(\ell_4) = \frac{\mu\{S*(q,\ell_4,A)\}}{\mu\{S*(q,\ell_4)\}} = \frac{0}{\pi\ell_4^2} = 0 \qquad (2.25)$$

Similarly to the distance density function, the road-area density function is decreasing as ℓ is increasing.

Example 4. The result with Manhattan distances in a rectangle (fig. 2.6) for the road-area distribution becomes:

$$nr_q(\ell_1) = 1 \qquad (2.26)$$

$$nr_q(\ell_2) = \frac{2\ell_2^2 - (q_2 + \ell_2 - b)^2 - (q_1 + \ell_2 - a)^2 - (\ell_2 - q_2)^2}{2\ell_2^2} \qquad (2.27)$$

$$nr_q(\ell_3) = \frac{\ell_3^2 - \frac{1}{2}(q_2 + \ell_3 - b)^2 - \frac{1}{2}(\ell_3 - q_2)^2}{2\ell_3^2} \qquad (2.28)$$

$$nr_q(\ell_4) = 0. \qquad (2.29)$$

2.3.3. Measuring the contact distribution

Point q is located in R^2; $S(q,\ell) \triangleq \{x; d(q,x) = \ell\}$ is the set of points at distance ℓ. This set S consists of a bounded number of locations, each location (point) has a non-zero area measure. Now consider the set $S(q,\ell,A) = \{x; d(q,x) = \ell, x \in A\}$; this is the set of locations

at distance ℓ in A; this set is measurable, one can simply count this
number in order to find the number of contacts at distance ℓ starting in
q. So, in this case μ {S(q,ℓ,A)} is a measure of the number of contacts
at distance ℓ.

$$nc_q(\ell) \triangleq \mu \{S(q,\ell,A)\} \qquad\qquad (2.30)$$

This means that there is a direct relation between the number of contacts and the relative number of distances (see definition 2.12); the
contact density function is found by multiplying the relative number of
the distances by $\mu\{S(q,\ell)\}$ which is, in case p = 1, $4\ell \sqrt{2}$

$$p = 2, \ 2\pi\ell \text{ and}$$
$$p = \infty, \ 8\ell.$$

<u>Example 5</u>. The number of contacts depends on the length of the arc with
radius ℓ_1, ℓ_2, ℓ_3 and ℓ_4 as far as this is located inside A (fig. 2.7).

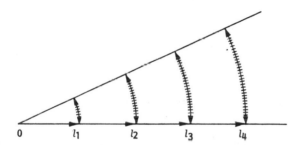

fig. 2.7. Increasing number of contacts as distances increase

According to fig (2.5) we have:
$$nc_q(\ell_1) = 2\pi\ell_1$$
$$nc_q(\ell_2) = \alpha_2\ell_2$$
$$nc_q(\ell_3) = \alpha_3\ell_3$$
$$nc_q(\ell_4) = 0 \qquad ; \text{ it is clear that one can find the contact density func-}$$
tion from the distance density function by multiplying the latter by
$2\pi\ell$.

Example 6. See fig. (2.6):

$nc_q(\ell_1) = 4\ell_1 \ \surd\ 2$

$nc_q(\ell_2) = 2b \ \surd\ 2 - 2(q_1 + \ell_2 - a)\surd 2$

$nc_q(\ell_3) = \ b \ \surd 2$

$nc_q(\ell_4) = 0$

2.4. Some examples

In a well-defined two-dimensional space a point q is chosen and a measure for the number of distances ℓ is defined. In order to find the complete distribution of all distances one has to determine this measure for each point. Considering each distance value ℓ and integrating over all points q in the set, the distribution of distances is found.

Example 1. Instead of working in two-dimensional space R^2, an interval in R^1 is now considered; let A be an interval [a,b] in R^1, b > a, and consider distances ℓ in A, so $0 < \ell < b-a$.

fig. 2.8.   Distances in a one-dimensional space

Looking for the distribution of all the distances in the interval, one can start at point a (fig. 2.8), the largest distance value that can be observed being $\ell = b-a$, the smallest zero (these are the extreme values of the distribution). Going to the right into the direction of b, considering each point x, one will always find only one distance of value ℓ as long as

$a < x < b-\ell \ (0 < \ell < b-x)$.

So the measure for the number of distances as mentioned in 2.3, is not relevant in the one dimensional space R^1: in this space there is only one distance ℓ for each point. The characteristic difference between the distance distribution, the road area distribution and the contact distribution has disappeared: all distributions are the same.

Now the number of points has to be measured:

$$\mu\ [a,\ b-\ell] = b-\ell-a \tag{2.31}$$

The density function is found by multiplying the measure for the number of points and the measure for the number of distances (1 in this case).

So, the distance density function, noted $df(\ell)$, becomes

$$df(\ell) = (b-a-\ell).1 = b-a-\ell \tag{2.32}$$

This function has to be multiplied by a constant in order to find $df^r(\ell)$, the relative distance density function, having the property;
$$\int_\ell df^r(\ell) = 1 \ ;$$

this yields $df^r(\ell) = \dfrac{2(b-a-\ell)}{(b-a)^2}$. $\tag{2.33}$

The expected distance $E\ell$ is found via $E\ell = \int_\ell \ell df^r(\ell) d\ell = \dfrac{1}{3}(b-a)$ $\quad(2.34)$

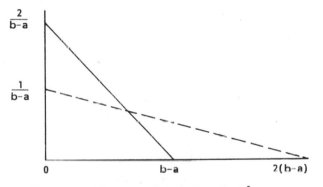

fig. 2.9. Distance distribution in R^1

In figure 2.9 two distance density functions are shown; they are linear declining functions. The function will be much flatter as the interval increases.

Example 2.

Consider a square (a x a) and Euclidean distance ℓ. In this two-dimensional space a distance density function, a road-area density function and a contact distribution will be (partly) derived (fig 2.10).

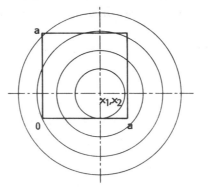

fig. 2.10. Euclidean distances in a square

First the measures for the number of distances have to be calculated for each point inside the square. The number of points inside the square is infinite and ℓ varies from 0 to $a\sqrt{2}$. Sets of points, having comparable measures with respect to the number of distances are grouped; therefore the distances ℓ have to be divided into several classes determined by the value of ℓ. First consider $0 < \ell < \frac{a}{2}$; it is possible to divide the square into a number of sets (fig. 2.11).

Set 1. This set contains points $x = (x_1, x_2)$, $\ell < x_i < a-\ell$, $i = 1,2$. The measure for the number of distances ℓ of each point equals 1, because every circle with radius ℓ is completely located inside the square. A measure for the number of points in set 1 is $(a - 2\ell)^2$ (the area of the set), so the share of this set in the distance density function $df_1(\ell)$ is:

$$df_1(\ell) = rf_1(\ell) = cf_1(\ell) = (a - 2\ell)^2 \cdot 1 = (a - 2\ell)^2, \qquad (2.35)$$
where $rf_1(\ell)$ indicates the road area density function, and
$cf_1(\ell)$ the contact density function in set 1.

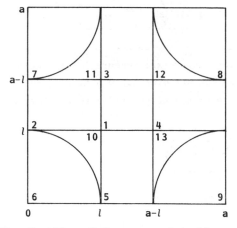

fig. 2.11. Partition of the square into 13 sets of points

<u>Set 2.</u> This set contains points $x = (x_1, x_2)$, $0 \leqslant x_1 \leqslant \ell$, $\ell \leqslant x_2 \leqslant a-\ell$

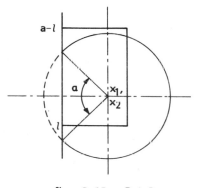

fig. 2.12. Set 2

First consider the distance density function looking at a point x the measure for the number of distances ℓ equals $n_x(\ell) = \dfrac{2\pi\ell - \alpha\ell}{2\pi\ell} = 1 - \dfrac{\alpha}{2\pi}$, α depending on the x_1 co-ordinate of x: when $x_1 = 0$, $\alpha = \pi$, and when $x_1 = \ell$, $\alpha = 0$ (the x_2 co-ordinate of x does not change this measure).

$$n_x(\ell) = 1 - \frac{\alpha}{2\pi} = 1 - \frac{2\cos^{-1}\frac{x_1}{\ell}}{2\pi} = 1 - \frac{\cos^{-1}\frac{x_1}{\ell}}{\pi} \tag{2.36}$$

In set 2 one can find an average measure for the number of distances ℓ by integrating this measure over x_1, $0 < x_1 < \ell$, and dividing this sum by a measure for the number of points in this interval, which is ℓ, so

$$\bar{n}_x(\ell) = \frac{\displaystyle\int_{x_1=0}^{\ell} 1 - \frac{\cos^{-1}\frac{x_1}{\ell}}{\pi}\, dx_1}{\ell} = 1 - \frac{1}{\pi} \tag{2.37}$$

The share of set 2 in the distance density function $df_2(\ell)$, is found by multiplying this average value by a measure for the number of points inside the set; this measure is equal to the area of the set e.g. $(a-2\ell)\ell$, so

$$df_2(\ell) = (a - 2\ell)\ell(1 - \frac{1}{\pi}) \tag{2.38}$$

Secondly, the road area density function is considered; a measure for the road area is:

$$n_x(\ell) = \frac{\pi\ell^2 - \frac{\alpha}{2}\ell^2}{\pi\ell^2} = 1 - \frac{\alpha}{2\pi} \text{ , this measure equals the "distance density}$$

function measure", so

$$rf_2(\ell) = (a - 2\ell)\ell(1 - \frac{1}{\pi}). \tag{2.39}$$

Finally the contact density function will be determined; a measure for the number of contacts at distance ℓ is: $2\pi\ell - \alpha\ell$

$n_x(\ell) = 2\pi\ell - \alpha\ell = 2\ell(\pi - \cos^{-1}\frac{x_1}{\ell})$; the average value of this measure considering all points x, $0 < x_1 < \ell$ becomes

$$\overline{n}_x(\ell) = \frac{\int\limits_{x_1=0}^{\ell} 2\ell(\pi - \cos^{-1}\frac{x_1}{\ell})dx_1}{\ell} = 2\ell(\pi-1) , \qquad (2.40)$$

this measure could have been found immediately because the contact density function is directly related to the distance density function; one can find the contact density function by multiplying the distance density function by $2\pi\ell$: $2\pi\ell(1 - \frac{1}{\pi}) = 2\ell(\pi-1)$.

The share of set 2 in the contact density function is:

$$cf_2(\ell) = (a-2\ell)\ell \cdot 2\ell(\pi-1) = 2(\pi-1)(a-2\ell)\ell^2; \qquad (2.41)$$

this set has the same properties concerning measures of distance as sets 3, 4, and 5, so

$df_2(\ell) = df_3(\ell) = df_4(\ell) = df_5(\ell)$ and
$rf_2(\ell) = rf_3(\ell) = rf_4(\ell) = rf_5(\ell)$ and
$cf_2(\ell) = cf_3(\ell) = cf_4(\ell) = cf_5(\ell)$.

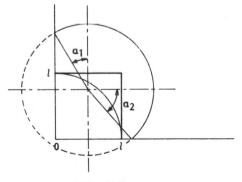

fig. 2.13. Set 6

Now look at set 6 (fig 2.13); set 6 contains points x with $0 < x_1 < \ell$, $0 < x_2 < \sqrt{\ell^2 - x_1^2}$.

A measure of the number of distances, looking for the distance density function, is:

$$n_x(\ell) = \frac{\alpha_1 \ell + \alpha_2 \ell + \frac{\pi}{2}\ell}{2\pi\ell} = \frac{\sin^{-1}\frac{x_1}{\ell} + \frac{\pi}{2} + \sin^{-1}\frac{x_2}{\ell}}{2\pi} \; .$$

The measure changes as the co-ordinates change, so for each point one will find another value. The share in the distance density function is found by simply summing (integrating) the measure for all points inside the set, so

$$df_6(\ell) = \int_{x_1=0}^{\ell} \int_{x_2=0}^{\sqrt{\ell^2-x_1^2}} \frac{\sin^{-1}\frac{x_1}{\ell} + \sin^{-1}\frac{x_2}{\ell} + \frac{\pi}{2}}{2\pi} \, dx_2 \, dx_1$$

$$= \frac{1}{2\pi} \int_{x_1=0}^{\ell} \frac{\pi}{2}\sqrt{\ell^2-x_1^2} + \sqrt{\ell^2-x_1^2}\sin^{-1}\frac{x_1}{1} + \sqrt{\ell^2-x_1^2}\sin^{-1}\frac{\sqrt{\ell^2-x_1^2}}{\ell} + x_1 - \ell dx_1$$

$$(2.42)$$

this result can be combined easily with $df_{10}(\ell)$.

The road area density function is found by defining a measure for the road area in point x;

$$n_x(\ell) = \frac{\frac{\alpha_1}{2}\ell^2 + \frac{\alpha_2}{2}\ell^2 + \frac{\pi}{4}\ell^2}{\pi\ell^2} = \frac{\alpha_1 + \alpha_2 + \frac{\pi}{2}}{2\pi}, \qquad (2.43)$$

this measure equals the measure for the number of distances , so $rf_6(\ell)$ = $df_6(\ell)$.

The contact density function is found directly by multiplying the distance density function by $2\pi\ell$ so

$$cf_6(\ell) = \ell \int_{x_1=0}^{\ell} \frac{\pi}{2}\sqrt{\ell^2-x_1^2} + \sqrt{\ell^2-x_1^2}\sin^{-1}\frac{x_1}{\ell} + \sqrt{\ell^2-x_1^2}\sin^{-1}\frac{\sqrt{\ell^2-x_1^2}}{\ell} + x_1 - \ell \, dx_1$$

$$(2.44)$$

Because of symmetry
$$df_6(\ell) = df_7(\ell) = df_8(\ell) = df_9(\ell) \text{ and}$$
$$rf_6(\ell) = rf_7(\ell) = rf_8(\ell) = rf_9(\ell) \text{ and}$$
$$cf_6(\ell) = cf_7(\ell) = cf_8(\ell) = cf_9(\ell).$$

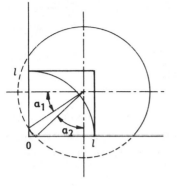

fig. 2.14. Set 10

Finally look at set 10 (fig. 2.14); $0 < x_1 < \ell$,
$$\sqrt{\ell^2 - x_1^2} < x_2 < \ell .$$

A measure of the number of distances is:

$$n_x(\ell) = \frac{2\pi\ell - 2\alpha_1\ell - 2\alpha_2\ell}{2\pi\ell} = 1 - \frac{1}{\pi}\cos^{-1}\frac{x_1}{\ell} - \frac{1}{\pi}\cos^{-1}\frac{x_2}{\ell} . \qquad (2.45)$$

This measure depends also on each co-ordinate of x, so integrating the measure over all points of the set gives the share in the distance density function.

$$df_{10}(\ell) = \int_{x_1=0}^{\ell} \int_{x_2=\sqrt{\ell^2-x_1^2}}^{\ell} 1 - \frac{1}{\pi}\cos^{-1}\frac{x_1}{\ell} - \frac{1}{\pi}\cos^{-1}\frac{x_2}{\ell} \, dx_2 dx_1 ,$$

$$= \int_{x_1=0}^{\ell} 1 - \frac{x_1}{\pi} - \frac{1}{\pi}\cos^{-1}\frac{x_1}{\ell} + \frac{\sqrt{\ell^2-x_1^2}}{\pi}\cos^{-1}\frac{\sqrt{\ell^2-x_1^2}}{\ell} \, dx_1 \qquad (2.46)$$

This result combined.with $df_6(\ell)$ yields:

$$df_6(\ell) + df_{10}(\ell) = \ell^2 - \frac{7\ell^2}{4\pi} \text{ , and because of symmetry we find,}$$

$$df_6(\ell) + df_{10}(\ell) = df_7(\ell) + df_{11}(\ell)$$

$$= df_8(\ell) + df_{12}(\ell) = df_9(\ell) + df_{13}(\ell).$$

In this case too, the road area density function equals the distance density function for all relevant sets; the contact density function is found by multiplying the distance density function by $2\pi\ell$, so

$$cf_6(\ell) + cf_{10}(\ell) = 2\pi\ell^3 - \frac{7}{2}\ell^3 \text{ and}$$

$$cf_6(\ell) + cf_{10}(\ell) = cf_7(\ell) + cf_{11}(\ell) = cf_8(\ell) + cf_{12}(\ell)$$

$$= cf_9(\ell) + cf_{13}(\ell)$$

Concluding: the general expression for the distance density function in a square (axa) using Eulidean distances and $0 < \ell < \frac{a}{2}$ is

$$df(\ell) = \sum_{i=1}^{13} df_i(\ell) = (a - 2\ell)^2 + 4\ell(a - 2\ell)(1 - \frac{1}{\pi}) + 4(\ell^2 - \frac{7\ell^2}{4\pi})$$

$$df(\ell) = a^2 - \frac{4a\ell}{\pi} + \frac{\ell^2}{\pi} \tag{2.47}$$

The road area density function shows the same result as

$$rf(\ell) = a^2 - \frac{4a\ell}{\pi} + \frac{\ell^2}{\pi} \tag{2.48}$$

The contact density function is

$$cf(\ell) = (a - 2\ell)^2 + 4. \; 2(\pi - 1) \; (a - 2\ell)\ell^2 + 4(2\pi\ell^3 - \frac{7}{2}\ell^3)$$

$$= 2\pi\ell \; (a^2 - \frac{4a\ell}{\pi} + \frac{\ell^2}{\pi})$$

$$= 2\pi a^2\ell - 8a\ell^2 + 2\ell^3$$

$$cf(\ell) = 2\ell(\pi a^2 - 4a\ell + \ell^2) \qquad\qquad (2.49)$$

Although just a small part of the whole function is now determined, one can conclude that
- both the distance and the road area density function are decreasing functions, the maximum valued being reached for

$$\ell = 0 \qquad\qquad df(0) = a^2 = rf(0).$$

If $\qquad \ell = \frac{a}{2} \qquad\qquad df(\frac{a}{2}) = a^2 - \frac{7a^2}{4\pi} = rf(\frac{a}{2}),$

- the contact density function is <u>increasing</u> first; $cf(0) = 0$, and reaches a maximum at $\ell = \dfrac{4a - a\sqrt{16 - 3\pi}}{3} = .48a.$

Conclusion

In the chapters 3, 4, and 5 a number of density functions will be calculated; this will be done for well-defined two-dimensional shapes, namely a square, a rectangle and a circle, while in chapter 6 functions in other intervals are also considered. The calculations of density functions in a square will be carried out extensively; since calculations in other shapes are basically the same, these will be less detailed, and just the essential results will be presented.

3 Distance distributions

In this chapter a number of distance density functions defined in 2.3 will be calculated; this is done for well-defined shapes, namely a square, a rectangle and a circle. Points inside these areas are considered to be continuously distributed.

3.1. The distance distribution in a square

As said before, the calculation of the distance density function in a square using resp. p = 1, p = 2 and p= ∞ will be carried out extensively.

3.1.1. p = 1

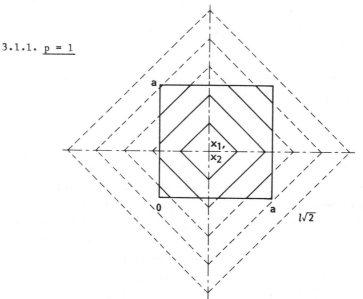

fig. 3.1.   Distances in a square

The measure for the number of distances ℓ, starting from a point (x_1, x_2) inside the square (axa) is defined as the fraction of the perimeter of the square $(\ell\sqrt{2} \ x \ \ell\sqrt{2})$ located inside the square (axa); the value of this measure is always between 0 and 1. If ℓ is small this value will be close to or equal to 1, if ℓ increases this value becomes smaller and becomes zero when all points are located outside the square (axa) (fig. 3.1).

As p=1 the domain of the distribution will be $0 < \ell < 2a$. As was the case with the calculation presented as example 2 in chapter 2.3 this domain has to be partitioned; first $0 < \ell < \frac{a}{2}$ can be analysed, the square having to be divided now in 13 sets of points; points inside each set having comparable properties with respect to the distances ℓ.

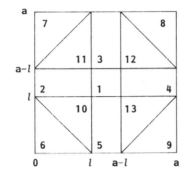

fig. 3.2. p=1; partition of the square $0 \leqslant 1 \leqslant \frac{a}{2}$

Set 1 (fig. 3.2) contains points $x = (x_1, x_2)$; $\ell < x_1 < a-\ell$, $i = 1, 2$. A measure for the number of distances in point x, is: $n_x(\ell) = 1$, because the square $(\ell\sqrt{2} \times \ell\sqrt{2})$ is completely situated inside the square (axa); each point x in this set has this property. A measure for this number of points is the area of the set, so

$$df_1(\ell) = (a-2\ell)^2 \cdot 1 = (a-2\ell)^2 \qquad (3.1)$$

Set 2 contains points $x = (x_1, x_2)$, $0 < x_1 < \ell$, $\ell < x_2 < a-\ell$.

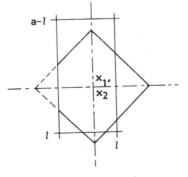

fig. 3.3. Set 2

$$n_x(\ell) = \frac{4\ell\sqrt{2} - 2(\ell-x_1)\sqrt{2}}{4\ell\sqrt{2}} \; ; \text{ this measure for the number of distances}$$

depends only on x_1; an average measure for the number of distances is found by integrating $n_x(\ell)$ over x_1.

$$\overline{n}_x(\ell) = \int_{x_1=0}^{\ell} 1 - \frac{(\ell - x_1)}{2\ell} \, dx_1$$

$$= \frac{3}{4} \ell$$

(3.2)

The density function in this set is found by multiplying this measure by a measure for the number of points x_2, so

$df_2(\ell) = \frac{3}{4} \ell(a-2\ell).$

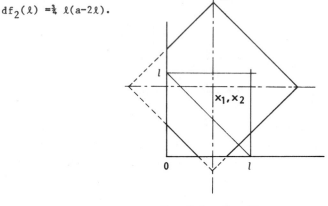

fig. 3.4. Set 10

<u>Set 10</u> contains points $x = (x_1, x_2)$, $0 < x_1 < \ell$, $\ell-x_1 < x_2 < \ell$.

$$n_x(\ell) = \frac{4\ell\sqrt{2} - 2(\ell-x_1)\sqrt{2} - 2(\ell-x_2)\sqrt{2}}{\ell 4\sqrt{2}}$$

$$= \frac{2x_1\sqrt{2} + 2x_2\sqrt{2}}{\ell 4\sqrt{2}} = \frac{x_1 + x_2}{2\ell}$$

(3.3)

The density function in this set is found by summing (integrating) this measure for all points inside the set, so

$$df_{10}(\ell) = \int_{x_1=0}^{\ell} \int_{x_2=\ell-x_1}^{\ell} \frac{x_1 + x_2}{2\ell}\, dx_2\, dx_1$$

$$= \frac{1}{3}\ell^2 \tag{3.4}$$

Finally consider <u>set 6</u>, containing points x; $0 < x_1 < \ell$, $0 < x_2 < \ell - x_1$.

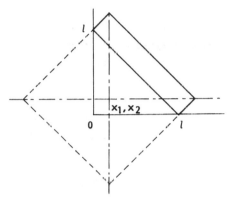

Fig. 3.5. Set 6

$$n_x(\ell) = \frac{4\ell\sqrt{2} - \ell\sqrt{2} - (\ell-x_1)\sqrt{2} - (\ell-x_2)\sqrt{2}}{4\ell\sqrt{2}}$$

$$= \frac{\ell\sqrt{2} + x_1\sqrt{2} + x_2\sqrt{2}}{4\ell\sqrt{2}} = \frac{x_1 + x_2 + \ell}{4\ell} \tag{3.5}$$

Analogously to the calculation of set 10, the density function is found by:

$$df_6(\ell) = \int_{x_1=0}^{\ell} \int_{x_1=0}^{\ell-x_1} \frac{x_1 + x_2 + \ell}{4\ell}\, dx_2\, dx_1$$

$$= \frac{5}{24}\ell^2. \tag{3.6}$$

Because of the symmetry $df_2(\ell) = df_3(\ell) = df_4(\ell) = df_5(\ell)$ and

$$df_{10}(\ell) = df_{11}(\ell) = df_{12}(\ell) = df_{13}(\ell) \text{ and}$$

$$df_6(\ell) = df_7(\ell) = df_8(\ell) = df_9(\ell).$$

The general expression for the density function considering $0 < \ell < \frac{a}{2}$ becomes:

$$
\begin{aligned}
df(\ell) &= \sum_{i=1}^{13} df_i(\ell) \\
&= (a-2\ell)^2 + 4 \cdot \frac{3}{4}\,\ell(a-2\ell) + 4\,\frac{5}{24}\,\ell^2 \\
&= a^2 - a\ell + \frac{1}{6}\,\ell^2
\end{aligned}
\tag{3.7}
$$

It is also possible to derive the distance density function in the following way; because of symmetry consider just a quarter of the square $(\ell\sqrt2 \times \ell\sqrt2)$ of possible distances from point $x = (x_1, x_2)$ (fig. 3.6).

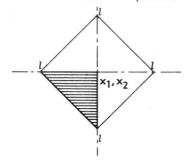

fig. 3.6.   Manhattan distances from point x

Consider $0 < \ell < a$; the square (axa) now has to be divided into 5 different sets (fig. 3.7).

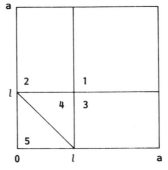

fig. 3.7.   5 sets $0 \leqslant \ell \leqslant a$, south-west oriented

Fig. 3.7 contains 5 sets of points, looking to the "south-west" distances starting in x. Of course, the same square would appear, considering only "north-west" distances; only fig. 3.7 has to be turned 90° to the right. Turning 90° ahead one finds the "north-east" distances and after turning once more 90° one has the "south-east" distances. This means that fig. 3.7 stands for all distances.

$$df_1(\ell) = (a-\ell)^2 \cdot 1 = (a-\ell)^2, \tag{3.8}$$

$$df_2(\ell) = (a-\ell) \cdot \int_{x_1=0}^{\ell} \frac{\ell\sqrt{2} - (\ell-x)\sqrt{2}}{\ell\sqrt{2}}\, dx_1 = \frac{1}{2}\ell(a-\ell), \tag{3.9}$$

$$df_3(\ell) = df_2(\ell) = \frac{1}{2}\,\ell(a-\ell), \tag{3.10}$$

$$df_4(\ell) = \int_{x_1=0}^{\ell} \int_{x_2=\ell-x_1}^{\ell} \frac{\ell\sqrt{2} - (\ell-x_1)\sqrt{2} - (\ell-x_2)\sqrt{2}}{\ell\sqrt{2}}\, dx_2\, dx_1 = \frac{1}{6}\,\ell^2, \tag{3.11}$$

$$df_5(\ell) = 0. \tag{3.12}$$

The complete density function $0 < \ell < a$ becomes:

$$df(\ell) = (a-\ell)^2 + 2\,\frac{1}{2}\,\ell(a-\ell) + \frac{1}{6}\,\ell^2$$

$$= a^2 - a\ell + \frac{1}{6}\,\ell^2 \tag{3.13}$$

These results agree with the results found earlier in (3.7).

Now assume that $a < \ell < 2a$; only two relevant sets remain (fig. 3.8).

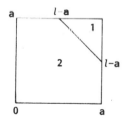

fig. 3.8. $a < \ell < 2a$ "south-west" distances

A measure for the number of distances of a point x in set 1 is found by

$$n_x(\ell) = \frac{\ell\sqrt{2} - (\ell-x_1)\sqrt{2} - (\ell-x_2)\sqrt{2}}{\ell\sqrt{2}} = \frac{x_1 + x_2 - \ell}{1} \qquad (3.14)$$

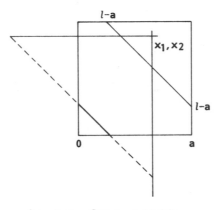

fig. 3.9.   Set 1; $a \leqslant \ell \leqslant 2a$

$$df_1(\ell) = \int_{x_1=\ell-a}^{a} \int_{x_2=\ell-x_1}^{a} \frac{x_1 + x_2 - \ell}{\ell} \, dx_2 \, dx_1$$

$$= \frac{1}{2} (2a-\ell)^2 \frac{2a-\ell}{3\ell} = \frac{(2a-\ell)^3}{6\ell} \qquad (3.15)$$

$$df_2(\ell) = 0 \qquad (3.16)$$

The distance density function for $a < \ell < 2a$ becomes $df(\ell) = \frac{(2a-\ell)^3}{6\ell}$.
Concluding we have for the distance density function in a square (axa)
using Manhattan distances (p=1):

$$df(\ell) = \begin{cases} a^2 - a\ell + \frac{1}{6} \ell^2 & 0 < \ell < a \\ \dfrac{(2a -)\ell^3}{6\ell} & a < \ell < 2a \\ 0 & \text{otherwise} \end{cases} \qquad (3.17)$$

To calculate the relative distance density function one has to require

$$\int_{\ell=0}^{2a} df(\ell) \, d\ell = 1 \; ; \; \text{so the relative distance density function } df^r(\ell)$$

is:

$$df^r(\ell) = \begin{cases} \dfrac{3(a^2 - a\ell + \frac{1}{6}\ell^2)}{a^3(4\log 2 - 1)} & ----- \quad 0 \leqslant \ell \leqslant a \\[3mm] \dfrac{(2a - \ell)^3}{2a^3(4\log 2 - 1)\ell} & ----- \quad a \leqslant \ell \leqslant 2a \\[3mm] 0 & ----- \quad \text{otherwise} \end{cases} \qquad (3.18)$$

It is interesting to plot a number of distributions for different values of a in one picture; this is done for a = 20, 40, 60, 80 and 100 (fig. 3.10); from this picture it is clear that density functions become flatter with increasing a.

Knowing the distance density function it is easy to calculate the expected value of ℓ, $E\ell$.

$$E\ell = \int_{\ell=0}^{2a} \ell \, df^r(\ell) \, d\ell = \frac{\frac{1}{4}a}{\frac{4}{3}\log 2 - \frac{1}{3}} = .423a \qquad (3.19)$$

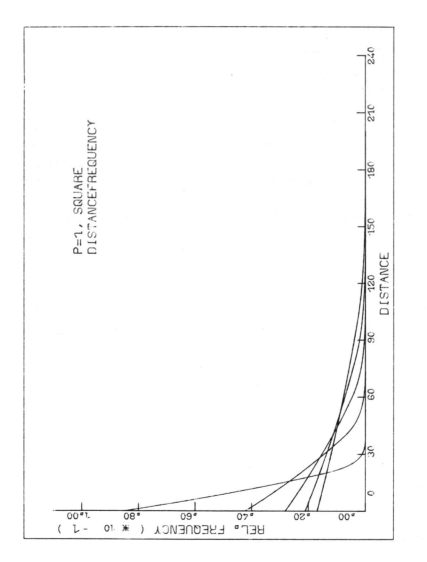

fig. 3.10   Relative distance distributions for a=20,40,60,80 and 100

3.1.2. p = 2

Now Euclidean distances are considered in a square (axa); from example 2 in chapter 2.3. we know the density function for $0 < \ell < \frac{a}{2}$

$$df(\ell) = a^2 - \frac{4a\ell}{\pi} + \frac{\ell^2}{\pi} \qquad\qquad 0 < \ell < \frac{a}{2} \qquad\qquad (3.20)$$

Also in this case it is possible to derive the distribution by considering just one quarter of all possible distances from point x inside the square (fig. 3.11).

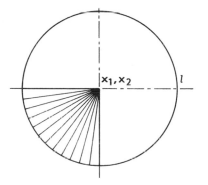

fig. 3.11. Euclidean distances from point x (= x_1, x_2)

Considering distances ℓ, $0 < \ell < a$ the distance density function can be calculated by dividing the square into 5 different sets of points (fully comparable with fig. 3.7).

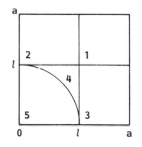

fig. 3.12. 5 sets $0 \leqslant \ell \leqslant a$, "south-west" distances

$$df_1(\ell) = (a-\ell)^2 \; , \tag{3.21}$$

$$df_2(\ell) = (a-\ell) \int\limits_{x=0}^{\ell} \frac{\frac{1}{2}\pi\ell - \ell\cos^{-1}\frac{x_1}{\ell}\; dx_1}{\frac{1}{2}\pi\ell} = (a-\ell)\; \ell(1-\frac{2}{\pi})\; , \tag{3.22}$$

$$df_3(\ell) = df_2(\ell) \; . \tag{3.23}$$

Looking at fig. 2.10 the density function of set 4 is found by

$$df_4(\ell) = \int\limits_{x_1=0}^{\ell} \int\limits_{x_2=\sqrt{\ell^2-x_1^2}}^{\ell} \frac{\frac{1}{2}\pi\ell - \ell\cos^{-1}\frac{x_1}{\ell} - \ell\cos^{-1}\frac{x_2}{\ell}}{}\; dx_2\; dx_1$$

$$= \ell^2 - \frac{3}{\pi}\; \ell^2, \text{ obviously,} \tag{3.24}$$

$$df_5(\ell) = 0. \tag{3.25}$$

The distance density function in a square using Euclidean distances with $0 < \ell < a$ becomes

$$df(\ell) = \sum\limits_{i=1}^{5} df_i(\ell)$$

$$= (a-\ell)^2 + 2(a-\ell)\ell(1-\frac{2}{\pi}) + \ell^2 - \frac{3}{\pi}\ell^2$$

$$= a^2 - \frac{4a\ell}{\pi} + \frac{\ell^2}{\pi} \; . \tag{3.26}$$

Consider $a < \ell < a\sqrt{2}$.

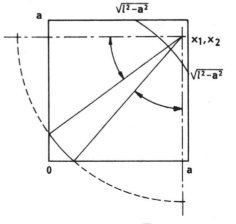

fig. 3.13. $a \leqslant l \leqslant a\sqrt{2}$, set 1

There are two sets of points of special interest; first set 1 is considered. Starting in x the measure for the number of distances

$$n_x(\ell) = \frac{\frac{1}{2}\pi\ell - \alpha\ell - \beta\ell}{\frac{1}{2}\pi\ell} = \frac{\frac{1}{2}\pi\ell - \ell\cos^{-1}\frac{x_1}{\ell} - \ell\cos^{-1}\frac{x_2}{\ell}}{\frac{1}{2}\pi\ell}, \qquad (3.27)$$

integrating this expression over all points x inside set 1, yields the distance density function.

$$df_1(\ell) = \int_{x_1=\sqrt{\ell^2-a^2}}^{a} \int_{x_2=\sqrt{\ell^2-x_1^2}}^{a} \frac{\frac{1}{2}\pi\ell - \ell\cos^{-1}\frac{x_1}{\ell} - \ell\cos^{-1}\frac{x_2}{\ell}}{\frac{1}{2}\pi\ell} dx_2\, dx_1$$

$$= a^2 + \frac{4a}{\pi}\sqrt{\ell^2-a^2} - \frac{2a^2}{\pi} - \frac{\ell^2}{\pi} - \frac{4a^2}{\pi}\cos^{-1}\frac{a}{\ell} \qquad (3.28)$$

$df_2(\ell) = 0$, so the general expression $df(\ell)$, $a < \ell < a\sqrt{2}$ becomes

$$df(\ell) = df_1(\ell) \ .$$

Summarising the distance density function in a square using Euclidean distances gives:

$$df(\ell) = \begin{cases} a^2 - \dfrac{4a\ell}{\pi} + \dfrac{\ell^2}{\pi} & 0 < \ell < a \\[2mm] a^2 + \dfrac{4a}{\pi}\sqrt{\ell^2-a^2} - \dfrac{2a^2}{\pi} - \dfrac{\ell^2}{\pi} - \dfrac{4a^2}{\pi}\cos^{-1}\dfrac{a}{\ell} & a < \ell < a\sqrt{2} \\[2mm] 0 & \text{otherwise} \end{cases}$$

$$(3.29)$$

with:

$$df(0) = a^2, \ df(a) = a^2 - \frac{3a^2}{\pi}, \ df(a\sqrt{2}) = 0$$

The relative distance density function $df^r(\ell)$ is:

$$df^r(\ell) = \left\{\frac{2}{3} - \frac{2}{3}\sqrt{3} + 2\log(\sqrt{2}+1)\ \frac{a^3}{\pi}\right\}^{-1} df(\ell) \tag{3.30}$$

The expected value $E\ell$ is found by:

$$E\ell = \int_{\ell=0}^{a\sqrt{2}} \ell\ df^r(\ell)\ d\ell = \frac{a}{4(\frac{1}{3} - \frac{\sqrt{3}}{3} + \log(\sqrt{2}+1)} = .336a \tag{3.31}$$

To get an impression of the shape of these functions, both $df(\ell)$ and $df^r(\ell)$ are plotted for a = 20, 40, 60, 80, 100 (fig. 3.14).

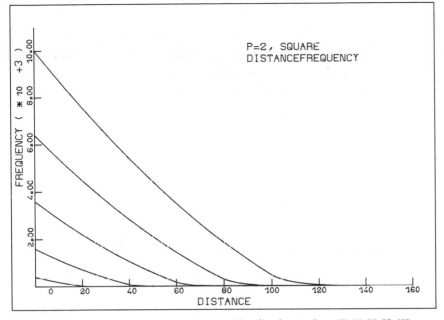

fig. 3.14 Absolute and relative distance distributions,p=2, a=20,40,60,80,100

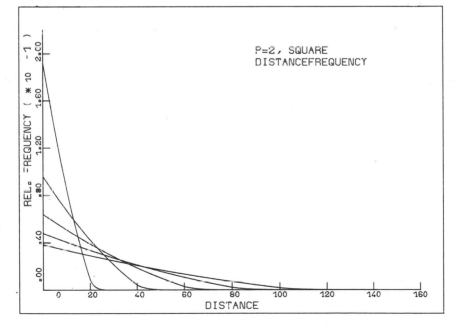

3.1.3. $p = \infty$

The distance is determined by the dominating value of the co-ordinates; so one will only find distance ℓ where $0 < \ell < a$. As before, consider just a quarter of all possible distances.

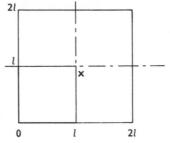

fig. 3.15. $p = \infty$, distances from point x

The square (axa) has to be divided into 4 sets of points according to fig. 3.16.

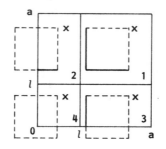

fig. 3.16. $p = \infty$ 4 sets

The distance density functions are calculated in the following way,

$0 < \ell < a;$

$$df_1(\ell) = (a-\ell)^2 \tag{3.32}$$

$$df_2(\ell) = (a-\ell) \int_{x_1=0}^{\ell} \frac{x_1}{2\ell} \, dx_1 = \frac{1}{4} \ell (a-\ell) \tag{3.33}$$

$$df_3(\ell) = df_2(\ell) \text{ and} \tag{3.34}$$

$$df_4(\ell) = 0 \qquad\qquad (3.35)$$

So, the complete distance density function becomes:

$$df(\ell) = (a-\ell)^2 + 2\,\frac{1}{4}\,\ell(a-\ell)$$

$$df(\ell) = (a-\ell)\,(a-\frac{1}{2}\ell) \qquad\qquad 0 < \ell < a \qquad\qquad (3.36)$$

The relative distance density function $df^r(\ell)$ becomes:

$$df^r(\ell) = \frac{12}{5a^3}\,(a-\ell)\,(a-\frac{1}{2}\ell) \qquad\qquad 0 < \ell < a\ ; \qquad\qquad (3.37)$$

this function is plotted for a = 20, 40, 60, 80 and 100 (fig. 3.17).

The expected value $E\ell$:

$$E\ell = \int_{\ell=0}^{a} \ell\,df^r(\ell)d\ell = .3a \qquad\qquad (3.38)$$

Resuming we found:

$E\ell_{p=1} = .432a$

$E\ell_{p=2} = .336a$

$\vdots$

$E\ell_{p=\infty} = .300a$, showing that the expected distance decreases as p increases.

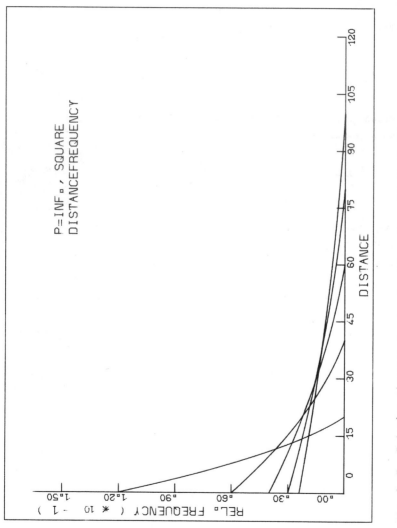

Fig. 3.17 Relative distance density functions for a=20,40,60,100.

3.2. Distance distribution in a rectangle

The distribution is determined in a similar way as in the previous section concerning a square; therefore only the most important results will be mentioned here. One can always compare the results found in a rectangle (a x b, a>b) with the results of the square by considering a=b.

3.2.1. p = 1

Assume $\ell < b$; there are now 5 sets of points of special interest now (fig. 3.18)

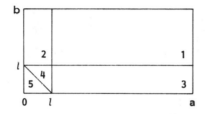

fig. 3.18. $0 \leqslant l \leqslant b$; p=1; 5 sets of points

Considering only "south-west" distances one finds

$$df_1(\ell) = (a-\ell)(b-\ell).1 = (a-\ell)(b-\ell) \qquad (3.39)$$

$$df_2(\ell) = \int_{x_1=0}^{\ell} \int_{x_2=0}^{b} \frac{\ell\sqrt{2} - (\ell-x)\sqrt{2}}{\ell\sqrt{2}} dx_2 \, dx_1 = \frac{1}{2} \ell \, (b-\ell) \qquad (3.40)$$

$$df_3(\ell) = \int_{x_1=\ell}^{a} \int_{x_2=0}^{\ell} \frac{\ell\sqrt{2} - (\ell-x_2)\sqrt{2}}{\ell\sqrt{2}} dx_2 \, dx_1 = \frac{1}{2} \ell \, (a-\ell) \qquad (3.41)$$

$$df_4(\ell) = \int_{x_1=0}^{\ell} \int_{x_2=\ell-x_1}^{\ell} \frac{\ell\sqrt{2} - (\ell-x_1)\sqrt{2} - (\ell-x_2)\sqrt{2}}{\ell\sqrt{2}} dx_2 \, dx_1 = \frac{1}{6} \ell^2$$
$$\qquad (3.42)$$

$$df_5(\ell) = 0.$$

The distance density function becomes:

$$df(\ell) = (a-\ell)(b-\ell) + \frac{1}{2}\ell(b-\ell) + \frac{1}{2}\ell(a-\ell) + \frac{1}{6}\ell^2$$

$$= ab - \frac{1}{2}(a+b)\ell + \frac{1}{6}\ell^2 \qquad\qquad 0 < \ell < b \qquad\qquad (3.43)$$

Assume $b < \ell < a$; there are three important sets inside the rectangle (fig. 3.19).

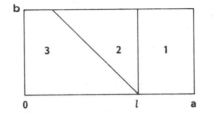

fig. 3.19. $b \leqslant \ell \leqslant a$; p=1, 3 sets of points

$$df_1(\ell) = \int_{x_1=\ell}^{x_1=a} \int_{x_2=0}^{x_2=b} \frac{\ell\sqrt{2} - (\ell-x_2)\sqrt{2}}{\ell\sqrt{2}} dx_2 dx_1 = b(a-\ell)\frac{b}{2\ell} \qquad (3.44)$$

$$df_2(\ell) = \int_{x_1=\ell-b}^{x_1=\ell} \int_{x_2=\ell-x_1}^{b} \frac{\ell\sqrt{2} - (\ell-x_1)\sqrt{2} - (\ell-x_2)\sqrt{2}}{\ell\sqrt{2}} dx_2 dx_1 = \frac{1}{2}b^2\frac{b}{3\ell} \quad (3.45)$$

$$df_3(\ell) = 0, \qquad\qquad\qquad\qquad\qquad\qquad\qquad\qquad (3.46)$$

so the distance density function in this case becomes:

$$df(\ell) = b(a-\ell)\frac{b}{2\ell} + \frac{b^3}{6\ell}$$

$$= \frac{b^2}{2\ell}(a-\ell + \frac{b}{3}) \qquad\qquad\qquad b < \ell < a \qquad\qquad (3.47)$$

Finally assume $a < \ell < a+b$; there are 2 sets of points left now.

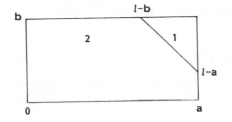

fig. 3.20. $a \leqslant l \leqslant a+b;$ $p=1$, 2 sets of points

$$df_1(l) = \int\limits_{x_1=l-b}^{a} \int\limits_{x_2=l-x_1}^{b} \frac{l\sqrt{2} - (l-x_1)\sqrt{2} - (l-x_2)\sqrt{2}}{l\sqrt{2}} \, dx_2 \, dx_1$$

$$= \frac{1}{6l} (b + a - l)^3 \tag{3.48}$$

$$df_2(l) = 0 \tag{3.49}$$

Summarising the distance density function in a rectangle (a x b) using $p=1$ norm (Manhattan distances) gives:

$$df(l) = \begin{cases} ab - \frac{1}{2}(a+b)l + \frac{1}{6}l^2 & 0 < l < b \\ (a - l + \frac{b}{3})\frac{b^2}{2l} & b \leqslant l \leqslant a \\ \dfrac{(b + a - l)^3}{6l} & a < l < a+b \\ 0 & \text{otherwise} \end{cases} \tag{3.50}$$

(If a = b one finds the result on a square)

The relative distance density function $df^r(l)$ having property

$\int\limits_{l=0}^{a+b} df^r(l) = 1$, is found by $df^r(l) = c^{-1} df(l)$,

with:

$$c = \frac{1}{6}(a+b)^3 \log(a+b) - \frac{1}{6} a^2(a+3b)\log a - \frac{1}{6} b^2(3a+b)\log b - \frac{1}{6} ab(a+b), \tag{3.51}$$

The expected value is found by $\int_{\ell=o}^{a+b} \ell df^r(\ell)$, the result being:

$$E\ell = \frac{\frac{3}{2} a^2 b^2}{(a+b)^3 \log(a+b) - b^2(3a+b)\log b - a^2(a+3b)\log a - ab(a+b)} \qquad (3.52)$$

If $a = b$ we find:

$$E\ell = \frac{\frac{3}{2} a^4}{8a^3\log 2a - 4a^3\log a - 4a^3\log a - \frac{1}{3} a^3} = \frac{\frac{3}{2} a}{2(8\log 2 - 2)} = .423a,$$

which is indeed the result found earlier in a square.

The function $df(\ell)$ is plotted for $a = 100$, $b = 20$ in fig. 3.21, and in one picture for $a = 100$, $b = 20$, 40, 60, 80, 100 (fig. 3.22); the same is done with respect to $df^r(\ell)$ in fig. 3.23.

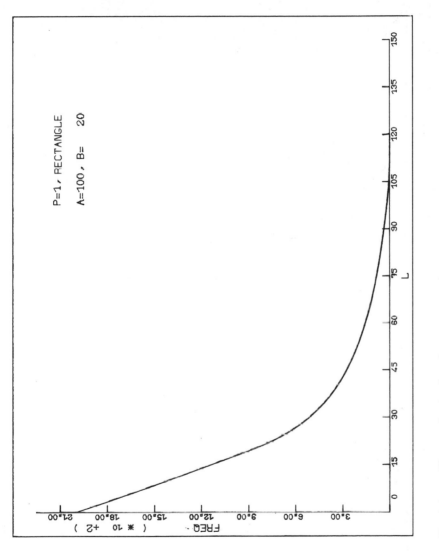

fig. 3.21   Distance density function on a rectangle

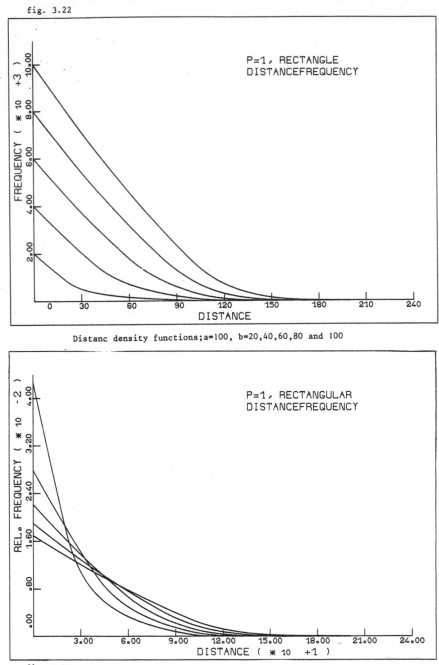

fig. 3.22

Distanc density functions;a=100, b=20,40,60,80 and 100

fig. 3.23

3.2.2. $\underline{p = 2}$

The calculations are to a large extent comparable with $p = 1$ (3.2.1). First assume $0 < \ell < b$; once again there are 5 relevant sets of points inside the rectangle.

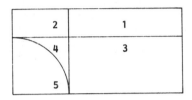

fig. 3.24. $0 \leqslant \ell \leqslant b$; p=2, 5 sets of points

$$df_2(\ell) = (b-\ell)\ell(1-\frac{2}{\pi}), \tag{3.54}$$

$$df_3(\ell) = (a-\ell)\ell(1-\frac{2}{\pi}), \tag{3.55}$$

$$df_4(\ell) = \int\limits_{x_1=0}^{\ell} \int\limits_{x_2=\sqrt{\ell^2-x_1^2}}^{\ell} \frac{\frac{1}{2}\pi\ell - \ell\cos^{-1}\frac{x_1}{\ell} - \ell\cos^{-1}\frac{x_2}{\ell}}{\frac{1}{2}\pi\ell}\, dx_2\, dx_1 = \ell^2 - \frac{3\ell^2}{\pi}$$

$$\tag{3.56}$$

$$df_5(\ell) = 0. \tag{3.57}$$

The complete distance density function is:

$$df(\ell) = ab - \frac{2}{\pi}(a+b)\ell + \frac{\ell^2}{\pi} \qquad\qquad 0 < \ell < b \tag{3.58}$$

Assume $b < \ell < a$:

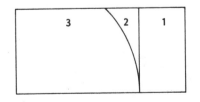

fig. 3.25. $b \leqslant \ell \leqslant a$; p=2, 3 sets of points

-55-

$$df_1(\ell) = \int_{x_1=\ell}^{a} \int_{x_2=0}^{b} \frac{\frac{1}{2}\pi\ell - \ell\cos^{-1}\frac{x_1}{\ell}}{\frac{1}{2}\pi\ell} \, dx_2 \, dx_1,$$

$$= b(a-\ell) - \frac{2b(a-\ell)}{\pi}\cos^{-1}\frac{b}{\ell} + \frac{2(a-\ell)}{\pi}\sqrt{\ell^2-b^2} - \frac{2\ell}{\pi}(a-\ell). \quad (3.59)$$

$$df_2(\ell) = \int_{x_1=\ell}^{a} \int_{x_2=0}^{b} \frac{\frac{1}{2}\pi\ell - \ell\cos^{-1}\frac{x_1}{\ell} - \ell\cos^{-1}\frac{x_2}{\ell}}{\frac{1}{2}\pi\ell} \, dx_2 \, dx_1,$$

$$= b\ell - \frac{2b\ell}{\pi}\cos^{-1}\frac{b}{\ell} + \frac{2\ell}{\pi}\sqrt{\ell^2-b^2} - \frac{2\ell^2}{\pi} - \frac{b^2}{\pi} \quad (3.60)$$

$$df_3(\ell) = 0. \quad (3.61)$$

The complete result in this case is:

$$df(\ell) = ab - \frac{2ab}{\pi}\cos^{-1}\frac{b}{\ell} + \frac{2a}{\pi}\sqrt{\ell^2-b^2} - \frac{2a\ell}{\pi} - \frac{b^2}{\pi} \qquad b \leqslant \ell \leqslant a$$
$$(3.62)$$

Finally, assume $a \leqslant \ell \leqslant \sqrt{a^2+b^2}$.; there are two relevant sets of points inside the rectangle.

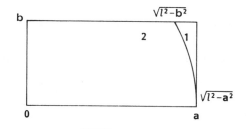

fig. 3.26. $a \leqslant l \leqslant \sqrt{a^2+b^2}$; p=2, 2 sets of points

$$df_1(\ell) = \int_{x_1=\sqrt{\ell^2-b^2}}^{a} \int_{x_2=\sqrt{\ell^2-x_1^2}}^{b} \frac{\frac{1}{2}\pi\ell - \ell\cos^{-1}\frac{x_1}{\ell} - \ell\cos^{-1}\frac{x_2}{\ell}}{\frac{1}{2}\pi\ell} \, dx_2 \, dx_1$$

$$= b(a-\ell) - \frac{2b(a-\ell)}{\pi}\cos^{-1}\frac{b}{\ell} + \frac{2(a-\ell)}{\pi}\sqrt{\ell^2-b^2} - \frac{2\ell}{\pi}(a-\ell). \quad (3.63)$$

$$df_2(\ell) = 0. \tag{3.64}$$

Summarising we have found the following distance density function in a rectangle (a x b), using Euclidean distances:

$$df(\ell) = \begin{cases} ab - \dfrac{2}{\pi}(a+b)\ell + \dfrac{\ell^2}{\pi} & 0 \leqslant \ell \leqslant b \\[2mm] ab - \dfrac{2ab}{\pi}\cos^{-1}\dfrac{b}{\ell} + \dfrac{2a}{\pi}\sqrt{\ell^2-b^2} - \dfrac{2a\ell}{\pi} - \dfrac{b^2}{\pi} & b \leqslant \ell \leqslant a \\[2mm] ab - \dfrac{2ab}{\pi}\left(\cos^{-1}\dfrac{b}{\ell} + \cos^{-1}\dfrac{a}{\ell}\right) + \dfrac{2}{\pi}(a\sqrt{\ell^2-b^2} + b\sqrt{\ell^2-a^2}) \\[2mm] \quad - \dfrac{a^2}{\pi} - \dfrac{b^2}{\pi}\dfrac{\ell^2}{\pi} & a \leqslant \ell \leqslant \sqrt{a^2+b^2} \\[2mm] 0 & \text{otherwise} \end{cases} \tag{3.65}$$

The relative density function $df^r(\ell)$ is found by multiplying $df(\ell)$ with a constant c^{-1}.

$$c^{-1} = \dfrac{a^3}{3\pi} + \dfrac{b^3}{3\pi} - \dfrac{(\sqrt{a^2+b^2})^3}{3\pi} + \dfrac{a^2\sqrt{a^2-b^2}}{\pi} + \dfrac{ab^2}{\pi}\log\left(\dfrac{a+\sqrt{a^2+b^2}}{b}\right) +$$

$$= \dfrac{a^2 b}{\pi}\log\left(\dfrac{b+\sqrt{a^2+b^2}}{a}\right) \tag{3.66}$$

(If $a = b$; $c^{-1} = \dfrac{2a^3}{\pi}\left(\dfrac{1}{3} - \dfrac{\sqrt{2}}{3} + \log(\sqrt{2}+1)\right)$; the result of the square).

The expected value of $E\ell$ is found by calculating

$$\int_{\ell=0}^{\sqrt{a^2+b^2}} \ell\, df^r(\ell)d\ell; \;;$$

after some calculations one gets:

$$E\ell = \dfrac{\dfrac{a^2b^2}{\pi} - \dfrac{2a^3b}{\pi}\cos^{-1}\dfrac{b}{a}}{\dfrac{a^3}{3\pi} + \dfrac{b^3}{3\pi} - \dfrac{(\sqrt{a^2+b^2})^3}{3\pi} + \dfrac{a^2}{\pi}\sqrt{a^2-b^2} + \dfrac{ab^2}{\pi}\log\left(\dfrac{a+\sqrt{a^2+b^2}}{b}\right) + \dfrac{a^2b}{\pi}\left(\log\dfrac{b+\sqrt{a^2+b^2}}{a}\right)}$$

$$\tag{3.67}$$

(remember the result of the square; $E\ell = \dfrac{a}{4(\frac{1}{3} - \frac{1}{3}\sqrt{2} + \log(\sqrt{2}+1)} =$

.336a).

Both $df(\ell)$ and $df^r(\ell)$ are plotted for $a = 100$ and $b = 20$, 40, 60, 80, and 100 (fig. 3.27 and 3.28).

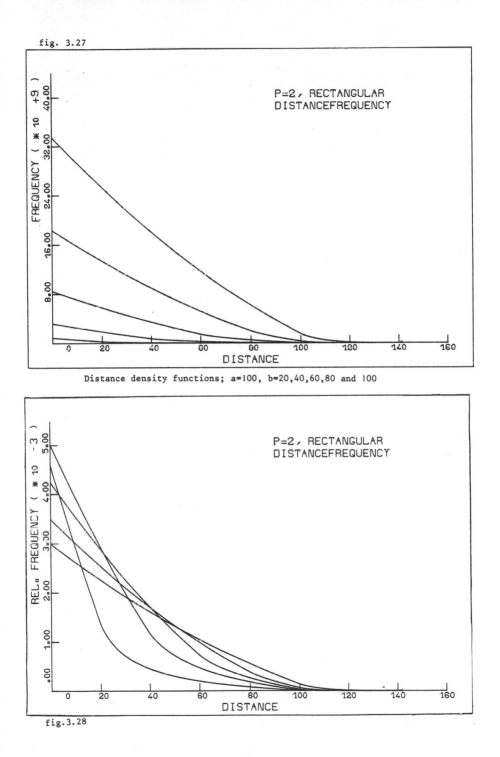

fig. 3.27

Distance density functions; a=100, b=20,40,60,80 and 100

fig.3.28

3.2.3. $p = \infty$

Assume $0 \leqslant \ell \leqslant b$; there are 4 relevant sets of points inside the rectangle (a x b) (fig. 3.29).

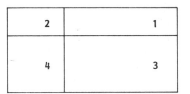

fig. 3.29. $0 \leqslant \ell \leqslant b$; $p=\infty$, 4 sets of points

$$df_1(\ell) = (a-\ell)(b-\ell) \tag{3.68}$$

$$df_2(\ell) = \int_{x_1=0}^{\ell} \int_{x_2=\ell}^{b} \frac{x_1}{2\ell} \, dx_2 \, dx_1 = \frac{1}{4} \ell \, (b-\ell) \, , \tag{3.69}$$

$$df_3(\ell) = \int_{x_1=0}^{\ell} \int_{x_2=\ell}^{a} \frac{x_2}{2\ell} \, dx_2 \, dx_1 = \frac{1}{4} \ell \, (a-\ell) \, ,$$

$df_4(\ell) = 0$; so the distance density function in this case becomes

$$df(\ell) = (a-\ell)(b-\ell) + \frac{1}{2} \ell \, (a+b-2\ell) \qquad 0 \leqslant \ell \leqslant b. \tag{3.70}$$

Assume $b \leqslant \ell \leqslant a$; now 2 sets of points have to be distinguished (fig. 3.30).

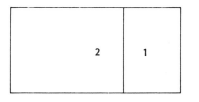

fig. 3.30. $b \leqslant \ell \leqslant a$; $p=\infty$, 2 sets of points

$$df_1(\ell) = \int_{x_1=\ell}^{a} \int_{x_2=0}^{b} \frac{x_2}{2\ell} \, dx_2 \, dx_1 = \frac{1}{4} \frac{b^2}{\ell} (a-\ell) , \qquad\qquad (3.71)$$

$$df_2(\ell) = 0; \qquad\qquad (3.72)$$

so the distance density function is:

$$df(\ell) = \frac{1}{4} \frac{b^2}{\ell} (a-\ell) \qquad\qquad b \leqslant \ell \leqslant a \quad . \qquad\qquad (3.73)$$

The complete distance density function in a rectangle using a Minkowski distance measure $p = \infty$ is:

$$df(\ell) = \begin{cases} (a-\ell)(b-\ell) + \frac{1}{4} \ell \, (a+b-2\ell) & 0 \leqslant \ell \leqslant b \\[2mm] \frac{1}{4} \frac{b^2}{\ell} (a-\ell) & b \leqslant \ell \leqslant a \qquad (3.74) \\[2mm] 0 & \text{otherwise} \end{cases}$$

The relative distance density function is

$$df^r(\ell) = \frac{1}{\frac{3}{8} ab^2 + \frac{1}{24} b^3 + \frac{1}{4} a \, b^2 \log \frac{a}{b}} \, df(\ell); \quad \text{the expected value } E\ell \text{ is:}$$

$$E\ell = \frac{\frac{1}{8} a^2 b^2}{\frac{3}{8} ab^2 + \frac{1}{24} b^3 + \frac{1}{4} ab^2 \log \frac{a}{b}} = \frac{\frac{1}{2} a^2}{\frac{3}{2} a + \frac{1}{6} b + a \log \frac{a}{b}} , \qquad\qquad (3.75)$$

(if a=b we find $E\ell = \dfrac{\frac{1}{2}a^2}{\frac{5}{3}a} = .3a$, the result on the square).

The distance density functions are plotted for a = 100, and b = 20, 40, 60, 80 and 100 (figs. 3.31 and 3.32).

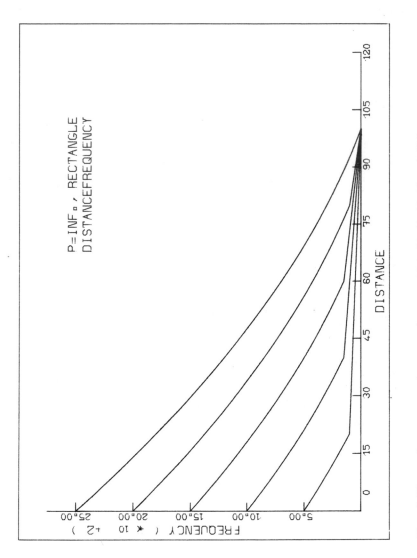

fig. 3.31   Distance density functions; a=100, b=20, 40, 60, 80 and 100

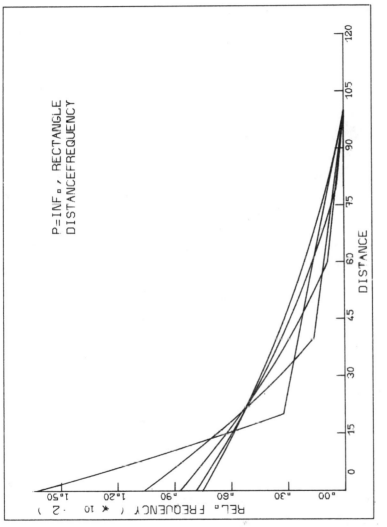

fig.3.32 Relative distance density functions; a=100, b=20,40,60,80 and 100

3.3. The distance distribution in a circle

3.3.1. $p = 2$.

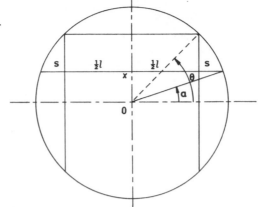

fig. 3.33. Euclidean distances in a circle

Consider distances ℓ, $0 < \ell < 2R$, inside a circular shape (radius R). ℓ is a metric on the real line inside the circle and parallel to the horizontal axis. The distribution of the distances located on all such real lines inside the circle represents the relative distance density function of the Euclidian distances inside a circle. Consider a line at distance x from 0 (centre of the circle) parallel to the horizontal axis, and a distance on this line. A measure for the number of distances ℓ on this line amounts to 2s (see also example 1, section 2, the distance distribution on a line), where $s = R\cos\alpha - \tfrac{1}{2}\ell$. So the total number of distances on the line at distance x from 0 is:

$$2(R\cos\alpha - \tfrac{1}{2}\ell)$$

$$= 2(R \sqrt{1 - \frac{x^2}{R^2}} - \tfrac{1}{2}\ell)$$

$$= 2\sqrt{R^2 - x^2} - \ell \qquad\qquad (3.76)$$

The total number of distances ℓ is:

$$2 \int_{x=0}^{x=R\sin\theta} 2\sqrt{R^2 - x^2} - \ell\,dx \quad \text{where } \theta = \arccos \frac{\ell}{2R}$$

$$= 2R\sin\theta \ \sqrt{R^2 - R^2\sin^2\theta} \ + R^2\theta - R\ell\sin\theta$$

$$= 2R^2\theta - R\ell\sin\theta$$

$$= 2R^2 \ arcos \ \frac{1}{2R} - \tfrac{1}{2}\ell \ \sqrt{4R^2 - \ell^2} \tag{3.77}$$

The distance density function $df(\ell)$ is:

$$df(\ell) = \begin{cases} \dfrac{2R^2\cos \dfrac{\ell}{2R} - \tfrac{1}{2}\ell \ \sqrt{4R^2 - \ell^2}}{\pi R^2} & 0 < \ell < 2R \\ 0 & \text{otherwise} \end{cases} \tag{3.78}$$

This distribution is plotted for R = 50 (fig. 3.34).

The relative distance density function is:

$$df^r(\ell) = \frac{3}{8\ R^3}\left(2R^2 arcos \ \frac{\ell}{2R} - \tfrac{1}{2}\ell \ \sqrt{4R^2 - \ell^2} \ \right) \qquad 0 < \ell < 2R \tag{3.79}$$

The expected distance is found by:

$$E \ \ell = \frac{\displaystyle\int_{\ell=0}^{2R} \ell\left(2R^2\cos_2\frac{\ell}{2R} - \tfrac{1}{2}\ell \ \sqrt{4R^2 - \ell^2}\right)d\ell}{\displaystyle\int_{\ell=0}^{2R} \left(2R^2\cos \frac{\ell}{2R} - \tfrac{1}{2}\ell \ \sqrt{4R^2 - \ell^2}\right)d\ell} = \frac{5}{16}\ \pi R = .981R \tag{3.80}$$

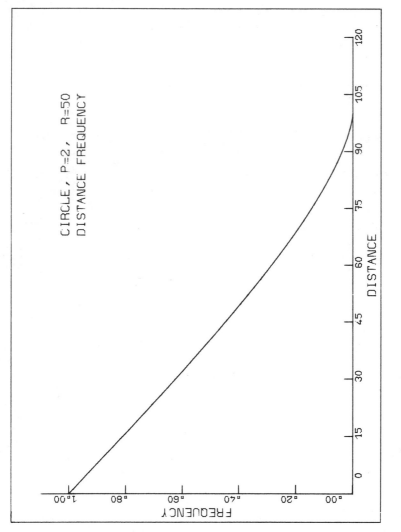

fig.3.34   Distance density function; R=50

4 The road-area distribution

In this chapter the road area distribution in a square, a rectangle and a circle will be derived for several p norms.

4.1. The road area density function in a square

4.4.1. p = 1

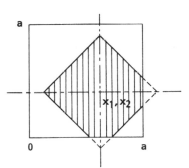

fig. 4.1.   Road area in a square, p=1

The measure for the number of roads is the fraction of the surface of the square ($\ell\sqrt{2}$ x $\ell\sqrt{2}$) that can be covered with roads (distance ℓ) inside the defined shape, the square (a x a). If ℓ is small all roads of distance ℓ are located inside the square (a x a) and therefore the measure will be 1; if ℓ increases the number of roads, distance ℓ will decrease and so does the measure for the number of roads; finally if $\ell >$ 2a, it becomes zero. As is the case with the distance density function the road area density function will decline starting from $\ell = 0$.

Because of the symmetry, the road area density function will be derived by considering a quarter of all roads; this makes it easier to divide the defined shape (a square (a x a)) in nice samples of points, which have comparable properties concerning the number of roads.

As shown in fig. 3.6 the south-west part of the square ($\ell\sqrt{2}$ x $\ell\sqrt{2}$) is considered. First consider distance ℓ, $0 < \ell < a$; five sets of points have to be distinguished inside the square (a x a), fig. 4.2.

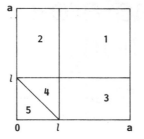

fig. 4.2. $0 \leqslant l \leqslant a$; 5 sets of points

$rf_i(l)$ is the road area density function in set i;

$$rf(l) = \sum_{i=1}^{5} rf_i(l)$$

$rf_1(l) = (a-l)^2 \cdot 1 = (a-l)^2$; from each point in set 1 roads of distance l are always completely located inside the square (a x a), so the measure of the road area for each point is 1; the number of points in set 1 is measured by $(a-l)^2$.

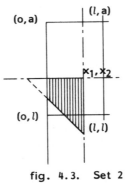

fig. 4.3.   Set 2

The road area density function in set 2 is calculated by:

$$rf_2(l) = (a-l) \int_{x_1=0}^{l} \frac{\frac{1}{2} l^2 - \frac{1}{2} (l-x_1)^2}{\frac{1}{2} l^2} \, dx_1,$$

$$= \frac{2}{3} l \, (a-l). \tag{4.1}$$

Because of symmetry $rf_3(\ell) = rf_2(\ell)$.

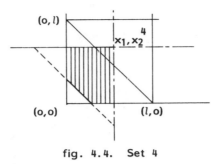

fig. 4.4. Set 4

The road area density function in set 4 is:

$$rf_4(\ell) = \int\limits_{x_1=0}^{\ell} \int\limits_{x_2=\ell-x_1}^{\ell} \frac{\frac{1}{2} \ell^2 - \frac{1}{2}(\ell-x_1)^2 - \frac{1}{2}(\ell-x_2)^2}{\frac{1}{2} \ell^2} \, dx_2 dx_1,$$

$$= \frac{1}{3} \ell^2. \tag{4.2}$$

$rf_5(\ell) = 0$; all roads, distance ℓ, are located outside the square. The road area density function, becomes:

$$rf(\ell) = (a-\ell)^2 + 2 \, \frac{2}{3}(a-\ell) + \frac{1}{3} \ell^2 \qquad 0 \leqslant \ell \leqslant a$$

$$= a^2 - \frac{2}{3} a\ell. \tag{4.3}$$

Now road distances ℓ, $a \leqslant \ell \leqslant 2a$, are considered. In this case two sets of points are of interest (fig. 4.5).

The road area density function in set 1 is calculated as follows (fig. 4.6):

$$rf_1(\ell) = \int\limits_{x_1=\ell-a}^{a} \int\limits_{x_2=\ell-x_1}^{a} \frac{\frac{1}{2} \ell^2 - \frac{1}{2}(\ell-x_1)^2 - \frac{1}{2}(\ell-x_2)^2}{\frac{1}{2} \ell^2} \, dx_2 dx_1,$$

$$= \frac{2a\ell^3 + 12a^3\ell - 9a^2\ell^2 - 4a^4}{3\ell^2}. \tag{4.4}$$

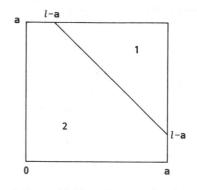

fig. 4.5. $a \leqslant l \leqslant 2a$; 2 sets of points

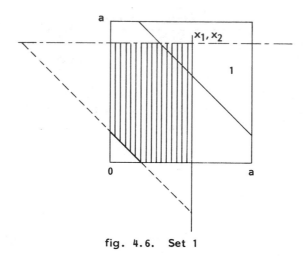

fig. 4.6. Set 1

So the road area density function for $a < \ell < 2a$ becomes:

$$rf(\ell) = \frac{2a\ell^3 + 12a^3\ell - 9a^2\ell^2 - 4a^4}{3\ell^2} \, .$$ (4.5)

The complete road area density function in a square (a x a) using Manhattan distances (p=1) gives:

$$rf(\ell) = \begin{cases} a^2 - \dfrac{2}{3}\, a\ell & 0 \leqslant \ell \leqslant a \\[2mm] \dfrac{2a\ell^3 + 12a^3\ell - 9a^2\ell^2 - 4a^4}{3\ell^2} & a < \ell < 2a \\[2mm] 0 & \text{otherwise} \end{cases} \qquad (4.6)$$

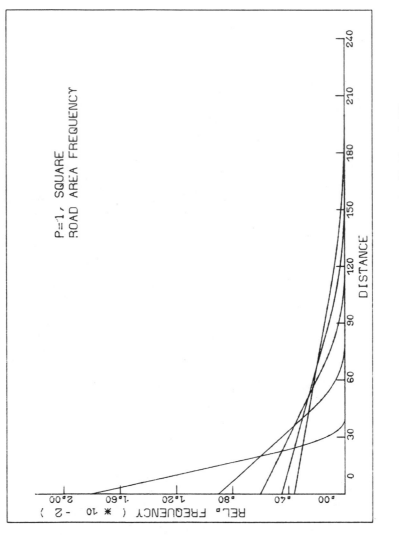

fig.4.7   Relative road area density functions;a=20,40,60,80 and 100

The relative road area density function $rf^r(\ell)$ is:

$$rf^r(\ell) = \frac{1}{4a^3\log2 - 2a^3} \, rf(\ell) = \frac{rf(\ell)}{2a^3(2\log2-1)} \quad (\text{fig. } 4.7). \qquad (4.7)$$

The expected road distance $E\ell$ belonging to the expected part of the area of the square that is covered with roads becomes:

$$E\ell = \int_\ell \ell rf^r(\ell) \, d\ell$$

$$= 2a \, \frac{(1-\log2)}{3(2\log2-1)} = .528 \; a \qquad (4.8)$$

4.1.2. $p = 2$

First consider road distance ℓ, $0 < \ell < a$. As with the derivation of the road area density function for $p = 1$, the square (a x a) in this case is divided into five sets of points (fig. 3.12) and just a quarter of all possible roads is considered (fig. 3.11).

$$rf_1(\ell) = (a-\ell)^2.$$

$$rf_2(\ell) = \int_{x_1=0}^{\ell} \int_{x_2=\ell}^{a} \frac{\ell^2 \cos^{-1}\frac{x_1}{\ell}}{\frac{1}{2}\pi} \, dx_1 \, dx_2,$$

$$= (a-\ell)\ell \left(1 - \frac{2}{\pi}\right) \quad (\text{fig. } 4.8). \qquad (4.10)$$

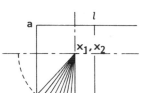

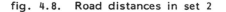

fig. 4.8. Road distances in set 2

$$rf_3(\ell) = rf_2(\ell).$$
(4.11)

$$rf_4(\ell) = \int_{x_1=0}^{\ell} \int_{x_2=\sqrt{\ell^2-x_1^2}}^{\ell} 1 - \frac{\cos^{-1}\frac{x_1}{\ell}}{\frac{1}{2}\pi} - \frac{\cos^{-1}\frac{x_2}{\ell}}{\frac{1}{2}\pi} \, dx_2 dx_1$$

$$= \ell^2 \left(1 - \frac{3}{\pi}\right) .$$
(4.12)

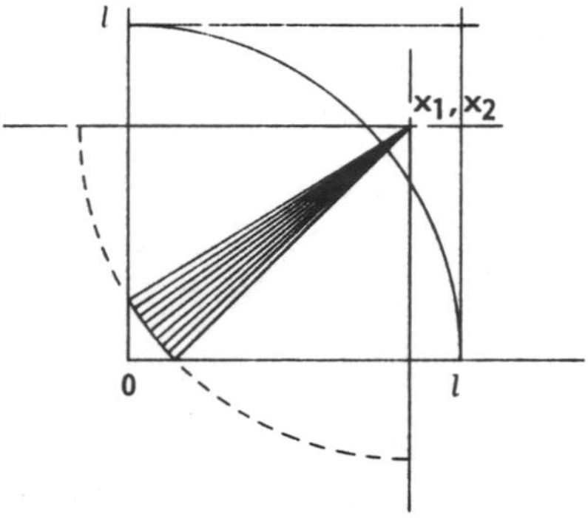

fig. 4.9.   Road distances in set 4

$$rf_5(\ell) = 0.$$

The road area density function is equal to the distance density function.

$$rf(\ell) = (a-\ell)^2 + 2\ell(a-\ell) \left(1-\frac{2}{\pi}\right) + \ell^2\left(1 - \frac{3}{\pi}\right) + 0$$

$$= a^2 - \frac{4a\ell}{\pi} + \frac{\ell^2}{\pi} \qquad\qquad 0 < \ell < a \qquad (4.13)$$

Now distances ℓ, $a < \ell < a\sqrt{2}$ are considered; 2 sets of points inside the square are of interest (fig 4.10).

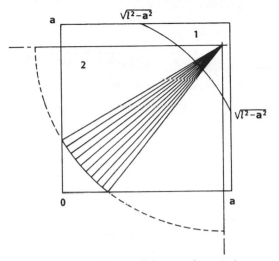

fig. 4.10. Road distances in set 1

$$rf_1(\ell) = \int_{x_1=\sqrt{\ell^2-a^2}}^{a} \int_{x_2=\sqrt{\ell^2-x_1^2}}^{a} \left(1 - \frac{\cos^{-1}\frac{x_1}{\ell}}{\frac{1}{2}\pi} - \frac{\cos^{-1}\frac{x_2}{\ell}}{\frac{1}{2}\pi}\right)dx_2\,dx_1,$$

$$= a^2 + \frac{4a}{\pi}\sqrt{\ell^2-a^2} - \frac{2a^2}{\pi} - \frac{\ell^2}{\pi} - 4a^2\cos^{-1}\frac{a}{\ell} \qquad (4.14)$$

$$rf_2(\ell) = 0. \qquad (4.15)$$

Concluding the road area density function in a square using an Euclidean distance measure is:

$$rf(\ell) = \begin{cases} a^2 - \frac{4a\ell}{\pi} + \frac{\ell^2}{\pi} & 0 \leqslant \ell \leqslant a \\[2mm] a^2 + \frac{4a}{\pi}\sqrt{\ell^2-a^2} - \frac{2a^2}{\pi} - \frac{\ell^2}{\pi} - 4a^2\cos^{-1}\frac{a}{\ell} & a \leqslant \ell \leqslant a\sqrt{2} \qquad (4.16) \\[2mm] 0 & \text{otherwise} \end{cases}$$

(this road area density function is completely equal to the distance density function in a square).

4.1.3. $p = \infty$

Fig. 3.15 and 3.16 are of interest for the calculation of the road area density function.

Considering $0 < \ell < a$ we find:

$$rf_1(\ell) = (a-\ell)^2. \tag{4.17}$$

$$rf_2(\ell) = \int_{x_1=0}^{\ell} \int_{x_2=\ell}^{a} \frac{x_1}{\ell}\, dx_1 dx_2 = (a-\ell)\frac{1}{2}\ell. \tag{4.18}$$

$$rf_3(\ell) = \int_{x_1=\ell}^{a} \int_{x_2=0}^{\ell} \frac{x_2}{\ell}\, dx_1 dx_2 = \frac{1}{2}\ell\,(a-\ell). \tag{4.19}$$

$$rf_4(\ell) = 0. \tag{4.20}$$

The road area density function in this case becomes:

$$rf(\ell) = \begin{cases} (a-\ell)^2 + 2.\frac{1}{2}\ell\,(a-\ell) = a(a-\ell) & 0 < \ell < a \\ 0 & \text{otherwise} \end{cases} \tag{4.21}$$

The relative road area density function is:

$$rf^r(\ell) = \begin{cases} \dfrac{2}{a^3}\,a(a-\ell) = \dfrac{2(a-\ell)}{a^2} & 0 < \ell < a \\ 0 & \text{otherwise} \end{cases} \tag{4.22}$$

The expected value $E\ell$ of the road distance related to the expected area that will be covered with roads is:

$$E\ell = \int_\ell \ell rf^r(\ell)d\ell = \frac{1}{3}a\ . \tag{4.23}$$

4.2. The road area density function in a rectangle

Consider a rectangle (a, b; b < a); density functions with Min-kowski distance measures for p = 1, p = 2 and p = ∞ are succesively cal-culated.

4.2.1. p = 1

First distances 0<ℓ<b are viewed; only a quarter of all possible road distances need to be considered because of symmetry.

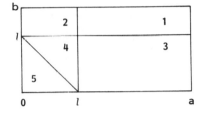

fig. 4.11. $0 \leqslant l \leqslant b$; 5 sets of points

Of course, the calculations for a rectangle differ not basically from the calculations in a square; only the results will be mentioned here.

$$rf_1(\ell) = (a-\ell)(b-\ell). \tag{4.24}$$

$$rf_2(\ell) = (b-\ell) \int_{x_1=0}^{\ell} \frac{\frac{1}{2}\ell^2 - \frac{1}{2}(\ell-x_1)^2}{\frac{1}{2}\ell^2} dx_1 = \frac{2}{3}\ell(b-\ell). \tag{4.25}$$

$$rf_3(\ell) = \frac{2}{3}\ell(a-\ell). \tag{4.26}$$

$$rf_4(\ell) = \int_{x_1=0}^{\ell} \int_{x_2=\ell-x_1}^{\ell} \frac{\frac{1}{2}\ell^2 - \frac{1}{2}(\ell-x_1)^2 - \frac{1}{2}(\ell-x_2)^2}{\frac{1}{2}\ell^2} dx_2 dx_1 = \frac{1}{3}\ell^2. \tag{4.27}$$

$$rf_5(\ell) = 0. \tag{4.28}$$

Summing these results gives:

$$rf(\ell) = ab - \frac{1}{3} \ell(a+b); \text{ if } \ell = 0 \ rf(0) = ab, \text{ if } \ell = b, \ rf(b) = \frac{1}{3} b(2a-b)$$

Now road distances ℓ, $b < \ell < a$ are considered.

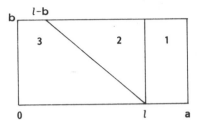

fig. 4.12. $b \leqslant l \leqslant a$; 3 sets of points

We have 3 sets of points in this case:

$$rf_1(\ell) = \int_{x_1=\ell}^{a} \int_{x_2=0}^{b} \frac{\frac{1}{2}\ell^2 - \frac{1}{2}(\ell-x_2)^2}{\frac{1}{2}\ell^2} \, dx_2 dx_1 =$$

$$= (a-\ell)b + \frac{(a-\ell)(\ell-b)^3}{3\ell^2} - \frac{1}{3}(a-\ell)\ell = \frac{(a-\ell)b^2(\ell-\frac{1}{3}b)}{\ell^2} \quad (4.29)$$

$$rf_2(\ell) = \int_{x_1=\ell-b}^{\ell} \int_{x_2=\ell-x_1}^{b} \frac{\frac{1}{2}\ell^2 - \frac{1}{2}(\ell-x_1)^2 - \frac{1}{2}(\ell-x_2)^2}{\frac{1}{2}\ell^2} \, dx_2 dx_1$$

$$= \frac{b^3(2\ell-b)}{3\ell^2}. \quad (4.30)$$

$$rf_3(\ell) = 0. \quad (4.31)$$

So the road area density function for $b < \ell < a$ is:

-78-

$$rf(\ell) = (a-\ell)b + \frac{(a-\ell)(\ell-b)^3}{3\ell^2} - \frac{1}{3}(a-\ell)\ell + \frac{b^3(2\ell-b)}{3\ell^2}$$

$$= \frac{b^2(3\ell-b)(a+b)}{3\ell^2} - b^2 \tag{4.32}$$

If $\ell=b$, $rf(b) = (a-b)b - \frac{1}{3}(a-b)b + \frac{b^3 b}{3b^2} =$

$$= ab-b^2 - \frac{1}{3}ab + \frac{1}{3}b^2 + \frac{1}{3}b^2 = \frac{1}{3}b(2a-b).$$

If $\ell=a$, $rf(a) = \frac{(2a-b)\,b^3}{3a^2}$.

Finally consider $a < \ell < a+b$; 2 sets of points have to be examined (fig. 4.13).

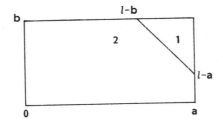

fig. 4.13. $a \leqslant l \leqslant a+b$, 2 sets of points

$$rf_1(\ell) = \int\limits_{x_1=\ell-b}^{a} \int\limits_{x_2=\ell-x_1}^{b} \frac{\frac{1}{2}\ell^2 - \frac{1}{2}(\ell-x_1)^2 - \frac{1}{2}(\ell-x_2)^2}{\frac{1}{2}\ell^2} \, dx_2 dx_1$$

$$= \frac{1}{3\ell^2}\left(b(\ell-a)^3 + a(\ell-b)^3 + 3ab\ell^2 - 3a^2\ell^2 - 3b^2\ell^2 + 3a^3\ell + 3b^3\ell -\right.$$

$$\left. - a^4 - b^4\right). \tag{4.33}$$

If $\ell = a$, $rf(a) = \frac{(2a - b)b^3}{3a^2}$; if $\ell = a+b$, $rf(a+b) = 0$.

$rf_2(\ell) = 0.$

Summarising:

$$rf(\ell) = \begin{cases} ab - \frac{1}{3}\ell(a+b) & 0 < \ell < b \\[2mm] \frac{b^2(a+b)(3\ell-b)}{3\ell^2} - b^2 & b < \ell < a \\[2mm] \frac{1}{3\ell^2}\left(b(\ell-a)^3 + a(\ell-b)^3 + 3ab\ell^2 - 3a^2\ell^2 - 3b^2\ell^2 \right. \\[2mm] \left. + 3a^3\ell + 3b^3\ell - a^4 - b^4\right) & a < \ell < a+b \\[2mm] 0 & \text{otherwise} \end{cases} \qquad (4.34)$$

The relative road area density function:

$$rf^r(\ell) = \frac{rf(\ell)}{-\frac{4}{9}a^3 + \frac{1}{9}b^3 - ab(a+b) + \frac{ab(a^2+b^2) + a^4 + b^4}{3(a+b)} - \frac{b^4}{3a} + b^2(a+b)\log\frac{a}{b} +}$$
$$+ (ab(a+b) + a^3b^3)\log\frac{a+b}{a}. \qquad (4.35)$$

If $a = b$ we find $rf^r(\ell) = \dfrac{rf(\ell)}{4a^3\log2 - 2a^3}$.

The expected value $E\ell$ of the road distance related to the expected area of the rectangle that will be covered with roads is: (c is the denominator of (4.35))

$$E\ell = \frac{1}{c}\left\{-\frac{1}{12}a^4 + \frac{1}{12}b^4 + \frac{2}{3}a^2b^2 + \frac{1}{3}ab(a^2+b^2) - \frac{1}{3}ab(a^2+b^2)\log(a+b) - \right.$$

$$\left. \frac{1}{3}(a^4+b^4)\log(a+b) + \frac{1}{3}b^4(\log a + \log b) + \frac{1}{3}a^3(a+b)\log a\right\}. \qquad (4.36)$$

if $a = b$, $E\ell = \dfrac{\frac{4}{3}a^4 - \frac{4}{3}a^4\log2}{4a^3\log2 - 2a^3} = \dfrac{\frac{2}{3}a(1-\log2)}{(2\log2 - 1)}$.

4.2.2. p = 2.

The road area density function is equal to the distance density function when Euclidean distances are used; these results are mentioned in 3.2.2.

4.2.3. p = ∞

Assume $0 < \ell < b$; there are 4 relevant sets of points inside the square (fig. 3.29). The results for each set are:

$$rf_1(\ell) = (a-\ell)(b-\ell). \tag{4.37}$$

$$rf_2(\ell) = \int_{x_1=0}^{\ell} \int_{x_2=\ell}^{b} \frac{x_1}{\ell} \, dx_1 dx_2 = \frac{1}{2}\ell(b-\ell). \tag{4.38}$$

$$rf_3(\ell) = \int_{x_1=\ell}^{x_1=a} \int_{x_2=0}^{\ell} \frac{x_2}{\ell} \, dx_1 dx_2 = \frac{1}{2}\ell(a-\ell). \tag{4.39}$$

$$rf_4(\ell) = 0. \tag{4.40}$$

So $rf(\ell)$, $0 < \ell < b$ is:

$$\tag{4.41}$$

$$rf(\ell) = (a-\ell)(b-\ell) + \frac{1}{2}\ell(a+b-2\ell).$$

$b < \ell < a$; the square contains 2 sets of interest (fig. 3.30).

$$rf_1(\ell) = \int_{x_1=\ell}^{a} \int_{x_2=0}^{b} \frac{x_2}{\ell} \, dx_2 dx_1 = \frac{1}{2}\frac{b^2}{\ell}(a-\ell). \tag{4.42}$$

$$rf_2(\ell) = 0. \tag{4.43}$$

Concluding the complete road area density function in a rectangle is:

$$
rf(\ell) = \begin{cases}
(a-\ell)(b-\ell) + \frac{1}{2}(a+b-2\ell) & 0 < \ell < b \\
\frac{b^2}{2\ell}(a-\ell) & b < \ell < a \\
0 & \text{otherwise}
\end{cases} \qquad (4.44)
$$

The relative road area density function $rf^r(\ell)$ is:

$$
rf^r(\ell) = \frac{1}{c} rf(\ell); \text{ where } c = \frac{1}{4} ab(b-a) + \frac{1}{2} b^3 + \frac{1}{2} ab^2 \log \frac{a}{b}; \qquad (4.45)
$$

and the expected value $E\ell$ of the road distance related to the expected area of the rectangle that will be covered with roads becomes

$$
E\ell = \int_\ell rf^r(\ell)\, \ell \, d\ell,
$$

$$
= \frac{1}{c}\left(\frac{1}{12} b^2(-2ab + 3a^2 + b^2)\right) = \frac{b(3a^2 - 2ab + b^2)}{3(2b^2 - a^2 + ab + 2ab \log \frac{a}{b})}, \qquad (4.46)
$$

if a=b one will find $E\ell = \frac{a.2a^2}{3.2a^2} = \frac{1}{3} a$; a result obtained earlier (4.23).

5 Contact distributions

In order to establish a contact, two different points are needed, each consuming a certain amount of space. According to (2.3.3.) there is a direct relation between our distance distribution and this contact distribution; one can find the contact density function by multiplying the distance density function by $\mu \{S(q, \ell)\}$ which is a measure for the number of points at distance ℓ from a point q, which is in the case of

p = 1: $4\ell\sqrt{2}$,

p = 2: $2\pi\ell$,

p = ∞: 8ℓ.

In this chapter the contact distribution will be calculated for a square, a rectangle and a circle continuously filled with points (5.1) and also filled with points in a discrete way (5.2).

5.1. Points continuously distributed

A measure for the number of contacts at distance ℓ, starting in a point is the length of the circumference of the circle (ℓ) (in case p = 2), as far as it is located inside the defined shape (fig. 5.1).

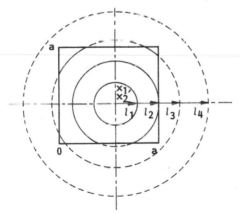

fig. 5.1. Contacts at distance l; from (x_1, x_2)

Using the results of the distance density function the contact density function will be presented for a square, a rectangle and a circle.

5.1.1. The square

5.1.1.1. p = 1.

The contact density function of (ℓ) on a square is calculated as follows:

$$cf(\ell) = \begin{cases} (a^2 - a\ell + \frac{1}{6}\ell^2)\ell\sqrt{2} & 0 < \ell < a \\[2mm] \dfrac{(2a-\ell)^3}{6\ell}\ell\sqrt{2} & a < \ell < 2a \\[2mm] 0 & \text{otherwise} \end{cases} \qquad (5.1)$$

The distance density function is multiplied by $\ell\sqrt{2}$ since one quarter of all possible distances are considered.

$$\int_{\ell=0}^{2a} cf(\ell)d\ell = \frac{a^4}{4} \text{ and therefore,}$$

$$cf^r(\ell) = \begin{cases} \dfrac{4\ell}{a^4}(a^2 - a\ell + \frac{1}{6}\ell^2)\sqrt{2} & 0 < \ell < a \\[2mm] \dfrac{2}{3a^4}(2a-\ell)^3\sqrt{2} & a < \ell < 2a \\[2mm] 0 & \text{otherwise} \end{cases} \qquad (5.2)$$

The expected value $E\ell$ is:

$$E\ell = \int_\ell \ell \, cf^r(\ell) \, d\ell = \frac{2}{3}a. \qquad (5.3)$$

In order to get an impression of the shape of this density function, it is plotted in one picture for a = 20, 40, 60, 80 and 100. One can observe clearly that the shape is becoming flatter as the square is increasing.

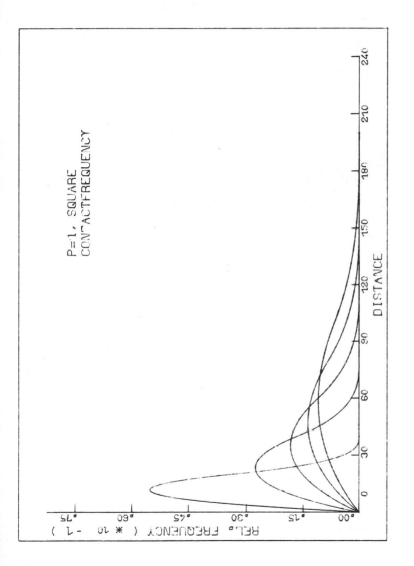

fig.5.2   Contact density functions; a=20,40,60,80 and 100

5.1.1.2. $\underline{p = 2}$.

The contact density function is found by multiplying the distance density function by $\frac{1}{2}\,\pi\ell$ (a quarter of all distances ℓ) so:

$$
cf(\ell) = \begin{cases}
\left(a^2 - \dfrac{4a\ell}{\pi} + \dfrac{\ell^2}{\pi}\right) \dfrac{\pi}{2}\,\ell & 0 \leqslant \ell \leqslant a \\[2ex]
\left(a^2 + \dfrac{4a}{\pi}\sqrt{\ell^2-a^2} - \dfrac{2a^2}{\pi} - \dfrac{\ell^2}{\pi} - \dfrac{4a^2}{\pi}\cos^{-1}\dfrac{a}{\ell}\right) \dfrac{\pi}{2}\,\ell & a \leqslant \ell \leqslant a\sqrt{2} \\[2ex]
0 & \text{otherwise,}
\end{cases}
$$

$$(5.4)$$

and

$$
cf^{r}(\ell) = \begin{cases}
\dfrac{4}{a^4}\left(a^2 - \dfrac{4a\ell}{\pi} + \dfrac{\ell^2}{\pi}\right) \dfrac{\pi}{2}\,\ell & 0 \leqslant \ell \leqslant a \\[2ex]
\dfrac{4}{a^4}\left(a^2 + \dfrac{4a}{\pi}\sqrt{\ell^2-a^2} - \dfrac{2a^2}{\pi} - \dfrac{\ell^2}{\pi} - \dfrac{4a^2}{\pi}\cos^{-1}\dfrac{a}{\ell}\right) \dfrac{\pi}{2}\,\ell & a \leqslant \ell \leqslant a\sqrt{2} \\[2ex]
0 & \text{otherwise.}
\end{cases}
$$

$$(5.5)$$

The expected value becomes:

$$
E\ell = 2a\left(\frac{1}{15} + \frac{1}{30}\sqrt{2} + \frac{1}{6}\log(\sqrt{2}+1)\right)
$$
$$
= .521a \text{ (this result was also obtained by De Smith (1977)).}
$$

5.1.1.3. $\underline{p = \infty}$.

$$
cf(\ell) = \begin{cases}
(a-\ell)(a-\frac{1}{2}\ell)\,2\ell & 0 \leqslant \ell \leqslant a \\[1ex]
0 & \text{otherwise,}
\end{cases}
$$

$$(5.7)$$

and

$$cf^r(\ell) = \begin{cases} \dfrac{4}{a^4}\,(a-\ell)\,(a-\tfrac{1}{2}\ell)\,2\ell & 0 \leqslant \ell \leqslant a \\ 0 & \text{otherwise.} \end{cases} \qquad (5.8)$$

Finally, the expected value becomes:

$$E\ell = \frac{7}{15}\,a = .466\ a. \qquad (5.9)$$

This function is also plotted for a = 20, 40, 60, 80 and 100 (fig. 5.3).

5.1.2. The rectangle

A somewhat more general case, discussed here, considers a rectangular shape (a x b; b ≤ a); only the results of a number of contact density functions will be presented.

5.1.2.1. p = 1.

$$cf(\ell) = \begin{cases} (ab - \tfrac{1}{2}(a+b)\ell + \tfrac{1}{6}\ell^2)\ \ell\sqrt{2} & 0 \leqslant \ell \leqslant b \\[2mm] (a - \ell + \tfrac{1}{3}b)\,\dfrac{b^2}{2\ell}\,\ell\sqrt{2} & b \leqslant \ell \leqslant a \\[2mm] \dfrac{(b+a-\ell)^3}{6\ell}\,\ell\sqrt{2} & a \leqslant \ell \leqslant a+b \\[2mm] 0 & \text{otherwise} \end{cases} \qquad (5.10)$$

$$cf^r(\ell) = \begin{cases} \dfrac{4\ell}{a^2b^2}\,(ab - \tfrac{1}{2}(a+b)\ell + \tfrac{1}{6}\ell^2)\ \sqrt{2} & 0 \leqslant \ell \leqslant b \\[2mm] (a - \ell + \tfrac{1}{3}b)\ \dfrac{2}{a^2}\cdot\sqrt{2} & b \leqslant \ell \leqslant a \\[2mm] \dfrac{(b+a-\ell)^3}{3}\,\dfrac{2}{a^2b^2}\,\sqrt{2} & a \leqslant \ell \leqslant a+b \\[2mm] 0 & \text{otherwise} \end{cases} \qquad (5.11)$$

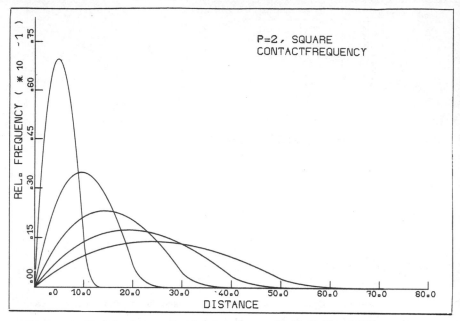

fig.5.3 Contact density functions;a=20,40,60,80 and 100

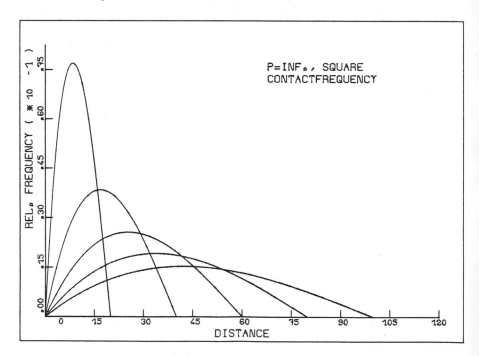

The expected distance contact in a rectangle is:

$$E\ell = \frac{1}{3} a + \frac{1}{3} b - \frac{a^3}{30b^2} + \frac{b^3}{30a^2}$$ (remember that, if a = b we found

$E\ell = \frac{2}{3} a$). (5.12)

This function is plotted for a = 100 and b =   20, 30, 40, 50, 60, 70, 80, 90 and 100 (fig. 5.4).

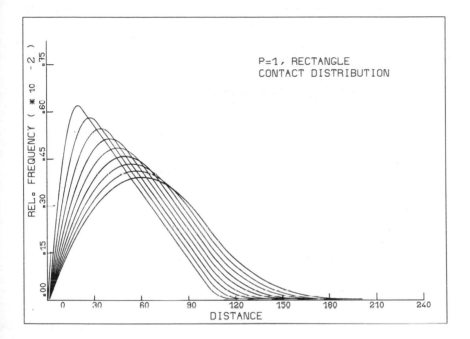

fig.5.4   Relative contact density functions, p=1

5.1.2.2. p = 2.

$$
cf(\ell) = \begin{cases}
(ab - \dfrac{2a\ell}{\pi} - \dfrac{2b\ell}{\pi} + \dfrac{\ell^2}{\pi}) \, \dfrac{\pi}{2} \, \ell & 0 < \ell < b \\[2ex]
(ab - \dfrac{2ab}{\pi} \cos^{-1} \dfrac{b}{\ell} + \dfrac{2a\sqrt{\ell^2-b^2}}{\pi} - \dfrac{2a\ell}{\pi} - \dfrac{b^2}{\pi}) \, \dfrac{\pi}{2} \, \ell & b < \ell < a \\[2ex]
(ab - \dfrac{2ab}{\pi} \cos^{-1} \dfrac{b}{\ell} + \dfrac{2a}{\pi} \sqrt{\ell^2-b^2} - \dfrac{2ab}{\pi} \cos^{-1} \dfrac{a}{\ell} + \dfrac{2b}{\pi} \sqrt{\ell^2-a^2} - \\[1ex]
\dfrac{a^2}{\pi} - \dfrac{b^2}{\pi} - \dfrac{\ell^2}{\pi}) \, \dfrac{\pi}{2} \, \ell & a < \ell < \sqrt{a^2+b^2} \\[2ex]
0 & \text{otherwise.}
\end{cases}
$$

(5.13)

$cf^r(\ell) = \dfrac{4}{a^2b^2}cf(\ell)$ (see De Smith (1977)).

The expected value is:

$$
E\ell = \frac{4}{a^2b^2} \left(\frac{a^5}{60} + \frac{b^5}{60} - \frac{(a^4+b^4)}{60} \sqrt{a^2+b^2} + \frac{a^2b^2}{20} \sqrt{a^2+b^2} + \frac{ab^4}{24} \log \left(\frac{a+\sqrt{a^2+b^2}}{a} \right) + \frac{a^4b}{24} \log \left(\frac{b+\sqrt{a^2+b^2}}{a} \right) \right) ;
$$

(5.14)

if a = b one finds indeed the result of a square, which is:

$$
E\ell = a(\frac{2}{15} + \frac{1}{15} \sqrt{2} + \frac{1}{3} \log(\sqrt{2}+1)) = .521a
$$

(5.15)

This function is plotted for a = 100 and b = 20, 40, 60, 80 and 100
(fig. 5.5).

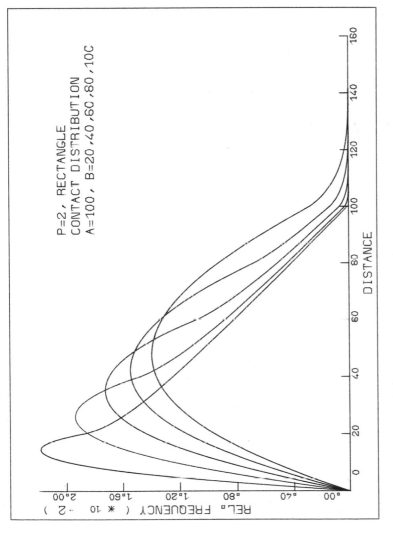

P=2, RECTANGLE
CONTACT DISTRIBUTION
A=100 , B=20,40,60,80,100

REL. FREQUENCY (* 10 ·· 2)

DISTANCE

fig.5.5   Relative contact density functions,p=2

5.1.2.3. $\underline{p = \infty}$

Using (3.74) the contact density function becomes:

$$
cf(\ell) = \begin{cases} (2ab - \frac{3}{2} a\ell - \frac{3}{2} b\ell + \ell^2)\ell & 0 \leq \ell \leq b \\[2mm] \dfrac{b^2}{2} (a-\ell) & b \leq \ell \leq a \\[2mm] 0 & \text{otherwise.} \end{cases} \tag{5.16}
$$

$$
cf^r(\ell) = \begin{cases} \dfrac{12}{3ab^3 - b^4 + a^3b} (2ab - \frac{3}{2} a\ell - \frac{3}{2} b\ell + \ell^2)\ell & 0 \leq \ell \leq b \\[2mm] \dfrac{12}{3ab^3 - b^4 + a^3b} \dfrac{1}{2} b\ell (a-\ell) & b \leq \ell \leq a \\[2mm] 0 & \text{otherwise} \end{cases} \tag{5.17}
$$

The expected value is:

$$
E\ell = \frac{\frac{3}{2} ab^3 - \frac{3}{5} b^4 + \frac{1}{2} a^4}{3ab^2 - b^3 + a^3} \; ;
$$

If $a = b$ we find $E\ell = \dfrac{7}{15} a$ (the result of the square). The function is plotted for $a = 100$, $b = 20$, 40, 60, 80 and 100 (fig. 5.6).

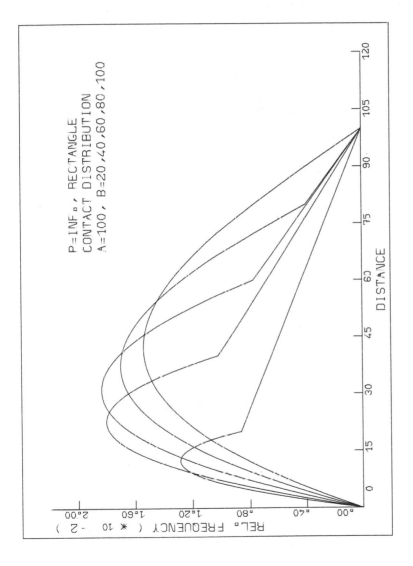

fig.5.6   Relative contact density functions, $p=\infty$

5.1.3. The contact distribution in a circle

5.1.3.1. p = 0

From 3.3.1 we know the distance density function in a circle with Euclidean distances; the contact density function is derived directly from the distance density function by multiplying the latter with $2\pi\ell$;

$$cf(\ell)_{p=2} = \frac{2\pi\ell}{\pi R^2} \left\{ 2R^2 \arccos\frac{\ell}{2R} - \frac{\ell}{2} \sqrt{4R^2-\ell^2} \right\} \tag{5.18}$$

$$= 4\ell \arccos\frac{\ell}{2R} - \frac{\ell^2}{R^2} \sqrt{4R^2-\ell^2} \qquad 0 < \ell < 2R$$

The relative contact density function is:

$$cf^r(\ell)_{p=2} = \frac{1}{\pi R^2} \left(4\ell \arccos\frac{\ell}{2R} - \sqrt{4R^2-\ell^2} \right) \qquad 0 < \ell < 2R \tag{5.19}$$

The expected value $E\ell$ is:

$$E\ell = \int_\ell \ell\, cf(\ell)^r\, d\ell = \frac{128R}{45\pi} = .905\ R \tag{5.20}$$

The contact distribution in a circle has been "reported" by many authors, e.g. Thanh, 1962; Hammersley, 1950; David and Fix, 1964; Lord, 1954; Fairthorne, 1964; Barton, David and Fix, 1963.

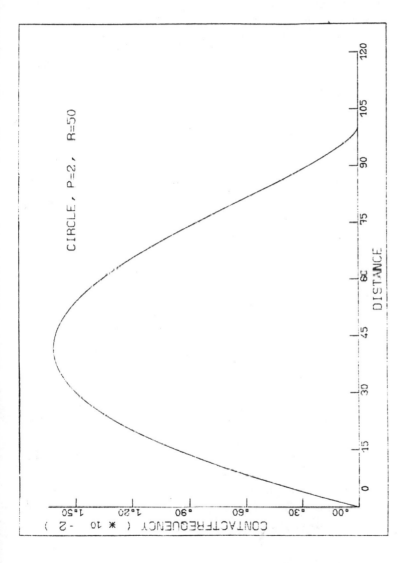

fig.5.7 Relative contact density functions. p=2

5.2. Points are distributed in a discrete way

In this section a number of special distributions of distances will be calculated. The square will be covered by a grid containing **equal** squared cells; each cell is represented by a point in the middle of it, and distances are measured between those points. The number of cells, so also the number of points, may vary. In order to define a distance 2 points are needed; all distances found between each pair should be arranged according to their value in order to produce a frequency distribution of distances. These distributions are only derived for p=1 and p=∞.

An example

Let us, as an example, consider a square (a x a); this square should be covered by a grid; two different grids are considered, one that divides the square into 4 equal cells, the other divides the square into 16 equal cells (figure 5.8).

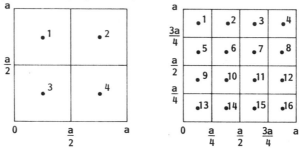

fig. 5.8. 2 squares with different grids

It depends on the grid how many cells, and therefore how many points and finally how many distances are found inside the square. The size of each cell is $\frac{a}{n}$ x $\frac{a}{n}$, so n^2 points are located inside the square.

In this example only Manhattan distances are considered; the distance between two points is d if the number of borders to be crossed in order to go from one point to another following rectangular roads amounts to d (see Kuiper, Paelinck, 1982). The following frequency distribution is obtained when all distances are counted:

1. Square with 4 points:

distance value $\downarrow$	point nr. $\rightarrow$	1	2	3	4	Total distances
	$\ell = 0$	1	1	1	1	4
	$\ell = 1$	2	2	2	2	8
	$\ell = 2$	1	1	1	1	4
	otherwise	0	0	0	0	$\dfrac{0}{16}+$

2. Square with 16 points:

distance value $\downarrow$	point nr $\rightarrow$	1	2	3	4	5	6	7	8	9	10	11	12	13	14	15	16	Total
	$\ell = 0$	1	1	1	1	1	1	1	1	1	1	1	1	1	1	1	1	16
	$\ell = 1$	2	3	3	2	3	4	4	3	3	4	4	3	2	3	3	2	48
	$\ell = 2$	3	4	4	3	4	6	6	4	4	6	6	4	3	4	4	3	68
	$\ell = 3$	4	4	4	4	4	4	4	4	4	4	4	4	4	4	4	4	64
	$\ell = 4$	3	3	3	3	3	1	1	3	3	1	1	3	3	3	3	3	40
	$\ell = 5$	2	1	1	2	1	0	0	1	1	0	0	1	2	1	1	2	16
	$\ell = 6$	1	0	0	1	0	0	0	0	0	0	0	0	1	0	0	1	4
	otherwise	0	0	0	0	0	0	0	0	0	0	0	0	0	0	0	0	$\dfrac{0}{256}+$

The total number of distances in case n=2 (4 points) is 16, if n=4 (16 points) there are 256 distances. In general one will find $(n^2)^2$ distances if n^2 points are located in the square.

In this case (with discrete points) it is also possible to derive, according to the definitions, both the distance distribution and the contact distribution.

Using definition (2.12) the distance frequency distribution is found by determining for each point in the relevant set the relative number of distances ℓ; summing over all points yields the complete distance frequency distribution. Consider point q, and (Manhattan) distance ℓ, $q \in A$ (fig. 5.9). The relative number of distances ℓ is calculated by

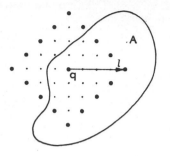

fig. 5.9.   Distribution of distances in the discrete case

counting the number of points at distance ℓ from q, located in A and
dividing this number by the total number of points at distance ℓ. Summing over all q, qϵA, yields the distance frequency distribution of ℓ.
According to definition (2.30) the number of contacts, starting in q, is
found by counting the number of points at distance ℓ from q located in
A. Summing this number for each q, qϵA, yields the absolute contact frequency distribution of ℓ.

Looking at both examples (with 4 points and 16 points), the distance frequency distribution and the contact frequency distribution will
be derived.

In example 1 the distance frequency is calculated as follows: $\ell=0$
was found 4 times; there are 4 points each having 1 point at distance
$\ell=0$, so the relative number of distances $\ell=0$ becomes $\frac{4}{4 \times 1} = 1$. $\ell=1$ was
found 8 times; for each point in the set the number of points at dis-
tance $\ell=1$ equals 4, so the distance frequency for $\ell=1$ becomes $\frac{8}{4 \times 4}$ and
for $\ell=2$, $\frac{4}{4 \times 8} = \frac{1}{8}$,   finally for $\ell \geqslant 3$ the frequency is 0.

For example 2 we find the distance frequencies:

$\ell=0$ $df(0) = \dfrac{16}{16 \times 1} = 1$

$\ell=1$ $df(1) = \dfrac{48}{16 \times 4} = \dfrac{3}{4}$

$\ell=2$ $df(2) = \dfrac{68}{16 \times 8} = \dfrac{17}{32}$

$\ell=3$ $df(3) = \dfrac{64}{16 \times 12} = \dfrac{1}{3}$

$\ell=4$ $df(4) = \dfrac{40}{16 \times 16} = \dfrac{5}{32}$

$\ell=5$ $df(\ell) = \dfrac{16}{16 \times 20} = \dfrac{1}{20}$

$\ell=6$ $df(\ell) = \dfrac{4}{16 \times 24} = \dfrac{1}{96}$

$\ell \geqslant 6$ $df(\ell) = 0$

The contact frequency distribution is mentioned in the last
column of both tables. The relative frequency is found by dividing the
absolute frequency by the total number of contacts which is $(n^2)^2=n^4$.
Both distance frequency distribution and the contact frequency distribution are plotted in fig. 5.10.

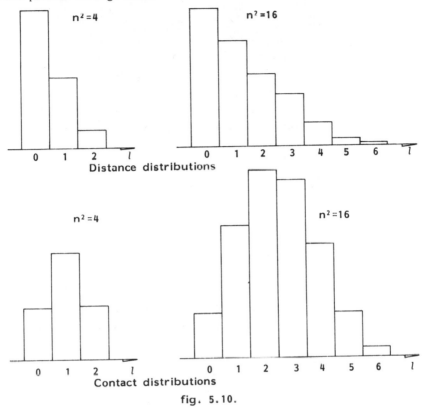

fig. 5.10.

After deriving the distance and contact frequency distribution for both
examples, these distributions will be derived in a more general way in a
square filled with n^2 points and a rectangle filled with mn points.

5.2.1. The square

In a square there are n^2 cells $(\frac{a}{n} \times \frac{a}{n})$. First the contact distribution will be derived; so all distances measured between points located

inside the square are arranged according to their value. After deriving
the contact frequency distribution the distance frequency distribution
can be found easily.

5.2.1.1. p = 1

Consider a point (i, j); the number of points (contacts) at distance ℓ amounts to 4ℓ if all points are situated inside the square. The
value of ℓ is restricted by the quotient $\frac{a}{n}$. Let α be the number of
steps $\frac{a}{n}$ between two points, then $\ell = \alpha \frac{a}{n}$. In fig. 5.11 there are 4 x 4
= 16 points at distance ℓ, $\ell = 4 \frac{a}{n}$ ($\alpha = 4$ in this example).

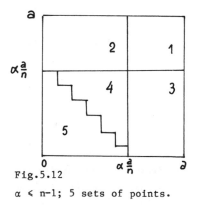

Fig. 5.11   points at distance $\ell = 4 \frac{a}{n}$.

The calculation of the exact distribution is done in 2 steps. Because of the symmetry only one quarter of all distances is considered
(fig. 5.12).
Step 1: $\alpha < n-1$.

Fig.5.12

$\alpha < n-1$; 5 sets of points.

A quarter of the possible
distances.

The square can be divided into 5 different sets.

set 1: all points α steps from each point in this set are located inside the square; so the number of distances becomes:

$$cf(\alpha) = \sum_{i=\alpha+1}^{n} \sum_{j=\alpha+1}^{n} \alpha = \alpha(n-\alpha)^2. \tag{5.21}$$

set 2: the number of distances α steps away from a point (i, j) in this set is computed by:

$$cf(\alpha) = \sum_{i=1}^{\alpha} \sum_{j=\alpha+1}^{n} i = (n-\alpha) \frac{1}{2} \alpha(\alpha+1). \tag{5.22}$$

set 3 is comparable with set 2:

$$cf(\alpha) = \sum_{i=\alpha+1}^{n} \sum_{j=1}^{\alpha} j - 1 = (n-\alpha) \frac{1}{2} \alpha(\alpha-1). \tag{5.23}$$

set 4:

$$cf(\alpha) = \sum_{i=2}^{\alpha} \sum_{j=\alpha-i+2}^{\alpha} i + j - \alpha - 1 = \frac{1}{6} \alpha(\alpha-1)(\alpha+1). \tag{5.24}$$

set 5: all points α steps away from all points in this set are located outside the square, so

$$cf(\alpha) = 0. \tag{5.25}$$

Since only one quarter of all distances starting in (i, j) are considered the contact frequency distribution $cf(\alpha)$ becomes:

$$cf(\alpha) = 4\{\alpha(n-\alpha)^2 + (n-\alpha) \frac{1}{2} \alpha(\alpha+1) + (n-\alpha) \frac{1}{2} \alpha(\alpha-1) + \frac{1}{6} \alpha(\alpha-1)(\alpha+1)\}$$

$$= 4\alpha\{(n-\alpha)^2 + (n-\alpha) \alpha + \frac{1}{6} (\alpha^2-1)\} \qquad \alpha \leqslant n-1. \tag{5.26}$$

$$cf(\alpha) = cf(\ell - \alpha \frac{a}{n}) \qquad \text{for } \alpha = 1, 2, \ldots, n-1.$$

Step 2: consider n < α < 2n-2; there are 2 relevant sets inside the square (fig. 5.13)

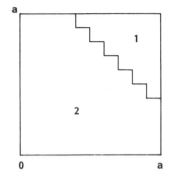

fig. 5.13.   2 sets of points; $n \leqslant a \leqslant 2n-2$

Set 1:

$$cf(\alpha) = \sum_{i=\alpha-n+2}^{n} \sum_{j=\alpha-1+2}^{n} i + j - \alpha - 1,$$

$$= \frac{1}{6} (2n-\alpha)(2n-\alpha-1)(2n-\alpha+1).$$

(5.27)

Set 2: all points at distance α steps from a point in this set, are located outside the square, so cf(α)= 0.

The result in this case is:

$$cf(\alpha) = \frac{2}{3} (2n-\alpha)(2n-\alpha-1)(2n-\alpha+1) \qquad n < \alpha < 2n-2,$$

$$cf(\ell = \alpha \frac{a}{n}) = cf(\alpha) \ , \ \alpha = n, n+1, \ldots, 2n-2.$$

(5.28)

The complete result of the whole square is (a x a) is:

$$
cf(\alpha) = \begin{cases}
n^2 & \alpha = 0 \\
4\alpha\left((n-\alpha)^2 + \alpha(n-\alpha) + \frac{1}{6}(\alpha^2-1)\right) & \alpha = 1, \ldots, n-1 \\
\frac{2}{3}(2n-\alpha)(2n-\alpha-1)(2n-\alpha+1) & \alpha = n, n+1, \ldots, 2n-2 \\
0 & \text{otherwise.}
\end{cases}
\tag{5.29}
$$

$$
cf(\ell = \alpha \frac{a}{n}) = cf(\alpha).
$$

We can use the result to check the outcomes of the example presented at the beginning of this section.

Example 1: $n = 2$, ($\frac{a}{n}$ was considered as 1 in that example), $\alpha = 0, 1, 2$.

$$
cf(\ell = 0) = 4.
$$

$$
cf(\ell = \frac{a}{2}) = 4. \; 1\left((2-1)^2 + 1 + \frac{1}{6}(1-1)\right) = 8.
$$

$$
cf(\ell = a) = \frac{2}{3}(4-2)(4-3)(4-1) = 4.
$$

$$
cf(\ell \neq \frac{a}{2}) = 0.
$$

Example 2: $n = 4$, $\alpha = 0, 1, 2, \ldots, 6$

$$
cf(\ell = 0) = n^2 = 16,
$$

$$
cf(\ell = \frac{a}{4}) = 4\left(3^2 + 3 + \frac{1}{6}(1-1)\right) = 48,
$$

$$
cf(\ell = \frac{a}{2}) = 8\left(2^2 + 4 + \frac{1}{6}3\right) = 68,
$$

$$
cf(\ell = \frac{3a}{4}) = 12\left(1 + 3 + \frac{1}{6}8\right) = 64,
$$

$$
cf(\ell = a) = \frac{2}{3}(8-4)(8-5)(8-3) = 40,
$$

$$cf(\ell = \frac{5a}{4}) = \frac{2}{3}(8-5)(8-6)(8-4) = 16,$$

$$cf(\ell = \frac{3a}{2}) = \frac{2}{3}(8-6)(8-7)(8-5) = 4,$$

$$cf(\ell > \frac{3a}{2}) = 0.$$

The results are equal to the results found by simply counting all distances.

If $n \to \infty$ all possible distances between 0 and 2a will appear because

$$0 \leqslant \alpha \leqslant 2n-2, \text{ so}$$

$$0 \frac{a}{n} \leqslant \alpha \frac{a}{n} \leqslant (2n-2)\frac{a}{n} \qquad \text{and as } \ell = \alpha \frac{a}{n}$$

$$0 \leqslant \ell \leqslant (2n-2)\frac{a}{n}$$

if $n \to \infty$, $0 \leqslant \ell \leqslant 2a$

If the number of points located inside the defined shape is increasing, the contact density function will approach the contact frequency distribution that is found if the space is continuously filled with points. This can be shown by considering a point (i,j) and the number of contacts at distance $\alpha \frac{a}{n}$, α being the number of steps and $\frac{a}{n}$ the distance value of each step; define $\ell \overset{\Delta}{=} \alpha \frac{a}{n}$.

Suppose the number of points between (i,j) and (i',j) (fig. 5.14) is increasing; then the value of $\frac{a}{n}$ will decrease and the number of steps will increase and so will the number of contacts represented by the number of points between (i,j') and (i',j) (in case Manhattan distances are considered those points are located on a straight line between (i,j') and (i',j); this is a quarter of all possible contacts).

If n approaches infinity, the number of contacts approaches infinity, being the number of points between (i,j') and (i',j). As a

measure for this number one can choose the distance between (i,j') and
(i',j) which equals $\ell\sqrt{2}$; this is exactly the same measure for the number
of contacts at distance ℓ from a point (i,j) as was defined by considering spaces continuously filled with points; the histograms of contact frequency distributions shown in this section illustrate this
point.

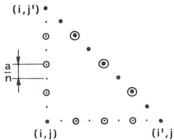

fig. 5.14. Contacts at distance $a\frac{a}{n}$ (a quarter of all contacts is shown)

As an illustration some contact distributions are shown; inside a
square (50 x 50) n^2 points are located, n = 10, 40 and 100 (fig. 5.15,
5.16, 5.17).

The relative distance frequency distribution is found by dividing
(5.29) by the total number of points that can be reached starting in
each point in the square; one can reach 4α points, α steps from each
point (this number equals 1 as $\alpha=0$), there are n^2 points inside the
square so (5.29) has to be divided by $4\alpha n^2$ in order to find the relative
distance frequency distribution:

$$df(\alpha) = \begin{cases} \dfrac{n^2}{n^2} & \alpha=0 \\[2ex] \dfrac{4\alpha\{(n-\alpha)^2 + \alpha(n-\alpha) + \frac{1}{6}(\alpha^2-1)\}}{4\alpha n^2} & \alpha=1,\ 2,\ \ldots,\ n-1 \\[2ex] \dfrac{\frac{2}{3}(2n+\alpha)(2n-\alpha-1)(2n-\alpha+1)}{4\alpha n^2} & \alpha=n,\ n+1,\ \ldots,\ 2n-2 \\[2ex] 0 & \text{otherwise} \end{cases}$$

(5.30)

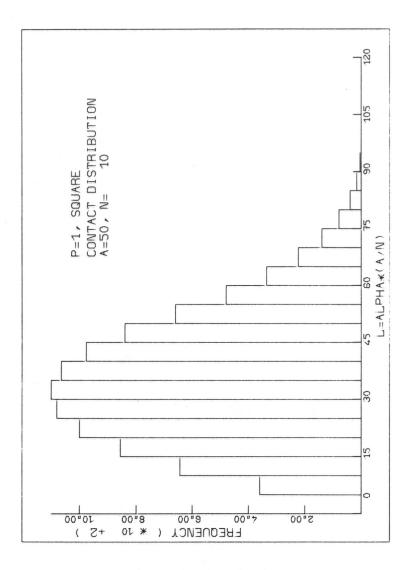

fig.5.15   Contact frequency distribution; 100 points

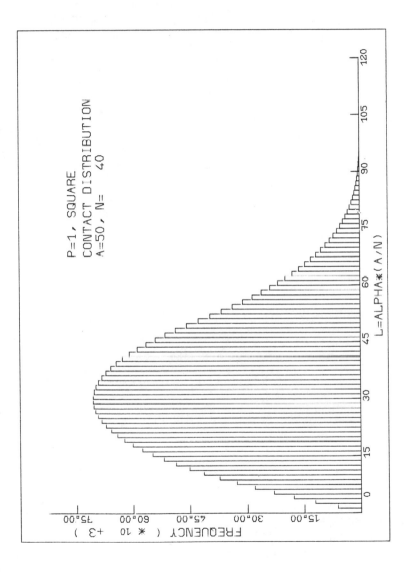

fig.5.16 Contact frequency distribution; 1600 points

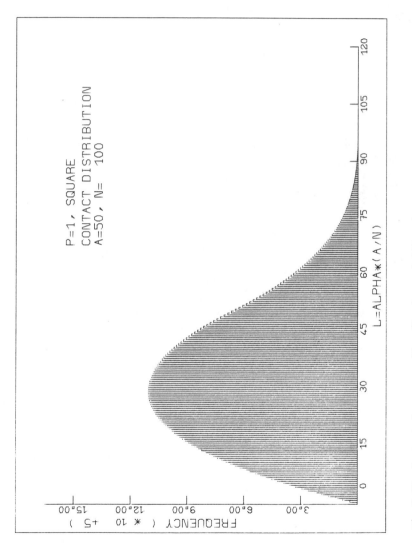

P=1, SQUARE
CONTACT DISTRIBUTION
A=50, N= 100

fig.5.17 Contact frequency distribution; 10,000 points

$$df(\alpha) = \begin{cases} 1 & \alpha=0 \\[2mm] \dfrac{1}{n^2}\{(n-\alpha)^2 + \alpha(n-\alpha) + \tfrac{1}{6}(\alpha^2-1)\} & \alpha=1,\ 2,\ \ldots,\ n-1 \\[3mm] \dfrac{(2n-\alpha)(2n-\alpha-1)(2n-\alpha+1)}{6\alpha n^2} & \alpha=n,\ n+1,\ \ldots,\ 2n-2. \\[3mm] 0 & \text{otherwise} \end{cases}$$

$$(5.31)$$

When the number of points is increasing this contact frequency distribution will approach (3.17), which is the distance density function in a square continuously filled with points. This can be proved in the following way:

$$df(\alpha) = \begin{cases} 1 & \alpha=0 \\[2mm] (1-\tfrac{\alpha}{n})^2 + \tfrac{\alpha}{n}(a-\tfrac{\alpha}{n}) + \tfrac{1}{n}((\tfrac{\alpha}{n})^2-\tfrac{1}{n^2}) & \alpha=1,\ 2,\ \ldots,\ n-1 \\[3mm] \tfrac{1}{6}(\tfrac{2n}{\alpha}-1)(2-\tfrac{\alpha}{n}-\tfrac{1}{n})(2-\tfrac{\alpha}{n}+\tfrac{1}{n}) & \alpha=n,\ n+1,\ \ldots,\ 2n-2. \end{cases}$$

$$(5.32)$$

$\ell = \alpha\,\dfrac{a}{n}$ and multiplying (5.32) by a^2 we find

$$df(\ell) = \begin{cases} a^2 & \ell=0 \\[2mm] (a-\ell)^2 + \ell(a-\ell) + \tfrac{1}{6}(\ell^2-(\tfrac{a}{n})^2) & \ell=\tfrac{a}{n},\ \ldots,\ a-\tfrac{a}{n} \\[3mm] \tfrac{1}{6}(\tfrac{2a-\ell}{\ell})(2a-\ell-\tfrac{a}{n})(2a-\ell+\tfrac{a}{n}) & \ell=a,\ \ldots,\ 2a-\tfrac{2a}{n} \end{cases}$$

$$(5.33)$$

As $n\to\infty$, $\dfrac{a}{n}\to 0$, so (5.33) = (3.17).

5.2.1.2. $p = \infty$

Considering a point (i, j) and a distance ℓ, the number of points at distance ℓ that can be visited amounts to 8ℓ (fig. 5.18).

fig. 5.18.   Points at distance L A quarter of all points

The contact frequency distribution is calculated by considering just a quarter of all distances ℓ.

The square should be divided into 4 sets of points (fig. 5.19)

Set 1: the number of points in this set is $(n-\alpha)^2$, so the distribution is:

$$cf(\alpha) = (n-\alpha)^2 \, 2\alpha. \tag{5.30}$$

Set 2: $cf(\alpha) = \sum_{i=1}^{\alpha} i \, \alpha(n-\alpha),$ $\tag{5.31}$

$$= \frac{1}{2} (n-\alpha) \, \alpha(\alpha+1).$$

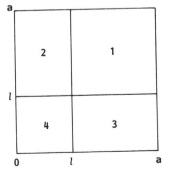

fig. 5.19.   p=∞; 4 sets of points

Set 3: $cf(\alpha) = (n-\alpha) \sum_{j=1}^{\alpha} j-1 = \frac{1}{2}(n-\alpha)\alpha(\alpha-1).$ (5.32)

Set 4 $cf(\alpha) = 0.$ (5.33)

Summing these results and multiplying by 4 yields the total contact frequency distribution:

$cf(\alpha) = n^2$ $\qquad\qquad \alpha = 0$

$cf(\alpha) = 4\alpha^3 - 8n^2\alpha - 12n\alpha^2,$
$\qquad = 4\alpha(n-\alpha)(2n-\alpha)$ $\qquad\qquad \alpha = 1, 2, \ldots, n-1.$
(5.34)

$cf(\ell) = cf(\ell = \alpha\frac{a}{n}) = cf(\alpha).$

This distribution shows the absolute number of distances; it is also possible to calculate the relative number, in which case

$cf^r(\alpha) = c\sum_{\alpha} cf(\alpha) = 1$
(5.35)

$cf^r(\alpha) = \frac{4\alpha(n-\alpha)(2n-\alpha) + n^2}{n^2(n-1)(n+1)}$ $\qquad\qquad \alpha = 0, 1, \ldots, n-1.$

The expected value of the contact distance can now be calculated.

$E\ell = E\alpha\frac{a}{n} = \frac{a}{n}E\alpha = \frac{a}{n}\frac{(n-1)(n+1)(7n^2+2)}{15n^3}$ (5.36)

$E\ell = \frac{7}{15}a - \frac{a}{3n^2} - \frac{2a}{15n^4} \; ; \; \text{if } n \to \infty \; E\ell = \frac{7}{15}a.$

This distribution is also plotted for n = 10, 40 and 100 (so 100, 1600 and 10,000 points respectively are located inside the square).

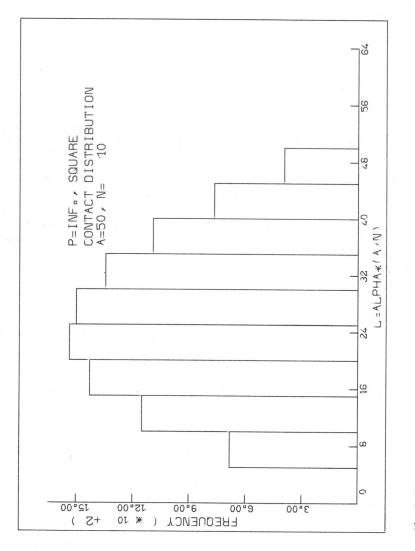

fig.5.20 Contact frequency distribution; 100 points

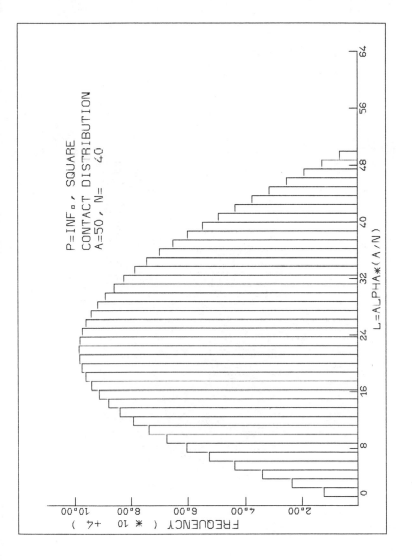

fig.5.21 Contact frequency distribution; 1600 points

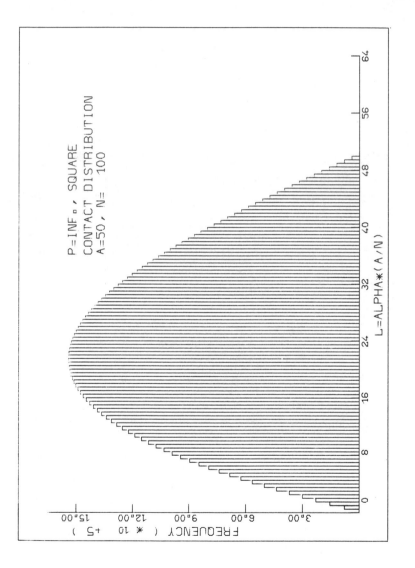

fig.5.22 Contact frequency distribution; 10,000 points

5.2.2. The rectangle

The rectangle (a x b, b < a) is covered by a grid containing cells of equal sizes; each cell should be located completely inside the rectangle so a relation exists between a and b depending on the number of cells inside the rectangle. Suppose the rectangle contains mn cells of equal size, so mn points (m < n); along the long axis there are n points, along the other axis there are m points (fig. 5.23).

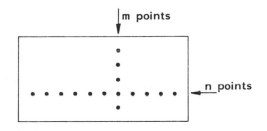

fig. 5.23.   mn cells inside the rectangle

Let us suppose the area of each cell is $(\frac{a}{n} \times \frac{a}{n})$; the rectangle is covered by equal cells so there are n cells on each row; the value of m is determined by the values of a and n and restricted by the value of b; m should be equal to the maximum number of cells that can be fitted on the rectangle vertically.

5.2.2.1. $\underline{p = 1}$

1. $\underline{\alpha \leqslant m-1}$

Consider just a quarter of all points that can be visited starting in (i, j), and first the south-west quarter. In this case there is a difference between the points in the south-west quarter in relation to the orientation of the rectangle; if the rectangle is turned 90 degrees, a shape is formed, different from the original with respect to the number of contacts. One has to consider both the south-west and the north-west quarter (the south-east and the north-east quarter yield the same result).

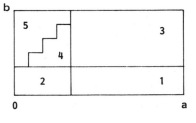

fig. 5.24. p=1; 5 sets of points   South-west quarter

set 1: $cf(\alpha) = \sum_{i=\alpha+1}^{n} \sum_{j=\alpha+1}^{m} \alpha$ $= (n-\alpha)(m-\alpha)\alpha,$ (5.37)

set 2: $cf(\alpha) = \sum_{i=1}^{\alpha} \sum_{j=\alpha+1}^{m} i$ $= (m-\alpha)\frac{1}{2}\alpha(\alpha+1),$ (5.38)

set 3: $cf(\alpha) = \sum_{i=\alpha+1}^{n} \sum_{j=1}^{\alpha} j-1$ $= (n-\alpha)\frac{1}{2}\alpha(\alpha-1),$ (5.39)

set 4: $cf(\alpha) = \sum_{i=2}^{\alpha} \sum_{j=\alpha-i+2}^{\alpha} i+j-\alpha-1$ $= \frac{1}{6}\alpha(\alpha-1)(\alpha+1),$ (5.40)

set 5: $cf(\alpha)$ $= 0.$ (5.41)

Now the north-west quarter is considered:

fig. 5.25.   North-west quarter

$$\text{set 1: } cf(\alpha) = \sum_{i=\alpha+1}^{n} \sum_{j=1}^{m-\alpha} \alpha = (n-\alpha)(m-\alpha)\,\alpha, \tag{5.42}$$

$$\text{set 2: } cf(\alpha) = \sum_{i=1}^{\alpha} \sum_{j=1}^{m-\alpha} i-1 = (m-\alpha)\,\frac{1}{2}\,\alpha(\alpha-1), \tag{5.43}$$

$$\text{set 3: } cf(\alpha) = \sum_{i=\alpha+1}^{n} \sum_{j=m-\alpha+1}^{m} m+1-j = (n-\alpha)\,\frac{1}{2}\,\alpha(\alpha+1), \tag{5.44}$$

$$\text{set 4: } cf(\alpha) = \sum_{i=2}^{\alpha} \sum_{j=m-\alpha+1}^{i-1+m-\alpha} i-j+m-\alpha = \frac{1}{6}\,\alpha(\alpha-1)(\alpha+1), \tag{5.45}$$

$$\text{set 5: } cf(\alpha) \qquad\qquad = 0. \tag{5.46}$$

The total contact frequency distribution is found by summing the results of all sets.

$$
\begin{aligned}
cf(\alpha) &= 4\,\alpha(n-\alpha)(m-\alpha) + 2(m-\alpha)\,\frac{1}{2}\,\alpha(\alpha-1) + 2(m-\alpha)\,\frac{1}{2}\,\alpha(\alpha+1) + 2(n-\alpha)\,\frac{1}{2}\,\alpha(\alpha+1) \\
&\quad + 2(n-\alpha)\,\frac{1}{2}\,\alpha(\alpha-1) + 4\,\frac{1}{6}\,\alpha(\alpha-1)(\alpha+1), \\
&= 4\alpha\{mn - \frac{1}{2}\,\alpha(m+n) + \frac{1}{6}\,(\alpha^2-1)\} \quad \alpha = 1, 2, \ldots, m-1.
\end{aligned}
\tag{5.47}
$$

$$cf(\ell = \alpha\,\frac{a}{n}) = cf(\alpha) \qquad \alpha = 1, \ldots, m-1.$$

2. $m \leqslant \alpha \leqslant n-1$

Also here, two quarters of possible contacts starting in (i, j) are considered separately; first the south-west quarter.

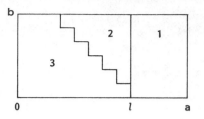

fig. 5.26. p=1; 3 sets of points (sw)

set 1: $cf(\alpha) = \sum\limits_{i=\alpha+1}^{n} \sum\limits_{j=1}^{m} j-1 = (n-\alpha)\frac{1}{2} m(m-1),$ (5.48)

set 2: $cf(\alpha) = \sum\limits_{i=\alpha-m+2}^{\alpha} \sum\limits_{j=\alpha+2-i}^{m} = \frac{1}{6} m^2 (m-1),$ (5.49)

set 3: $cf(\alpha) =$ $= 0.$ (5.50)

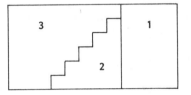

fig. 5.27. p=1; 3 sets of points (nw)

set 1: $cf(\alpha) = \sum\limits_{i=\alpha+1}^{n} \sum\limits_{j=1}^{m} m-j+1 = (n-\alpha)\frac{1}{2} m(m+1),$ (5.51)

set 2: $cf(\alpha) = \sum\limits_{i=\alpha-m+2}^{\alpha} \sum\limits_{j=1}^{i-\alpha+m-1} i-j+m-\alpha = \frac{1}{6} m^2(m-1),$ (5.52)

set 3: $cf(\alpha) =$ $= 0.$ (5.53)

The total contact frequency distribution becomes:

$cf(\alpha) = 2m^2(n-\alpha+ \frac{1}{3} (m-1))$ $\qquad \alpha = m,\ m+1,\ \ldots,\ n-1.$ (5.54)

$cf(\ell) = cf(\ell=\alpha \frac{a}{n}) = cf(\alpha)$ $\qquad \alpha = m,\ m+1,\ \ldots,\ n-1\ .$ (5.55)

3. $n \leqslant \alpha \leqslant m+n-1$

In this case just one quarter of all distances starting in (i, j) needs to be considered; the results are equal for each quarter one observes. (fig. 5.28).

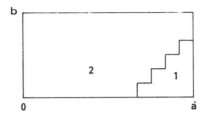

$$\text{fig. 5.28.} \quad p=1; \quad 2 \text{ sets of points}$$

set 1: $cf(\alpha) = \sum_{i=m+\alpha+2}^{n} \sum_{j=1}^{m-\alpha+i-1} i - j + m - \alpha = \frac{1}{6}(m+n-\alpha)(m+n-\alpha+1)(m+n-\alpha-1),$

$$(5.56)$$

set 2: $cf(\alpha) = \qquad\qquad\qquad\qquad 0. \qquad\qquad (5.57)$

So in this case

$$cf(\alpha) = \frac{2}{3}(m+n-\alpha)(m+n-\alpha+1)(m+n-\alpha-1) \quad \alpha=n, n+1, \ldots, m+n-1. \qquad (5.58)$$

Concluding: the contact frequency distribution in a rectangle $(a \times b)$ using a rectangular distance measure with mn points located in it in a very regular way is:

$$cf(\alpha) = \begin{cases} mn & \alpha = 0 \\ 4\alpha(mn - \frac{1}{2}(m+n) \; \alpha + \frac{1}{6}(\alpha^2 - 1)) & \alpha = 1, 2, \ldots, m-1 \\ 2m^2 (n-\alpha + \frac{1}{3}(m-1)) & \alpha = m, m+1, \ldots, n-1 \\ \frac{2}{3}(m+n-\alpha)(m+n-\alpha+1)(m+n-\alpha-1) & \alpha = n, n+1, \ldots, m+n-2 \\ 0 & \text{otherwise} \end{cases}$$

$$(5.59)$$

If m = n we find

$$cf(\alpha) = \begin{cases} n^2 & \alpha = 0 \\ 4\alpha \ (n^2 - n\alpha + \frac{1}{6} \ (\alpha^2-1)) & \alpha = 1, \ 2, \ \ldots, \ n-1 \\ \frac{2}{3} \ (2n-\alpha) \ (2n-\alpha-1) \ (2n-\alpha+1) & \alpha = n, \ n+1. \ \ldots, \ 2n-2 \\ 0 & \text{otherwise} \end{cases}$$

i.e. the result for a square. (5.60)

This result is plotted for a few examples:
a = 200, b = 50, m = 10, n = 40
a = 100, b = 25, m = 5, n = 20
a = 400, b = 100, m = 20, n = 80
a = 300, b = 75, m = 15, n = 60 (fig. 5.30, 5.31, 5.32, and 5.33).

5.2.2.2. p = ∞

1. α ⩽ m-1

The south-west and north-west quarter of all possible distances should be considered again separately; first the south-west quarter.

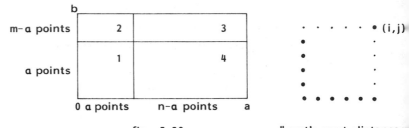

fig. 5.29.   "south-west distances"

set 1: cf(α) = = 0, (5.61)

set 2: $cf(\alpha) = \sum\limits_{i=1}^{\alpha} \ \sum\limits_{j=\alpha+1}^{m} i = (m-\alpha) \ \frac{1}{2} \ \alpha \ (\alpha+1),$ (5.62)

-120-

set 3: $cf(\alpha) = \sum\limits_{i=\alpha+1}^{n} 2\alpha\,(m-\alpha)$ $= (n-\alpha)\,2\alpha(m-\alpha),$ (5.63)

set 4: $cf(_a) = \sum\limits_{j=1}^{\alpha} (j-1)(n-\alpha)$ $= (n-\alpha)\,\dfrac{1}{2}\,\alpha\,(\alpha-1).$ (5.64)

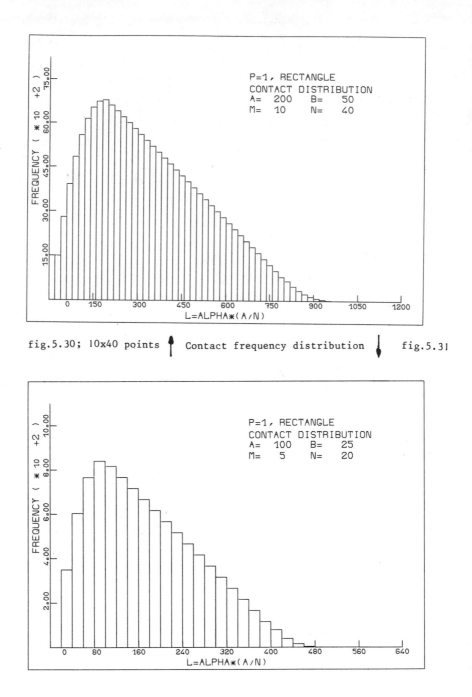

fig.5.30; 10x40 points ⬆ Contact frequency distribution ⬇ fig.5.31

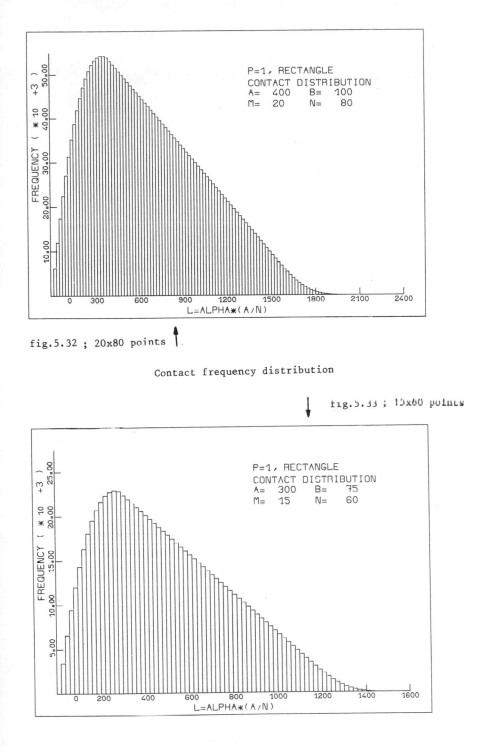

fig.5.32 ; 20x80 points ↑.

Contact frequency distribution

↓ fig.5.33 ; 15x60 points

Now the north-west quarter of possible distances is examined.

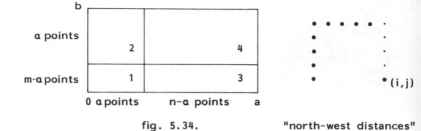

fig. 5.34.   "north-west distances"

set 1: $cf(\alpha) = \sum\limits_{i=1}^{\alpha} (i-1)(m-\alpha)$ $= (m-\alpha)\frac{1}{2}\alpha(\alpha-1),$ (5.65)

set 2: $cf(\alpha) =$ $= 0,$ (5.66)

set 3: $cf(\alpha) = \sum\limits_{j=m-\alpha+1}^{m} (m-j+1)(n-\alpha)$ $= (n-\alpha)\frac{1}{2}\alpha(\alpha+1),$ (5.67)

set 4: $cf(\alpha) = \sum\limits_{i=\alpha+1}^{n} 2\alpha(m-\alpha)$ $= (n-\alpha)(m-\alpha)2\alpha.$ (5.68)

The total contact distribution is:

$$cf(\alpha) = 4\alpha(2mn - \frac{3}{2}\alpha(m+n) + \alpha^2) \qquad \alpha = 1, 2, \ldots, m-1. \qquad (5.69)$$

2. $m \leqslant \alpha \leqslant n - 1$

The contribution of the south-west quarter to the contact frequency distribution is:

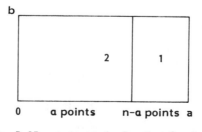

fig. 5.35. $m \leqslant a \leqslant n-1$; 2 sets of points

set 1: $cf(\alpha) = \sum\limits_{j=1}^{m} (n-\alpha)(j-1) = (n-\alpha)\dfrac{1}{2} m (m-1),$ \hfill (5.70)

set 2: $cf(\alpha) = 0$ \hfill (5.71)

The north-west quarter: (fig. 5.33)

set 1: $cf(\alpha) = \sum\limits_{j=1}^{m} (n-\alpha)(m-j+1) = (n-\alpha)\dfrac{1}{2} m (m-1),$ \hfill (5.72)

set 2: $cf(\alpha) = 0$ \hfill (5.73)

So the contact frequency distribution is:

$$cf(\alpha) = 2(n-\alpha)\dfrac{1}{2} m (m-1) + 2(n-\alpha)\dfrac{1}{2} m (m+1),$$

$$= 2 m^2 (n-\alpha) \qquad \alpha = m,\ m+1,\ \ldots,\ n-1. \hfill (5.74)$$

Finally, the complete contact distribution in a rectangle covered with mn equal cells, using $p = \infty$ is:

$$cf(\alpha) = \begin{cases} mn & \alpha = 0 \\ 4\alpha\ (2mn - \dfrac{3}{2}\alpha\ (m+n) + \alpha^2) & \alpha = 1,\ 2,\ \ldots,\ m-1 \\ 2m^2\ (n-\alpha) & \alpha = m,\ m+1,\ \ldots,\ n-1 \\ 0 & \text{otherwise} \end{cases} \hfill (5.75)$$

As an illustration some of these contact distributions are plotted:

$a = 400 \quad b = 100$

$n = 80 \quad m = 20 \quad$, and

$a = 100 \quad b = 25$

$n = 20 \quad m = 5$, fig. 5.36 and 5.37.

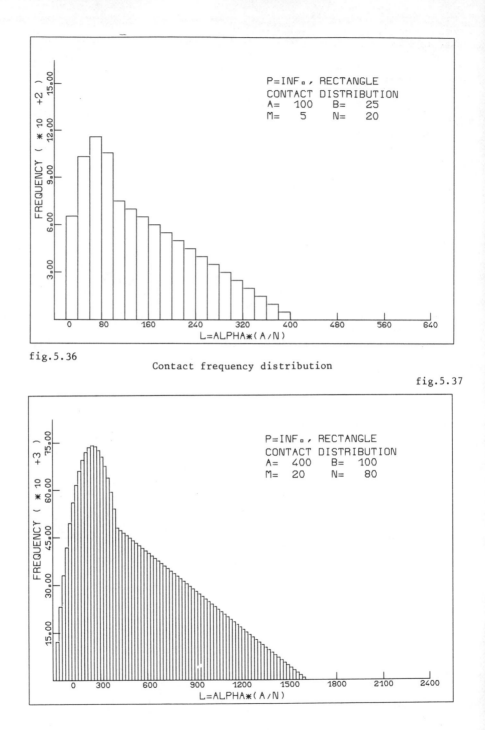

fig.5.36

Contact frequency distribution

fig.5.37

6 Distributions of distances in some special cases

6.1 The distance density function in two squares

It can be interesting to know something about the distribution of distances between separate areas; one can think of commuting or distribution problems. In two or more separate areas a number of objects are considered, which are related to a number of other objects on another spot. Between those groups one can use just one value for the distance between each individual object of each group; this should be, in a way, an average distance. For example one can think of the distance between two cities, for which a distance often the length of the road between both city centres is chosen. Especially when big cities are concerned, not too far away from each other, there will be a large inaccuracy in using one value for the distance: here the whole distribution of distances between each individual in each group to all others has to be analytically determined.

In order not to complicate things, two equal squares (a x a) are considered, containing an equal number of places, the distance between the squares being d (fig. 6.1), d>0. The distance frequency function inside each square is already computed; it is interesting now to calculate the distribution of distances between points in separate squares, the intersquare distances.

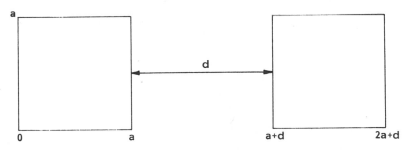

fig. 6.1. Distances between two squares

6.1.1. p = 1

In all cases the points inside the square are continuously distributed. If $\ell < d$ only distances inside both squares are relevant. The calculation will be carried out in 5 steps; only "inter-square distances" are considered here:

1. $d < \ell < \frac{1}{2}a + d$ $(d > 0)$

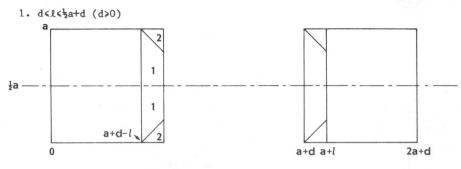

fig. 6.2. $d \leqslant \ell \leqslant \frac{1}{2}a + d$; 2 sets

There are 2 sets of interest in this case (fig. 6.2); the distance frequency function in set 1 is calculated via:

$$df_{p=1}(\ell)_1 = 2 \int_{x_1=a+d-\ell}^{x_1=a} \int_{x_2=x_1-a-d+\ell}^{x_2=\frac{1}{2}a} \frac{2 \cdot (x_1+\ell-a-d)\sqrt{2}}{4\ell\sqrt{2}} \, dx_2 \, dx_1$$

$$= \frac{1}{\ell} \left\{ \frac{1}{2}a(\ell-d)^2 - \frac{1}{3}(\ell-d)^3 \right\} \tag{6.1}$$

$$df_{p=1}(\ell)_2 = 2 \int_{x_1=a+d-\ell}^{x_1=a} \int_{x_2=0}^{x_2=x_1-d-a+\ell} \frac{(x+\ell-a-d)\sqrt{2}+x_2\sqrt{2}}{4\ell\sqrt{2}} \, dx_2 \, dx_1$$

$$= \frac{1}{4\ell}(\ell-d)^3 \tag{6.2}$$

So $df_{p=1}(\ell) = \frac{1}{12\ell}\left(3a(\ell-d)^2-(\ell-d)^3\right)$ $d < \ell < \frac{1}{2}a+d$ $\tag{6.3}$

If $\ell = d$, $df_{p=1}(\ell) = 0$ which was expected,

if $\ell = \frac{1}{2}a+d$, $df_{p=1}(\ell) = \frac{1}{12\ell}(3a \cdot \frac{1}{4}a^2 - \frac{1}{8}a^3) = \frac{5}{96\ell}a^3$

2. $\frac{1}{2}a+d \leqslant l \leqslant a+d$

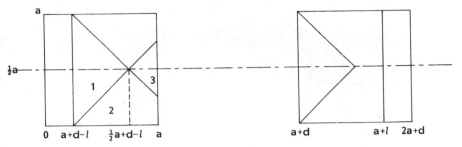

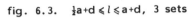

fig. 6.3. $\frac{1}{2}a+d \leqslant l \leqslant a+d$, 3 sets

$$df_{p=1}(l)_1 = 2 \int_{x_1=a+d-l}^{x_1=\frac{3}{2}a+d-l} \int_{x_2=x_1-a-d+l}^{x_2 \frac{1}{2}a} \frac{2 \cdot (x_1+l-a-d)\sqrt{2}}{4l\sqrt{2}} \, dx_2 dx_1$$

$$= \frac{a^3}{48l} \tag{6.4}$$

$$df_{p=1}(l)_2 = 2 \int_{x_1=a+d-l}^{x_1=\frac{3}{2}a+d-l} \int_{x_2=0}^{x_2=x_1-a-d+l} \frac{x_2\sqrt{2}}{4l\sqrt{2}} + \frac{(x_1+l-a-d)\sqrt{2}}{4l\sqrt{2}} \, dx_2 dx_1 \ +$$

$$2 \int_{x_1=\frac{3}{2}a+d-l}^{x_1=a} \int_{x_2=0}^{x_2=2a-x_1+d-l} \frac{x_2\sqrt{2}}{4l\sqrt{2}} + \frac{(x_1+l-a-d)\sqrt{2}}{4l\sqrt{2}} \, dx_2 dx_1$$

$$= \frac{1}{12l}(a+d-l-\frac{a}{4l}(a+d-l)^2+\frac{1}{12l}a^3)$$
$$= \frac{1}{12l}\{(a+d-l)^3-3a(a+d-l)^2+a^3\} \tag{6.5}$$

$$df_{p=1}(l)_3 = 2 \int_{x_1=\frac{3}{2}a+d-l}^{x_1=a} \int_{x_2=2a-x+d-l}^{x_2=\frac{1}{2}a} \frac{x_2\sqrt{2}}{4l\sqrt{2}} + \frac{(a-y)\sqrt{2}}{4l\sqrt{2}} \, dx_2 dx_1$$

$$= \frac{a}{4l}(l-d-\frac{1}{2}a)^2 \tag{6.6}$$

Concluding:

$$df_{p=1}(l) = \frac{a^3}{48l} + \frac{1}{12l}(a+d-l)^3 - \frac{a}{4l}(a+d-l)^2 + \frac{1}{12l}a^3 + \frac{a}{4l}(l-d-\frac{1}{2}a)^2 \tag{6.7}$$

If $\ell=a+d$, $df_{p=1}(\ell) = \frac{5}{48\ell}a^3 + \frac{a}{4\ell}(\frac{1}{2}a)^2 = \frac{1}{6\ell}a^3$,

if $\ell=\frac{1}{2}a+d$, $df_{p=1}(\ell) = \frac{5}{48\ell}a^3 + \frac{1}{12\ell}\frac{1}{8}a^3 - \frac{a}{4\ell}\frac{1}{4}a^2 = \frac{5}{96\ell}a^3$

3. Consider $a+d<\ell<\frac{3}{2}a+d$

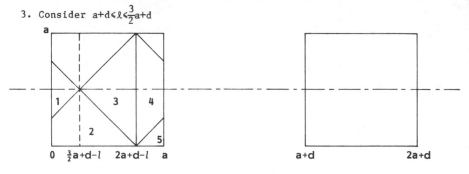

fig. 6.4. $a+d \leqslant l \leqslant \frac{3}{2}a+d$, 5 sets

There are 5 sets of interest in this case (fig. 6.4)

$$df_{p=1}(\ell)_1 = 2 \int_{x_1=0}^{x_1=\frac{3}{2}a+d-\ell} \int_{x_2=x_1+\ell-a-d}^{x_2=\frac{1}{2}a} \frac{2(x_1+\ell-a-d)\sqrt{2}}{4\ell\sqrt{2}} dx_2 dx_1$$

$$= \frac{a^3}{48\ell} + \frac{1}{3\ell}(\ell-a-d)^3 - \frac{a}{4\ell}(\ell-a-d)^2 \qquad (6.8)$$

$$df_{p=1}(\ell)_2 = 2 \int_{x_1=0}^{x_1=\frac{3}{2}a+d-\ell} \int_{x_2=0}^{x_2=\ell+x-a-d} \frac{x_2\sqrt{2}}{4\ell\sqrt{2}} + \frac{(x_1+\ell-a-d)\sqrt{2}}{4\ell\sqrt{2}} dx_2 dx_1 =$$

$$\int_{x_1=\frac{3}{2}a+d-\ell}^{x_1=2a+d-\ell} \int_{x_2=0}^{x_2=2a+d-\ell-x_1} \frac{(x_1+\ell-a-d)\sqrt{2}}{4\ell\sqrt{2}} + \frac{x_2\sqrt{2}}{4\ell\sqrt{2}} dx_2 x_1$$

$$= \frac{a^3}{12\ell} - \frac{1}{4\ell}(\ell-a-d)^3 \qquad (6.9)$$

$$df_{p=1}(\ell)_3 = \int_{x_1=\frac{3}{2}a+d-\ell}^{x_1=2a+d-\ell} \int_{x_2=2a+d-\ell-x_1}^{x_2=\frac{1}{2}a} \frac{a\sqrt{2}}{4\ell\sqrt{2}} dx_2 dx_1$$

$$= \frac{a^3}{16\ell} \qquad (6.10)$$

$$df_{p=1}(\ell)_4 = 2 \int_{x_1=2a+d-\ell}^{x_1=a} \int_{x_2=2a+d-\ell-x_1}^{x_2=\frac{1}{2}a} \frac{a\sqrt{2}-2(x_1-\ell-2a-d)\sqrt{2}}{4\ell\sqrt{2}} \, dx_2 dx_1$$

$$= \frac{a^3}{24\ell} - \frac{1}{3\ell}(\tfrac{3}{2}a-\ell+d)^3 \qquad\qquad (6.11)$$

$$df_{p=1}(\ell)_5 = 2 \int_{x_1=2a+d-\ell}^{x_1=a} \int_{x_2=0}^{x_2=x_1-2a-d+\ell} \frac{(a-x_2)\sqrt{2}}{4\ell\sqrt{2}} - \frac{(x_1+\ell-2a-d)\sqrt{2}}{4\ell\sqrt{2}} \, dx_2 dx_1$$

$$= \frac{a}{4\ell}(\ell-a-d)^2 - \frac{1}{4\ell}(\ell-a-d)^3 \qquad\qquad (6.12)$$

Concluding:

$$df_{p=1}(\ell) = \frac{a^3}{48\ell} + \frac{1}{3\ell}(\ell-a-d)^3 - \frac{3}{4\ell}(\ell-a-d)^2 + \frac{a^3}{12\ell} - \frac{1}{4\ell}(\ell-a-d)^3 + \frac{a^3}{16\ell} +$$

$$\frac{a^3}{24\ell} - \frac{1}{3\ell}(\tfrac{3}{2}a-\ell+d)^3 + \frac{a}{4\ell}(\ell-a-d)^2 - \frac{1}{4\ell}(\ell-a-d)^3$$

$$= \frac{10}{48\ell}a^3 - \frac{2}{12\ell}(\ell-a-d)^3 - \frac{1}{3\ell}(\tfrac{3}{2}a-\ell+d)^3$$

$$= \frac{5}{24\ell}a^3 - \frac{1}{6\ell}(\ell-a-d)^3 - \frac{1}{3\ell}(\tfrac{3}{2}a-\ell+d)^3 \qquad\qquad (6.13)$$

$$df_{p=1}(a+d) = \frac{5}{24\ell}a^3 - \frac{1}{3\ell}(\tfrac{1}{2}a)^3 = \frac{a^3}{6\ell}$$

$$df_{p=1}(\tfrac{3}{2}a+d) = \frac{5}{24\ell}a^3 - \frac{1}{6\ell}(\tfrac{1}{2}a)^3 = \frac{3}{16\ell}a^3 = \frac{3a^3}{16(\tfrac{3}{2}a+d)}$$

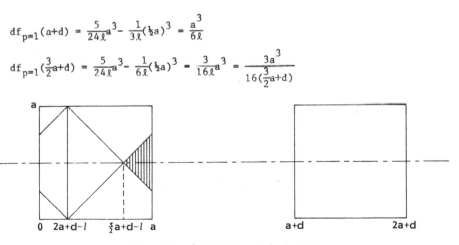

fig. 6.5. $\tfrac{3}{2}a+d \leqslant \ell \leqslant 2a+d$, 4 sets

4. $\frac{3}{2}a+d \leqslant \ell < 2a+d$

$$df_{p=1}(\ell)_1 = 2 \int\limits_{x_1=0}^{2a+d-\ell} \int\limits_{x_2=0}^{2a+d-\ell-x_1} \frac{x_2\sqrt{2}}{4\ell\sqrt{2}} + \frac{(x_1+\ell-a-d)\sqrt{2}}{4\ell\sqrt{2}} \; dx_2 dx_1$$

$$= -\frac{1}{12\ell}(2a+d-\ell)^3 + \frac{a}{4\ell}(2a+d-\ell)^2 \qquad (6.14)$$

$$df_{p=1}(\ell)_2 = 2 \int\limits_{x_1=0}^{x_1=2a+d-\ell} \int\limits_{x_2=2a+d-\ell-x_1}^{x_2=\frac{1}{2}a} \frac{x_2\sqrt{2}}{4\ell\sqrt{2}} + \frac{(a-x_2)\sqrt{2}}{4\ell\sqrt{2}} \; dx_2 dx_1$$

$$= \frac{a^3}{16\ell} - \frac{a}{4\ell}(\ell-\frac{3}{2}a-d)^2 \qquad (6.15)$$

$$df_{p=1}(\ell)_3 = 2 \int\limits_{x_1=2a+d-\ell}^{\frac{5}{2}a+d-\ell} \int\limits_{x_2=x_1-2a-d+\ell}^{x_2=\frac{1}{2}a} \frac{x_2\sqrt{2}}{4\ell\sqrt{2}} - \frac{2(x_1+\ell-2a-d)\sqrt{2}}{4\ell\sqrt{2}} \; dx_2 dx_1$$

$$= \frac{a^3}{24\ell} \qquad (6.16)$$

$$df_{p=1}(\ell)_4 \quad \int\limits_{x_1=2a+d-\ell}^{\frac{5}{2}a+d-\ell} \int\limits_{x_2=0}^{x_1-2a-d+\ell} \frac{(a-x_2)\sqrt{2}}{4\ell\sqrt{2}} - \frac{(x_1+\ell-2a-d)\sqrt{2}}{4\ell\sqrt{2}} \; dx_2 dx_1 \; +$$

$$\int\limits_{x_1=\frac{5}{2}a+d-\ell}^{a} \int\limits_{x_2=0}^{3a+d-\ell-x_1} \frac{(a-x_2)\sqrt{2}}{4\ell\sqrt{2}} - \frac{(x_1+\ell-2a-d)\sqrt{2}}{4\ell\sqrt{2}} \; dx_2 dx_1$$

$$= \frac{a^3}{24\ell} - \frac{1}{12\ell}(2a+d-\ell)^3 \qquad (6.17)$$

Concluding:

$$df_{p=1}(\ell) = \frac{a^3}{16\ell} - \frac{a}{4\ell}(\ell-\frac{3}{2}a-d)^2 + \frac{a}{4\ell}(2a+d-\ell)^2 - \frac{1}{12\ell}(2a+d-\ell)^3 +$$

$$+ \frac{a^3}{24\ell} - \frac{1}{12\ell}(2a+d-\ell)^3$$

$$= \frac{7a^3}{48\ell} - \frac{a}{4\ell}(\ell-\frac{3}{2}a-d)^2 + \frac{a}{4\ell}(2a+d-\ell)^2 - \frac{1}{6\ell}(2a+d-\ell)^3 \qquad (6.18)$$

$$df_{p+1}(2a+d) = \frac{7a^3}{48\ell} - \frac{a}{4\ell}\frac{a^2}{4} = \frac{(7-3)a^3}{48\ell} = \frac{a^3}{12(2a+d)}$$

5. $2a+d \leqslant \ell \leqslant \frac{5}{2}a+d$

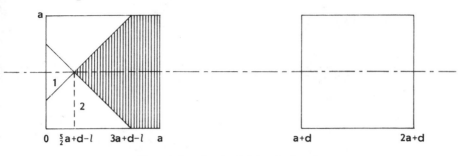

$$\quad 0 \quad \tfrac{5}{2}a+d-\ell \quad 3a+d-\ell \quad a \qquad\qquad a+d \qquad\qquad 2a+d$$

fig. 6.6. $2a+d \leqslant \ell \leqslant \frac{5}{2}a+d$, 2 sets

$$df_{p=1}(\ell)_1 =$$

$$2 \int_{x_1=0}^{\frac{5}{2}a+d-\ell} \int_{x_2=x_1+\ell-d-2a}^{\frac{1}{2}a} \frac{x_2\sqrt{2}-(x_1+\ell-2a-d)\sqrt{2}}{4\ell\sqrt{2}} + \frac{(a-x_2)\sqrt{2}-(x_1+\ell-2a-d)\sqrt{2}}{4\ell\sqrt{2}}\, dx_2 dx_1$$

$$= \frac{1}{3\ell}(\tfrac{3}{2}a-\ell+d)^3 \tag{6.19}$$

$$df_{p=1}(\ell)_2 = 2 \int_{x_1=0}^{\frac{5}{2}a+d-\ell} \int_{x_2=0}^{x_1+\ell-d-2a} \frac{-x_2\sqrt{2}+(3a-x_1+d-\ell)\sqrt{2}}{4\ell\sqrt{2}}\, dx_2 dx_1 \; +$$

$$\int_{x_1=\frac{5}{2}a+d-\ell}^{3a+d-\ell} \int_{x_2=0}^{3a-x_1+d-\ell} \frac{-x_2\sqrt{2}+(3a-x_1+d-\ell)\sqrt{2}}{4\ell\sqrt{2}}\, dx_2 dx_1$$

$$= \frac{-1}{32\ell}a^3 + \frac{a^3}{16\ell} + \frac{(\ell-d-2a)^3}{4\ell} - \frac{a}{4\ell}(\ell-d-2a)^2 + \frac{1}{96\ell}a^3$$

$$= \frac{1}{24\ell}a^3 + \frac{(\ell-d-2a)^3}{4\ell} - \frac{a(\ell-d-2a)^2}{4\ell} \tag{6.20}$$

$$df_{p=1}(2a+d) = \frac{a^3}{24\ell} + \frac{1}{3\ell}\frac{a^3}{8} = \frac{a^3}{12\ell} = \frac{a^3}{12(2a+d)}$$

$$df_{p=1}(\tfrac{5}{2}a+d) = \frac{a^3}{24\ell} + \frac{a^3}{32\ell} - a\frac{a^2}{16\ell} = \frac{(4+3-6)a^3}{96\ell} = \qquad =$$

6. $\tfrac{5}{2}a+d \leqslant \ell < 3a+d$

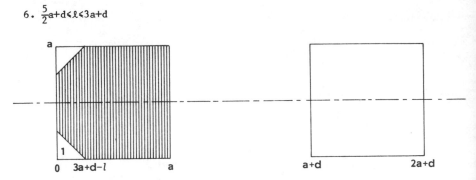

fig. 6.7. $\tfrac{5}{2}a+d \leqslant l \leqslant 3a+d$, 1 set

$$df_{p=1}(\ell) = 2 \int_{x_1=0}^{3a+d-\ell} \int_{x_2=0}^{3a+d-\ell-x_1} \frac{(a-x_2)\sqrt{2}-(x_1+\ell-2a-d)\sqrt{2}}{4\ell\sqrt{2}} \, dx_2 \, dx_1$$

$$= \frac{1}{12\ell}(3a+d-\ell)^3 \qquad\qquad (6.21)$$

$$df_{p=1}(\tfrac{5}{2}a+d) = \frac{1}{12\ell}\cdot\frac{a^3}{8} = \frac{a^3}{96\ell} = \frac{a^3}{96(\tfrac{5}{2}a+d)}$$

$$df_{p=1}(3a+d) = 0$$

The complete result of the distance frequency function between two squares using Manhattan distances is:

$$
df_{p=1}(\ell) =
\begin{cases}
\dfrac{1}{12\ell}\left\{3a(\ell-d)^2-(\ell-d)^3\right\} & d<\ell<\tfrac{1}{2}a+d \\[2em]
\dfrac{5a^3}{48\ell}+\dfrac{(a+d-\ell)^3}{12\ell}-\dfrac{a(a+d-\ell)^2}{4\ell}+\dfrac{a(\ell-d-\tfrac{1}{2}a)^2}{4\ell} & \tfrac{1}{2}a+d<\ell<a+d \\[2em]
\dfrac{5a^3}{24\ell}-\dfrac{(\ell-a-d)^3}{6\ell}-\dfrac{(\tfrac{3}{2}a-\ell+d)^3}{3\ell} & a+d<\ell<\tfrac{3}{2}a+d \\[2em]
\dfrac{7a^3}{48\ell}-\dfrac{a(\ell-\tfrac{3}{2}a-d)^2}{4\ell}+\dfrac{(2a+d-\ell)^2a}{4\ell}-\dfrac{(2a+d-\ell)^3}{6\ell} & \tfrac{3}{2}a+d<\ell<2a+d \\[2em]
\dfrac{7a^3}{24\ell}+\dfrac{(\ell-d-2a)^2}{4\ell}-\dfrac{a(\ell-d-2a)^2}{4\ell}+\dfrac{(\tfrac{5}{2}a-\ell+d)^3}{3\ell} & 2a+d<\ell<\tfrac{5}{2}a+d \\[2em]
\dfrac{(3a+d-\ell)^3}{12\ell} & \tfrac{5}{2}a+d<\ell<3a+d \\[2em]
0 & \text{otherwise}
\end{cases}
$$

$$(6.22)$$

A check on this result is to calculate the distance frequency function for d=0; one should obtain a result equal to the function of a rectangle (2a x a) keeping in mind that the distances inside each of the two squares should be added, because in this section only the "inter-square" distances are calculated.

First some previous results; the distance density function for a square is:

$$
df_{p=1}(\ell) =
\begin{cases}
(a^2-\ell+\tfrac{1}{6}\ell^2) & 0<\ell<a \\[1.5em]
\dfrac{(2a-\ell)^3}{6\ell} & a<\ell<2a
\end{cases}
$$

and the distance density function for a rectangle (2a x a),

$$
df_{p=1}(\ell) = \begin{cases}
(2a^2 - \frac{3}{2}a\ell + \frac{1}{6}\ell^2) & 0 < \ell < a \\[2mm]
(\frac{7}{3}a - \ell)\frac{a^2}{2\ell} & a < \ell < 2a \\[2mm]
\frac{(3a - \ell)^3}{6\ell} & 2a < \ell < 3a
\end{cases}
$$

The "intersquare" distance distribution, d=0, is:

$$0 < \ell < \tfrac{1}{2}a \; : \quad df_{p=1}(\ell) = \frac{1}{12\ell}(3a\ell^2 - \ell^3) = \frac{1}{4}a\ell - \frac{1}{12}\ell^2 = \frac{1}{12}\ell(3a - \ell)$$

$$\tfrac{1}{2}a < \ell < a \; : \quad df_{p=1}(\ell) = \frac{5a^3}{48\ell} + \frac{(a-\ell)^3}{12\ell} - \frac{a(a-\ell)^2}{4\ell} + \frac{a(\ell - \frac{1}{2}a)^2}{4\ell} = \frac{1}{12}\ell(3a - \ell)$$

so for $0 < \ell < a$ $\quad df_{p=1}(\ell) = \frac{1}{2}a\ell - \frac{\ell^2}{6}$

Inside two squares (a x a) this frequency
is $df_{p=1}(\ell) = 2(a^2 - a\ell + \frac{1}{6}\ell^2)$; combining the two results yields:

1. $0 < \ell < a$: $\quad df_{p=1}(\ell) = 2(a^2 - a\ell + \frac{1}{6}\ell^2) + \frac{1}{2}a\ell - \frac{\ell^2}{6}$

$$= 2a^2 - \frac{3}{2}a\ell + \frac{1}{6}\ell^2,$$

which is indeed the result for a rectangle (2a x a).

2. $a < \ell < 2a$:
The inter-square distances are:

$$df_{p=1}(\ell) = \frac{5a^3}{24\ell} - \frac{(\ell - a)^3}{6\ell} - \frac{(\frac{3}{2}a - \ell)^3}{3\ell} + \frac{7a^3}{48\ell} - \frac{a(\ell - \frac{3}{2}a)^2}{4\ell} +$$

$$\frac{a(2a - \ell)^2}{4\ell} - \frac{(2a - \ell)^3}{6\ell} = -\frac{3a^3}{2\ell} - 2a\ell + \frac{1}{3}\ell^2 + \frac{7}{2}a^2;$$

and the number of distances inside the squares is:

$$2\,\frac{(2a-\ell)^3}{6\ell} = \frac{16a^2}{6\ell} - 4a^2 + 2a\ell - \tfrac{1}{3}\ell^2;$$

adding both results yields: $df_{p=1}(\ell) = \dfrac{7a^3}{6\ell} - \tfrac{1}{2}\ell^2$; this result is equal to the distance frequency function for a rectangle (2a x a), using Manhattan distances.

3. $2a<\ell<3a$; in this case only intersquare distances are relevant:

$$
\begin{aligned}
df_{p=1}(\ell) &= \frac{a^3}{24\ell} + \frac{(\ell-2a)^3}{4\ell} - \frac{a(\ell-2a)^2}{4\ell} + \frac{(3a-\ell)^3}{12\ell} + \frac{(\tfrac{5}{2}a-\ell)^3}{3\ell} \\
&= \frac{9a^3}{2\ell} - \tfrac{1}{6}\ell^2 + \tfrac{3}{2}a\ell - \tfrac{9}{2}a^2,
\end{aligned}
$$

which is indeed equal to $\dfrac{(3a-\ell)^3}{6\ell}$ (the result for the rectangle).

In fig. 6.8 and 6.9 the distance frequency function is presented graphically; first only the function of inter-square distances is shown for d=0 and d=100; especially when d is small one can see clearly that this distribution is asymmetric. In fig. 6.10 some complete distance frequency functions are shown (d=0, 20, 40, 60, 80, and 100).

6.1.2. p=2

Comparable with the procedure for Manhattan distances, the calculation will be carried out in 5 steps.

1. Consider $d < \ell < \sqrt{a^2+d^2}$.

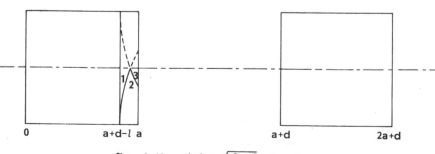

fig. 6.11. $d \leqslant l \leqslant \sqrt{a^2+d^2}$, 3 sets

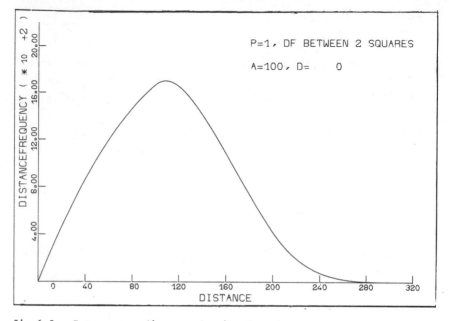

fig.6.8   Intersquare distance density function; d=0

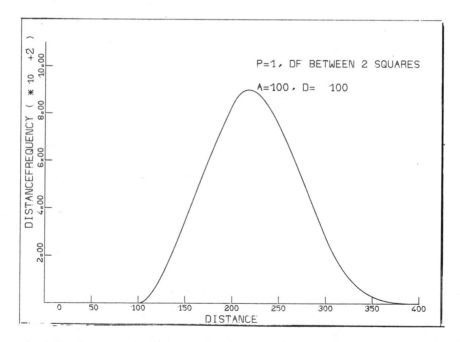

fig.6.9   Intersquare distance density function; d=100

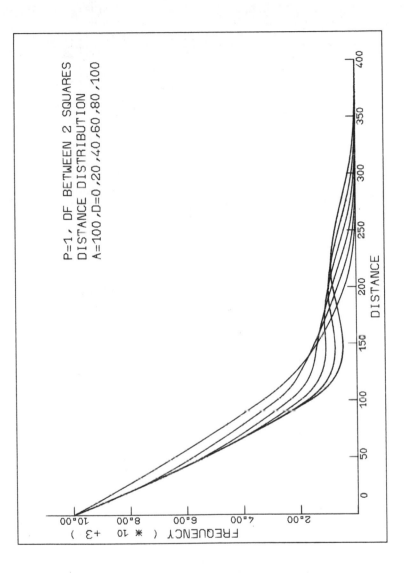

P=1, DF BETWEEN 2 SQUARES
DISTANCE DISTRIBUTION
A=100,D=0,20,40,60,80,100

FREQUENCY (* 10 +3)

DISTANCE

fig.6.10 Distance density functions on 2 squares

There are 3 relevant sets (fig. 6.11):

$$1. \quad df_{p=2}(\ell)_1 = 2 \int_{x_1=a+d-\ell}^{a+d-\sqrt{\ell^2-\frac{1}{4}a^2}} \int_{x_2=\sqrt{\ell^2-(x_1-(a+d)^2}}^{\frac{1}{2}a} \frac{2\ell \cos^{-1}\frac{a+d-x_1}{\ell}}{2\pi\ell} \, dx_2 dx_1$$

$$2. \quad df_{p=2}(\ell)_2 = 2 \int_{x_1=a+d-\ell}^{a+d-\sqrt{\ell^2-\frac{1}{4}a^2}} \int_{x_2=0}^{\sqrt{\ell^2-(x_1-(a+d))^2}} \frac{\ell\cos^{-1}\frac{a+d-x_1}{\ell} + \ell\sin^{-1}\frac{x_2}{\ell}}{2\pi\ell} \, dx_2 dx_1$$

$$+ \; 2 \int_{x_1=a+d-\sqrt{\ell^2-\frac{1}{4}a^2}}^{a} \int_{x_2=0}^{a-\sqrt{\ell^2-(x_1-(a+d))^2}} \frac{\ell\cos^{-1}\frac{a+d-x_1}{\ell}+\ell\sin^{-1}\frac{x_2}{\ell}}{2\pi\ell} \, dx_2 dx$$

$$3. \quad df_{p=2}(\ell)_3 = 2 \int_{x_1=a+d-\sqrt{\ell^3-\frac{1}{4}a^2}}^{a} \int_{x_2=a-\sqrt{\ell^2-(x_1-(a+d))^2}}^{\frac{1}{2}a} \frac{\ell\sin^{-1}\frac{x_2}{\ell}+\ell\sin^{-1}\frac{a-x_2}{\ell}}{2\pi\ell} \, dx_2 dx$$

The sum of these 3 integrals is equal to:

$$df_{p=2}(\ell) = \frac{1}{\pi} \int_{x_1=a+d-\ell}^{a} a \cos^{-1}\frac{a+d-x_1}{\ell} + a+d-x_1-\ell \; dx_1$$

$$= \frac{1}{\pi} \left\{ -ad \cos^{-1}\frac{d}{\ell} + a\sqrt{\ell^2-d^2} - \frac{1}{2}d^2+d\ell- \frac{1}{2}\ell^2 \right\} \quad d<\ell<\sqrt{a^2+d^2} \tag{6.23}$$

2. $\sqrt{a^2+d^2} < \ell < a+d$

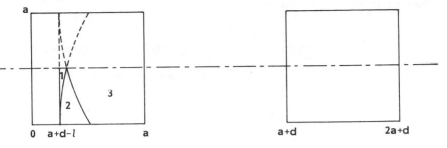

fig. 6.12. $\sqrt{a^2+d^2} \leqslant l \leqslant a+d$, 3 sets

1. $df_{p=2}(l)_1 = 2 \int\limits_{x_1=a+d-l}^{a+d-\sqrt{l^2-\frac{1}{4}a^2}} \int\limits_{x_2=\sqrt{l^2-(x_1-(a+d)^2}}^{x_2=\frac{1}{2}a} \dfrac{2l \cos^{-1}\dfrac{a+d-x_1}{l}}{2\pi l} dx_2 dx_1$

2. $df_{p=2}(l)_2 = 2 \int\limits_{x_1=a+d-l}^{a+d-\sqrt{l^2-\frac{1}{4}a^2}} \int\limits_{x_2=0}^{\sqrt{l^2-(x_1-(a+d))^2}} \dfrac{l\cos^{-1}\dfrac{a+d-x_1}{l}+l\sin^{-1}\dfrac{x_2}{l}}{2\pi l}dx_2 dx_1$

$+ 2 \int\limits_{x_1=a+d-\sqrt{l^2-\frac{1}{4}a^2}}^{a+d-\sqrt{l^2-a^2}} \int\limits_{x_2=0}^{x_2=a-\sqrt{l^2-(x_1-(a+d))^2}} \dfrac{l\cos^{-1}\dfrac{a+d-x_1}{l}+l\sin^{-1}\dfrac{x_1}{l}}{2\pi l}dx_2 dx_1$

3. $df_{p=2}(l)_3 = 2 \int\limits_{x_1=a+d-\sqrt{l^2-\frac{1}{4}a^2}}^{a+d-\sqrt{l^2-a^2}} \int\limits_{x_2=a-\sqrt{l^2-(x_1-(a+d))^2}}^{\frac{1}{2}a} \dfrac{l\sin^{-1}\dfrac{x_2}{l}+l\sin^{-1}\dfrac{a-x_2}{l}}{2\pi l}dx_2 dx_1$

$+ 2 \int\limits_{x_1=a+d-\sqrt{l^2-a^2}}^{a} \int\limits_{x_2=0}^{\frac{1}{2}a} \dfrac{l\sin^{-1}\dfrac{x_2}{l}+l\sin^{-1}\dfrac{a-x_2}{l}}{2\pi l} dx_2 dx_1$

Summing these 3 integrals yields:

$$df_{p=2}(\ell) = \frac{1}{\pi} \int_{x_1=a+d-\ell}^{a+d-\sqrt{\ell^2-a^2}} a \cos^{-1} \frac{a+d-x_1}{\ell} + a+d-x_1 - \ell \; dx_1 +$$

$$\frac{1}{\pi} \int_{x_1=a+d-\sqrt{\ell^2-a^2}} a \sin^{-1} \frac{a}{\ell} + \sqrt{\ell^2-a^2} - \ell \; dx_1$$

$$= -ad \sin^{-1} \frac{a}{\ell} - d\sqrt{\ell^2-a^2} + \tfrac{1}{2}a^2 + d\ell \qquad \sqrt{(a^2+d^2)} < \ell < a+d \quad (6.24)$$

3. $a+d < \ell < \sqrt{a^2+(a+d)^2}$.

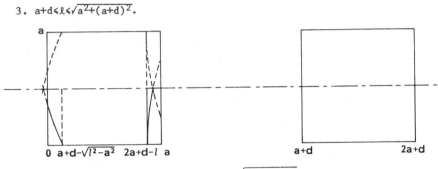

fig. 6.13. $a+d \leqslant l \leqslant \sqrt{a^2+(a+d)^2}$, 5 sets

Now there are 5 sets (fig. 6.13):

1. $$df_{p=2}(\ell)_1 = 2 \int_{x_1=0}^{a+d-\sqrt{\ell^2-a^2}} \int_{x_2=0}^{a-\sqrt{\ell^2-(a+d-x_1{}^2)}} \frac{\ell\cos^{-1} \frac{a+d-x_1}{\ell} + \ell\sin^{-1} \frac{x_2}{\ell}}{2\pi\ell} dx_2 dx_1$$

2. $$df_{p=2}(\ell)_2 = 2 \int_{x_1=0}^{a+d-\sqrt{\ell^2-a^2}} \int_{x_2=a-\sqrt{\ell^2(a+d-x_1)^2}}^{\tfrac{1}{2}a} \frac{\ell\sin^{-1} \frac{a-x_2}{\ell} + \ell\sin^{-1} \frac{x_2}{\ell}}{2\pi\ell} dx_2 dx_1$$

3. $df_{p=2}(\ell)_3 = 2 \int\limits_{x_1=a+d-\sqrt{\ell^2-a^2}}^{2a+d-\ell} \int\limits_{x_2=0}^{\frac{1}{2}a} \frac{\ell\sin^{-1}\dfrac{a-x_2}{\ell}+\ell\sin^{-1}\dfrac{x_2}{\ell}}{2\pi\ell}\, dx_2\,dx_1$

4. $df_{p=2}(\ell)_4 = 2 \int\limits_{x_1=2a+d-\ell}^{2a+d-\sqrt{\ell^2-\frac{1}{4}a^2}} \int\limits_{x_2=\sqrt{\ell^2-(2a+d-x_1)^2}}^{\frac{1}{2}a} \frac{\ell\sin^{-1}\dfrac{a-x_2}{\ell}-2\ell\cos^{-1}\dfrac{2a+d-x_1}{\ell}+\ell\sin^{-1}\dfrac{x_2}{\ell}}{2\pi\ell}\, dx_2\,dx_1$

5. $df_{p=2}(\ell)_5 = 2 \int\limits_{x_1=2a+d-\ell}^{2a+d-\sqrt{\ell^2-\frac{1}{4}a^2}} \int\limits_{x_2=0}^{\sqrt{\ell^2-(2a+d-x_1)^2}} \frac{\ell\sin^{-1}\dfrac{a-x_2}{\ell}\,\ell\cos^{-1}\dfrac{2a+d-x_2}{\ell}}{2\pi\ell}\, dx_2\,dx_1$

$+\ 2 \int\limits_{x_1=2a+d-\sqrt{\ell^2-\frac{1}{4}a^2}}^{a} \int\limits_{x_2=0}^{a-\sqrt{\ell^2-(2a+d-x_1)^2}} \frac{\ell\sin^{-1}\dfrac{a-x_2}{\ell}-\ell\cos^{-1}\dfrac{2a+d-x_1}{\ell}}{2\pi\ell}\, dx_2\,dx_1$

Summing these 5 integrals:

$$df_{p=2}(\ell) = \frac{1}{\pi}\int\limits_{x_1=0}^{a+d-\sqrt{\ell^2-a^2}} a\cos^{-1}\frac{a+d-x_1}{\ell}+a+d-x_1-\ell\ dx_1\ +$$

$$\frac{1}{\pi}\int\limits_{x_1=a+d-\sqrt{\ell^2-a^2}}^{a} a\sin^{-1}\frac{a}{\ell}+\sqrt{(\ell^2-a^2)}-\ell\ dx_1\ +$$

$$\frac{1}{\pi}\int\limits_{x_1=2a+d-\ell}^{a} a\cos^{-1}\frac{2a+d-x_1}{\ell}+2a+d-x_1-\ell\ dx_1\ .$$

-143-

$$df_{p=2}(\ell) = \frac{1}{\pi} \{\frac{1}{2}a^2 + \ell^2 + 2a(a+d)\cos^{-1}\frac{a+d}{\ell} - 2a\sqrt{\ell^2-(a+d)^2} + (a+d)^2 - 2\ell(a+d)$$
$$-ad\,\sin^{-1}\frac{a}{\ell} - d\sqrt{\ell^2-a^2} + d\ell\} \tag{6.25}$$

4. $\sqrt{(a+d)^2+a^2} \leqslant \ell \leqslant 2a+d$

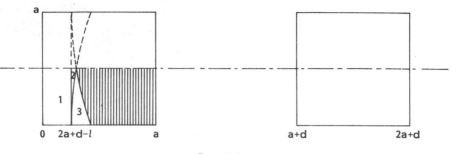

fig. 6.14.

There are three sets (fig. 6.14):

$$df_{p=2}(\ell)_1 = 2 \int_{x_1=0}^{2a+d-\ell} \int_{x_2=0}^{\frac{1}{2}a} \frac{\ell\sin^{-1}\frac{a-x_2}{\ell} + \ell\sin^{-1}\frac{x_2}{\ell}}{2\pi\ell} dx_2 dx_1$$

$$df_{p=2}(\ell)_2 = 2 \int_{x_1=2a+d-\ell}^{2a+d-\sqrt{\ell^2-\frac{1}{4}a^2}} \int_{x_2=\sqrt{\ell^2-(2a+d-x_1)^2}}^{\frac{1}{2}} \frac{\ell\sin^{-1}\frac{a-x_2}{\ell} - \ell\cos^{-1}\frac{2a+d-x_1}{\ell}}{2\pi\ell} +$$

$$+ \frac{\ell\sin^{-1}\frac{x_2}{\ell} - \ell\cos^{-1}\frac{2a+d-x_1}{\ell}}{2\pi\ell} dx_2 dx_1$$

$$df_{p=2}(\ell)_3 = 2 \int_{x_1=2a+d-\ell}^{2a+d-\sqrt{\ell^2-\frac{1}{4}a^2}} \int_{x_2=0}^{\sqrt{\ell^2-(2a+d-x_1)^2}} \frac{\ell\sin^{-1}\frac{a-x_2}{\ell} - \ell\cos^{-1}\frac{2a+d-x_1}{\ell}}{2\pi\ell} dx_2 dx_1$$

$$+ 2 \int_{x_1=2a+d-\sqrt{\ell^2-\frac{1}{4}a^2}}^{2a+d-\sqrt{\ell^2-a^2}} \int_{x_2=0}^{x_2=a-\sqrt{\ell^2-(2a+d-x_1)^2}} \frac{\ell\sin^{-1}\frac{a-x_2}{\ell} - \ell\cos^{-1}\frac{2a+d-x_1}{\ell}}{2\pi\ell} dx_2 dx_1$$

Summing these integrals yields:

$$df_{p=2}(\ell) = \frac{1}{\pi} \int_{x_1=0}^{2a+d-\sqrt{\ell^2-a^2}} a\sin^{-1}\frac{a}{\ell} + \sqrt{\ell^2-a^2} - \ell dx_1 +$$

$$\frac{1}{\pi} \int_{x_1=2a+d-\ell}^{2a+d-\sqrt{\ell^2-a^2}} a\cos^{-1}\frac{2a+d-x_1}{\ell} + 2a+d-x_1-\ell \; dx_1$$

$$\frac{1}{\pi} \{2a^2\sin^{-1}\frac{a}{\ell} +2a\sqrt{\ell^2-a^2}-2a\ell+ad\sin^{-1}\frac{a}{\ell} +d\sqrt{\ell^2-a^2}-d\ell-\frac{1}{2}a^2\}$$

$$\sqrt{(a+d)^2+a^2}<\ell<2a+d \quad (6.26)$$

5. $2a+d<\ell<\sqrt{(2a+d)^2+a^2}$

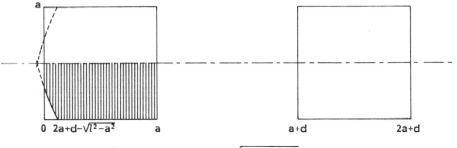

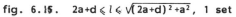

0    $2a+d-\sqrt{l^2-a^2}$ a   a+d   2a+d

fig. 6.15. $2a+d \leqslant l \leqslant \sqrt{(2a+d)^2+a^2}$, 1 set

$$df_{p=2}(\ell)=2\int_{x_1=0}^{2a+d-\sqrt{\ell^2-a^2}}\int_{x_2=0}^{a-\sqrt{\ell^2-(2a+d-x_1)^2}}\frac{\ell\sin^{-1}\dfrac{a-x_2}{\ell}-\ell\cos^{-1}\dfrac{2a+d-x_1}{\ell}}{2\pi\ell}dx_2\,dx_1$$

$$\frac{1}{\pi}\int_{x_1=0}^{2a+d-\sqrt{\ell^2-a^2}}a\sin^{-1}\frac{a}{\ell}+\sqrt{\ell^2-a^2}-\ell\;dx\;\overline{1}\;a\cos^{-1}\frac{2a+d-x_1}{\ell}$$
$$+\,2a+d-x_1-\ell\;dx_1$$

$$=\frac{1}{\pi}\left\{a(2a+d)\sin^{-1}\frac{a}{\ell}+(2a+d)\sqrt{\ell^2-a^2}-a(2a+d)\cos^{-1}\frac{2a+d}{\ell}-\frac{1}{2}(2a+d)^2\right.$$
$$\left.+a\sqrt{\ell^2-(2a+d)^2}-\frac{1}{2}\ell^2-\frac{1}{2}a^2\right\}\qquad(6.27)$$

The complete result is:

$$
df_{p=2}(\ell) = \begin{cases}
\frac{1}{\pi}\{-adcos^{-1}\frac{d}{\ell} + a\sqrt{(\ell^2-d^2)}-\frac{1}{2}d^2+d\ell-\frac{1}{2}\ell^2\} & d<\ell<\sqrt{(a^2+d^2)} \\[2em]
\frac{1}{\pi}\{-adsin^{-1}\frac{a}{\ell} -d\sqrt{(\ell^2-a^2)}+\frac{1}{2}a^2+d\ell\} & \sqrt{(a^2+d^2)}<\ell<a+d \\[2em]
\frac{1}{\pi}\{-adsin^{-1}\frac{a}{\ell} -d\sqrt{(\ell^2-a^2)}+\frac{1}{2}a^2+d\ell+\ell^2+2a(a+d)cos^{-1}\frac{a+d}{\ell} \\ \qquad -2a\sqrt{(\ell^2-(a+d)^2)}+(a+d)^2-2\ell(a+d)\} \\ \qquad\qquad\qquad\qquad\qquad\qquad a+d<\ell<\sqrt{a^2+(a+d)^2} \\[2em]
\frac{1}{\pi}\{a(2a+d)sin^{-1}\frac{a}{\ell}+(2a+d)\sqrt{(\ell^2-a^2)}-\frac{1}{2}a^2-2a\ell-d\ell\} \quad \sqrt{(a+d)^2+a^2}<\ell<2a+d \\[2em]
\frac{1}{\pi}\{a(2a+d)sin^{-1}\frac{a}{\ell}+(2a+d)\sqrt{(\ell^2-a^2)}-a(2a+d)cos^{-1}\frac{2a+d}{\ell}\frac{1}{2}(2a+d)^2 \\ \qquad +a\sqrt{(\ell^2-(2a+d)^2)}-\frac{1}{2}\ell^2-\frac{1}{2}a^2\} \quad 2a+d<\ell<\sqrt{(2a+d)^2+a^2} \\[2em]
0 & \text{otherwise}
\end{cases}
$$

$$(6.28)$$

A set of these complete density functions is plotted for a=100; d=0, 20, 40, 60, 80, and 100 in fig. 6.16. In fig. 6.17 and 6.18 only the density function of "intersquare-distances" are presented. A check on these results is the following;

the distance density function in a rectangle (2a x a), with Eucledian distances appeared to be:

$$df_{p=2}(\ell)= \begin{cases} 2a^2 - \dfrac{6a\ell}{\pi} - \dfrac{\ell^2}{\pi} & 0<\ell<a \\[20pt] 2a^2 - \dfrac{4a^2}{\pi}\cos^{-1}\dfrac{a}{\ell} + \dfrac{4a}{\pi}\sqrt{(\ell^2-a^2)} - \dfrac{4a\ell}{\pi} - \dfrac{a^2}{\pi} & a<\ell<2a \\[20pt] 2a^2 - \dfrac{4a^2}{\pi}\cos^{-1}\dfrac{a}{\ell} + \dfrac{4a}{\pi}\sqrt{(\ell^2-a^2)} - \dfrac{4a^2}{\pi}\cos^{-1}\dfrac{2a}{\ell} \\[10pt] \quad + \dfrac{2a}{\pi}\sqrt{(\ell^2-4a^2)} - \dfrac{5a^2}{\pi} - \dfrac{\ell^2}{\pi} & 2a<\ell<a \end{cases}$$

If we consider two squares with distance d=0, we should obtain the same result.

The result for one square (a x a) was:

$$df_{p=2}(\ell) = \begin{cases} a^2 - \dfrac{4a\ell}{\pi} + \dfrac{\ell^2}{\pi} & 0<\ell<a \\[20pt] a^2 + \dfrac{4a}{\pi}\sqrt{(\ell^2-a^2)} - \dfrac{2a^2}{\pi} - \dfrac{\ell^2}{\pi} - \dfrac{4a^2}{\pi}\cos^{-1}\dfrac{a}{\ell} & a<\ell<a\sqrt{2} \end{cases}$$

The extra distances, being the "inter square distances", are:

$$df_{p=2}(\ell) = \begin{cases} \dfrac{1}{\pi}(a\ell - \dfrac{1}{2}\ell^2) & 0<\ell<a \\[20pt] \dfrac{1}{\pi}(\dfrac{1}{2}a^2+\ell^2+2a^2\cos^{-1}\dfrac{a}{\ell} - 2a\sqrt{(\ell^2-a^2)}+a^2-2a\ell & a<\ell<a\sqrt{2} \\[20pt] \dfrac{1}{\pi}(2a^2\sin^{-1}\dfrac{a}{\ell} + 2a\sqrt{(\ell^2-a^2)} - \dfrac{1}{2}a^2-2a\ell) & a\sqrt{2}<\ell<2a \\[20pt] \dfrac{1}{\pi}(2a^2\sin^{-1}\dfrac{a}{\ell} + 2a\sqrt{(\ell^2-a^2)}-2a^2\cos^{-1}\dfrac{2a}{\ell} - 2a^2 \\[10pt] \quad + a\sqrt{(\ell^2-4a^2)} - \dfrac{1}{2}\ell^2 - \dfrac{1}{2}a^2) & 2a<\ell<a\sqrt{5} \end{cases}$$

Comparing both results yields:

1. $0 < \ell < a$ $\quad df(\ell)_{p=2}$ = intradistances + interdistances

$$= 2(a^2 - \frac{4a\ell}{\pi} + \frac{\ell^2}{\pi}) + 2 \cdot \frac{1}{\pi}\{a\ell - \frac{1}{2}\ell^2\}$$

$$= 2a^2 - \frac{6a\ell}{\pi} + \frac{\ell^2}{\pi}$$

2. $a < \ell < a\sqrt{2}$ $\quad df(\ell)_{p=2} = 2(a^2 + \frac{4a}{\pi}\sqrt{(\ell^2-a^2)} - \frac{2a^2}{\pi} - \frac{\ell^2}{\pi} - \frac{4a^2}{\pi}\cos^{-1}\frac{a}{\ell}) +$

$$2\frac{1}{\pi}(\frac{1}{2}a^2 + \ell^2 + 2a^2\cos^{-1}\frac{a}{\ell} - 2a\sqrt{(\ell^2-a^2)} + a^2 - 2a\ell)$$

$$= 2a^2 - \frac{4a^2}{\pi}\cos^{-1}\frac{a}{\ell} + \frac{4a}{\pi}\sqrt{\ell^2-a^2} - \frac{a^2}{\pi} - \frac{4a\ell}{\pi}$$

3. $a\sqrt{2} < \ell < 2a$ $\quad df(\ell)_{p=2}$ (only "inter square distances") =

$$= 2\frac{1}{\pi}(2a^2\sin^{-1}\frac{a}{\ell} + 2a\sqrt{(\ell^2-a^2)} - \frac{1}{2}a^2 - 2a\ell)$$

$$= \frac{4a^2}{\pi}\sin^{-1}\frac{a}{\ell} + \frac{4a}{\pi}\sqrt{(\ell^2-a^2)} - \frac{a^2}{\pi} - \frac{4a\ell}{\pi}$$

$$= 2a^2 - \frac{4a^2}{\pi}\cos^{-1}\frac{a}{\ell} + \frac{4a}{\pi}\sqrt{(\ell^2-a^2)} - \frac{a^2}{\pi} - \frac{4a\ell}{\pi}$$

and finally,

4. $2a < \ell < a\sqrt{5}$ $\quad df(\ell)_{p=2}$ = (only "inter square distances")

$$= 2\frac{1}{\pi}(2a^2\sin^{-1}\frac{a}{\ell} - 2a\sqrt{(\ell^2-a^2)} - 2a^2\cos^{-1}\frac{2a}{\ell}$$

$$- 2a^2 + a\sqrt{(\ell^2-4a^2)} - \frac{1}{2}\ell^2 - \frac{1}{2}a^2)$$

$$= 2a^2 - \frac{4a^2}{\pi}\cos^{-1}\frac{a}{\ell} + \frac{4a}{\pi}\sqrt{(\ell^2-a^2)} - \frac{4a^2}{\pi}\cos^{-1}\frac{2a}{\ell} - \frac{5a^2}{\pi}$$

$$+ \frac{2a}{\pi}\sqrt{(\ell^2-4a^2)} - \frac{\ell^2}{\pi}$$

which are indeed the results for a rectangle (2a x a).

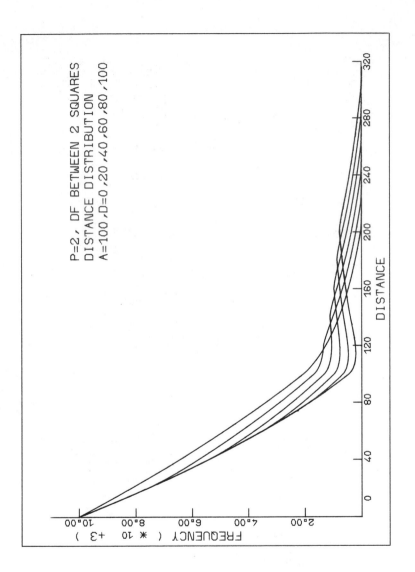

fig.6.16 Distance density functions

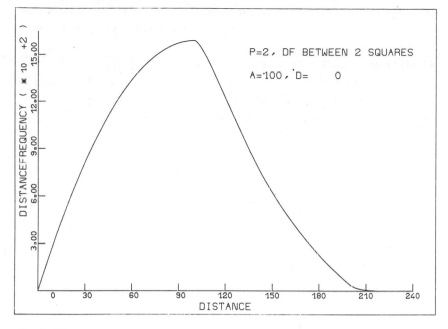

fig.6.17   Intersquare distance density function

fig.6.18

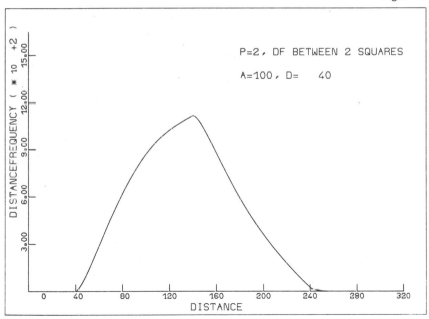

6.1.3. $p=\infty$

The calculation, in this case, is carried out in 4 steps, depending on the distance ℓ considered.

1. $\ell < d$;   here only the distances inside the squares are relevant; there being no intersquare distances.

2. $d < \ell < a$; assume $d < a$.

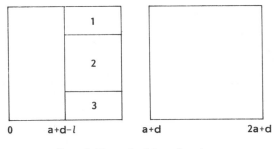

fig. 6.19.. $d \leqslant l \leqslant a$, 3 sets

There are 3 sets containing points which can be connected with points in the other square at distance ℓ (fig. 6.19):

set 1.
$$df_{p=\infty}(\ell)_1 = \int_{x_1=a+d-\ell}^{x_1=a} \int_{x_2=\ell}^{a} \frac{a-x_2+\ell+x_1+\ell-a-d}{8\ell} \, dx_2 dx_1 \tag{6.29}$$
$$= \frac{1}{2} \frac{(a-\ell)(\ell-d)(2\ell-d+a)}{8\ell}$$

set 3.
$$df_{p=\infty}(\ell)_3 = df_{p=\infty}(\ell)_1 \tag{6.30}$$

set 2.
$$df_{p=\infty}(\ell)_2 = \int_{x_1=a+d-\ell}^{a} \int_{x_2=a-\ell}^{\ell} \frac{a}{8\ell} \, dx_2 dx_1 = \frac{a(\ell-d)(2\ell-a)}{8\ell} \tag{6.31}$$

So the total distance density function in this case becomes:

$$df_{p=\infty}(\ell) = \frac{(\ell-d)(-2\ell^2+3a\ell-ad+d\ell)}{4\ell} \qquad (6.32)$$

3. $a<\ell<a+d$.

Inside each square there are no such distances ℓ; only distances that connect both squares are relevant in this case.

$$df_{p=\infty}(\ell) = 2 \int\limits_{x_1=a+d-\ell}^{a} \int\limits_{x_2=0}^{a} \frac{a}{8\ell}\ dx_2 dx_1 = \frac{a^2(\ell-d)}{4\ell} \qquad (6.33)$$

4. $a+d<\ell<2a+d$; there is one interesting zone (fig. 6.20):

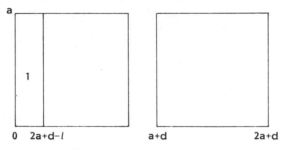

fig. 6.20 $a+d<\ell<2a+d$, 1 set.

$$df_{p=\infty}(\ell)_1 = 2 \int\limits_{x_1=0}^{2a+d-\ell} \int\limits_{x_2=0}^{\ell} \frac{a}{8\ell}\ dx_2 dx_1 ,$$

$$= \frac{a^2}{4\ell}(2a+d-\ell) \qquad (6.34)$$

Concluding:

$$df_{p=\infty}(\ell) = \begin{cases} \frac{1}{4}(\frac{\ell-d}{\ell})(-2\ell^2+3a\ell-ad+d\ell) & d<\ell<a \\[3mm] \frac{a^2}{4\ell}(\ell-d) & a<\ell<a+d \\[3mm] \frac{a^2}{4\ell}(2a+d-\ell) & a+d<\ell<2a+d \\[3mm] 0 & \text{otherwise} \end{cases}$$

$$(6.35)$$

(only intersquare distances are counted)

If d=0 one will find the results of a rectangle (a x 2a), namely

$$df_{p=\infty}(\ell) = \begin{cases} (a-\ell)(2a-\ell) + \frac{1}{4}\ell(3a-2\ell) & 0<\ell<a \\[3mm] \frac{a^2}{4\ell}(2a-\ell) & a<\ell<2a \end{cases}$$

The expected distance can be calculated as follows:

$$E\ell = \Big\{ \int_{\ell=0}^{d}(a-\ell)(2a-\ell)\ell d\ell + \int_{\ell=d}^{a}(a-\ell)(2a-\ell)\ell + \frac{1}{4}\ell(\frac{\ell-d}{\ell})(-2\ell^2+3a\ell-ad+d\ell)d\ell$$

$$+ \int_{\ell=a}^{a+d}\frac{a^2}{8\ell}\ell(\ell-d)d\ell + \int_{\ell=a+d}^{\ell=2a+d}\frac{a^2}{8\ell}(2a+d-\ell)\ell d\ell \Big\}$$

$$\Big\{ \int_{\ell=0}^{d}(a-\ell)(2a-\ell)d\ell + \int_{\ell=d}^{a}(a-\ell)(2a-\ell)+\frac{1}{4}\frac{(\ell-d)}{\ell}(-2\ell^2+3a\ell-ad+d\ell)d\ell +$$

$$\int_{\ell=a}^{a+d}\frac{a^2}{8\ell}(\ell-d)d\ell + \int_{\ell=a+d}^{2a+d}\frac{a^2}{8\ell}(\ell-d)d\ell \Big\},$$

and after some calculations,

$$E\ell = \frac{\frac{1}{2}a^4 + \frac{3}{16}a^2d^2 - \frac{3}{8}a^3d}{\frac{19}{24}a^3 - \frac{3}{8}a^2d + \frac{3}{8}ad^2 + \frac{1}{24}d^3 + \frac{1}{4}a^2d\log\frac{a(2a+d)}{(a+d)^2} + \frac{1}{4}ad^2\log\frac{a}{d} + \frac{1}{2}a^3\log\frac{2a+d}{a+d}} \qquad (6.36)$$

If d=0 we find $E\ell = \dfrac{\frac{1}{2}a^4}{\frac{19}{24}a^3 + \frac{1}{2}a^3\log2}$ which is the same result as the

expected value in case of a rectangle (a x 2a)

On fig 6.21, 6.22 and 6.23 some intersquare distance density functions are shown and in fig. 6.24 some complete density functions can be observed.

6.2. The contact distribution between two squares

6.2.1 p=1.

Once the distance density function is known, the contact density function can be derived by multiplying the distance density function by the circumference of a circle ($2\pi\ell$) in case Euclidean distances are involved, a square ($4\ell\sqrt{2}$) for Manhattan distances, or (8ℓ) for p=∞.

Only the results for Manhattan distances are presented here; the others can be derived similarly.

The results for the distance density function are

1. intrasquare distances:

$$A(\ell) = a^2 - a\ell + \frac{1}{6}\ell^2 \qquad\qquad 0 < \ell < a$$

$$B(\ell) = \frac{(2a-\ell)^3}{6\ell} \qquad\qquad a < \ell < 2a$$

2. intersquare distance:

$$C(\ell) = \frac{1}{12\ell}\{3a(\ell-d)^2 - (\ell-d)^3\} \qquad\qquad d<\ell<\tfrac{1}{2}a+d$$

$$D(\ell) = \frac{5a^3}{48\ell} + \frac{(\ell-a-d)^3}{12\ell} - \frac{a(a+d-\ell)^2}{4\ell}$$
$$+ \frac{a(\ell-d-\tfrac{1}{2}a)^2}{4\ell} \qquad\qquad \tfrac{1}{2}a+d<\ell<a+d$$

$$F(\ell) = \frac{5a^3}{24\ell} - \frac{(\ell-a-d)^3}{6\ell} - \frac{(\tfrac{3}{2}a-\ell+d)^3}{3\ell} \qquad\qquad a+d<\ell<\tfrac{3}{2}a+d$$

$$G(\ell) = \frac{7a^3}{48\ell} - \frac{a(\ell-\tfrac{3}{2}a-d)^2}{4\ell} + \frac{(2a+d-\ell)^2 a}{4\ell}$$
$$- \frac{(2a+d-\ell)^3}{6\ell} \qquad\qquad \tfrac{3}{2}a+d<\ell<2a+d$$

$$H(\ell) = \frac{a^3}{24\ell} + \frac{(\ell-d-2a)^3}{4\ell} - \frac{a(\ell-d-2a)^2}{3\ell}$$
$$+ \frac{(\tfrac{5}{2}a-\ell+d)^3}{3\ell} \qquad\qquad 2a+d<\ell<\tfrac{5}{2}a+d$$

$$I(\ell) = \frac{(3a+d-\ell)^3}{12\ell} \qquad\qquad \tfrac{5}{2}a+d<\ell<3a+d$$

The contact density function in two squares (a x a) at distance d becomes: (5 sets have to be distinguished)

1. $0<d<\tfrac{1}{2}a$

$$cf(\ell) = \begin{cases} 2A(\ell)\ell\sqrt{2} & 0<\ell<d \\ 2A(\ell)\ell\sqrt{2} + 2C(\ell)\ell\sqrt{2} & d<\ell<\tfrac{1}{2}a+d \\ 2A(\ell)\ell\sqrt{2} + 2E(\ell)\ell\sqrt{2} & \tfrac{1}{2}a+d<\ell<a \\ 2B(\ell)\ell\sqrt{2} + 2E(\ell)\ell\sqrt{2} & a<\ell<a+d \\ 2B(\ell)\ell\sqrt{2} + 2F(\ell)\ell\sqrt{2} & a+d<\ell<\tfrac{3}{2}a+d \\ 2B(\ell)\ell\sqrt{2} + 2G(\ell)\ell\sqrt{2} & \tfrac{3}{2}a+d<\ell<2a \end{cases}$$

$$\left[\begin{array}{ll}
2G(\ell)\ell\sqrt{2} & 2a<\ell<2a+d \\
2H(\ell)\ell\sqrt{2} & 2a+d<\ell<\frac{5}{2}a+d \\
2I(\ell)\ell\sqrt{2} & \frac{5}{2}a+d<\ell<3a+d
\end{array}\right.$$

$$(6.37)$$

2. $\frac{1}{2}a<d<a$

$$cf(\ell) = \left\{\begin{array}{ll}
2A(\ell)\ell\sqrt{2} & 0<\ell<d \\
2A(\ell)\ell\sqrt{2} + 2C(\ell)\ell\sqrt{2} & d<\ell<a \\
2B(\ell)\ell\sqrt{2} + 2C(\ell)\ell\sqrt{2} & a<\ell<\frac{1}{2}a+d \\
2B(\ell)\ell\sqrt{2} + 2E(\ell)\ell\sqrt{2} & \frac{1}{2}a+d<\ell<a+d \\
2B(\ell)\ell\sqrt{2} + 2F(\ell)\ell\sqrt{2} & a+d<\ell<2a \\
2F(\ell)\ell\sqrt{2} & 2a<\ell<\frac{3}{2}a+d \\
2G(\ell)\ell\sqrt{2} & \frac{3}{2}a+d<\ell<2a+d \\
2H(\ell)\ell\sqrt{2} & 2a+d<\ell<\frac{5}{2}a+d \\
I(\ell)\ell\sqrt{2} & \frac{5}{2}a+d<\ell<3a+d
\end{array}\right.$$

$$(6.38)$$

3. $a<d<\frac{3}{2}a$

$$cf(\ell) = \left\{\begin{array}{ll}
2A(\ell)\ell\sqrt{2} & 0<\ell<a \\
2B(\ell)\ell\sqrt{2} & a<\ell<d \\
2B(\ell)\ell\sqrt{2} + 2C(\ell)\ell\sqrt{2} & d<\ell<\frac{1}{2}a+d \\
2B(\ell)\ell\sqrt{2} + 2E(\ell)\ell\sqrt{2} & \frac{1}{2}a+d<\ell<2a \\
2E(\ell)\ell\sqrt{2} & 2a<\ell<a+d \\
2F(\ell)\ell\sqrt{2} & a+d<\ell<\frac{3}{2}a+d \\
G(\ell)\ell\sqrt{2} & \frac{3}{2}a+d<\ell<2a+d \\
2H(\ell)\ell\sqrt{2} & 2a+d<\ell<\frac{5}{2}a+d \\
2I(\ell)\ell\sqrt{2} & \frac{5}{2}a+d<\ell<3a+d
\end{array}\right.$$

$$(6.39)$$

4. $\frac{3}{2}a<d<2a$

$$\left[\begin{array}{ll}
2A(\ell)\ell\sqrt{2} & 0<\ell<a \\
2B(\ell)\ell\sqrt{2} & a<\ell<d
\end{array}\right.$$

$$cf(\ell)=\begin{cases} 2B(\ell)\ell\sqrt{2} + 2C(\ell)\ell\sqrt{2} & d<\ell<2a \\ 2C(\ell)\ell\sqrt{2} & 2a<\ell<\frac{1}{2}a+d \\ 2E(\ell)\ell\sqrt{2} & \frac{1}{2}a+d<\ell<a+d \\ 2F(\ell)\ell\sqrt{2} & a+d<\ell<\frac{3}{2}a+d \\ 2G(\ell)\ell\sqrt{2} & \frac{3}{2}a+d<\ell<2a+d \\ 2H(\ell)\ell\sqrt{2} & 2a+d<\ell<\frac{5}{2}a+d \\ 2I(\ell)\ell\sqrt{2} & \frac{5}{2}a+d<\ell<3a+d \end{cases}$$

$$(6.40)$$

5. $2a<d$

$$cf(\ell)=\begin{cases} 2A(\ell)\ell\sqrt{2} & 0<\ell<a \\ 2B(\ell)\ell\sqrt{2} & a<\ell<2a \\ 0 & 2a<\ell<d \\ 2C(\ell)\ell\sqrt{2} & d<\ell<\frac{1}{2}a+d \\ 2E(\ell)\ell\sqrt{2} & \frac{1}{2}a+d<\ell<a+d \\ 2F(\ell)\ell\sqrt{2} & a+d<\ell<\frac{3}{2}a+d \\ 2G(\ell)\ell\sqrt{2} & \frac{3}{2}a+d<\ell<2a+d \\ 2H(\ell)\ell\sqrt{2} & 2a+d<\ell<\frac{5}{2}a+d \\ 2I(\ell)\ell\sqrt{2} & \frac{5}{2}a+d<\ell<3a+d \end{cases}$$

$$(6.41)$$

It can easily be checked that in case d=0 the results of a contact density function in a rectangle (2a x a) are found. The complete function is plotted for d=0,1,2,3,4,5,6,7,10,20,30,40, and 50; (a=10) fig. 6.25, ..., fig. 6.37.

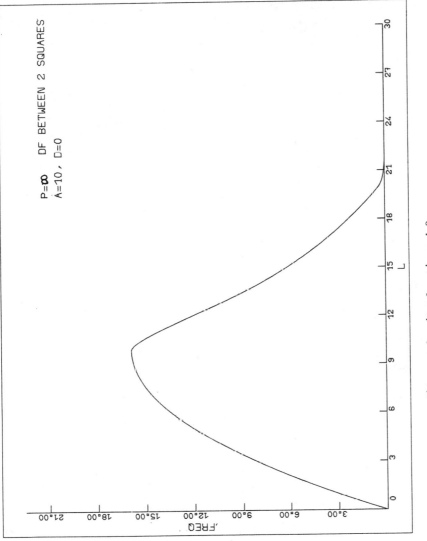

fig.6.21 Intersquare distance density function; d=0

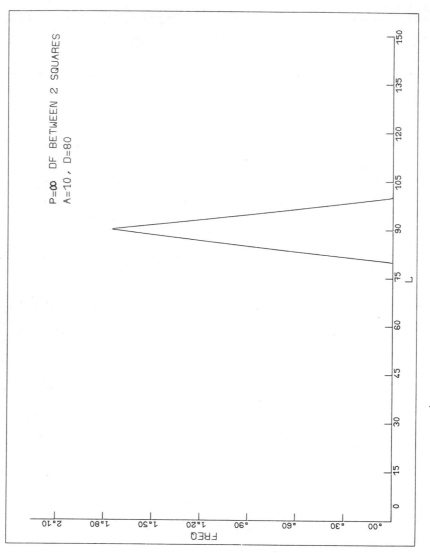

fig.6.22 Intersquare distance density function; d=80

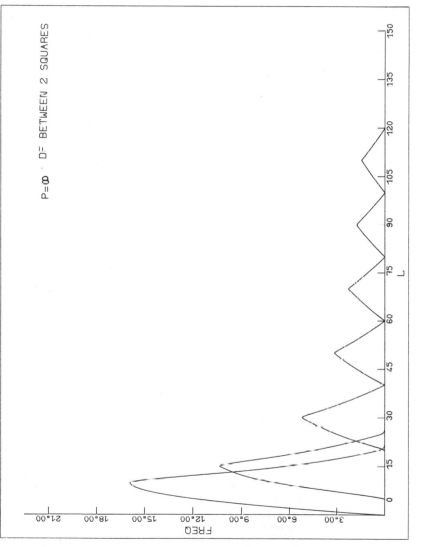

fig.6.23   Intersqare distance density functions; d=0,10,20,40,60,80,100

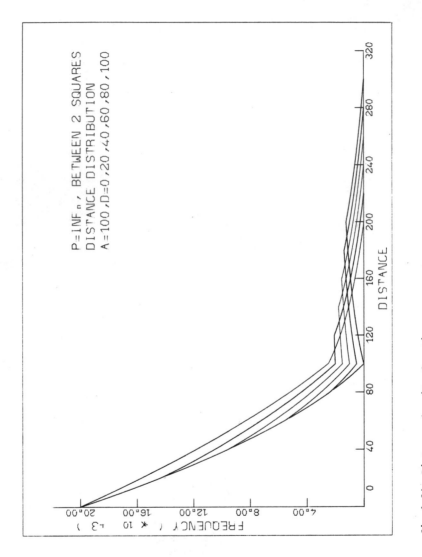

fig.6.24 Distance density functions

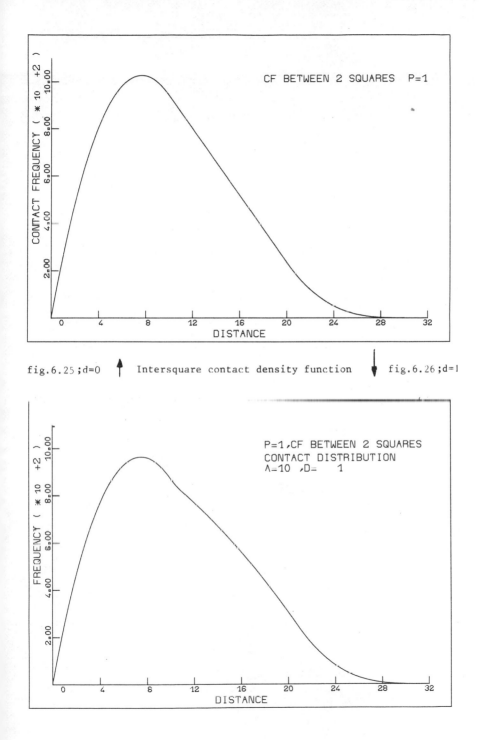

fig.6.25;d=0 ↑ Intersquare contact density function ↓ fig.6.26;d=1

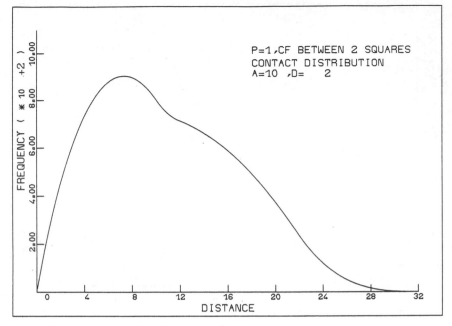

fig,6.27   Contact density function;d=2

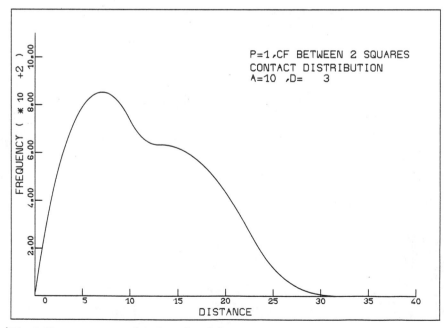

Fig.6.28   Contact density function;d=3

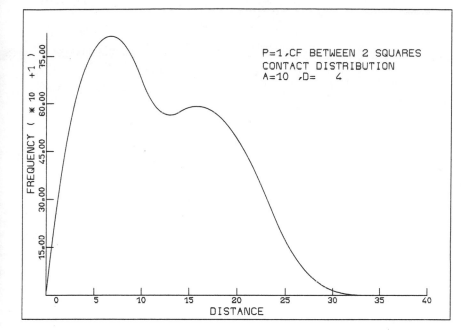

fig.6.29 Contact density function;d=4

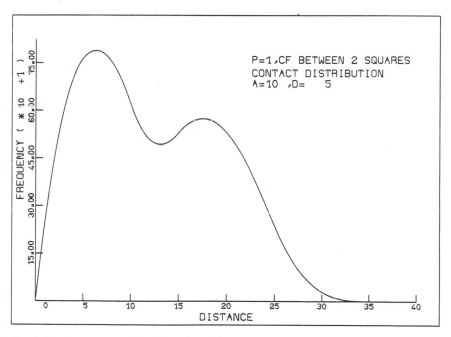

fig.6.30 Contact density function;d=5

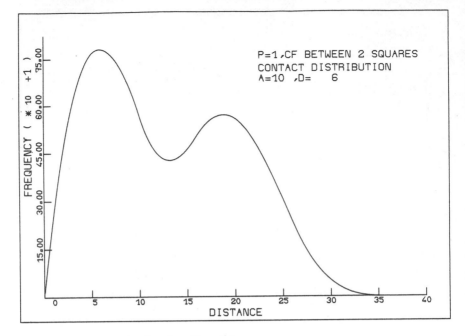

fig.6.31   Contact density function;d=6

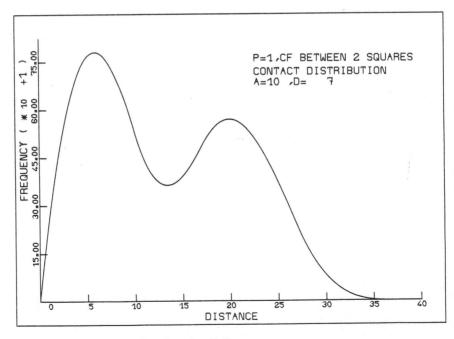

fig.6.32   Contact density function;d=7

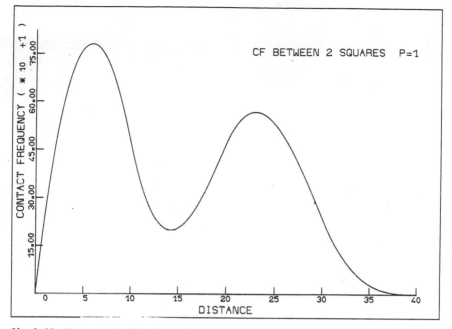

fig.6.33   Contact density function;d=10

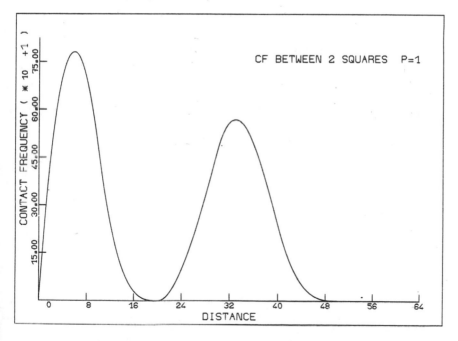

fig. 6.34   Contact density function; d=20

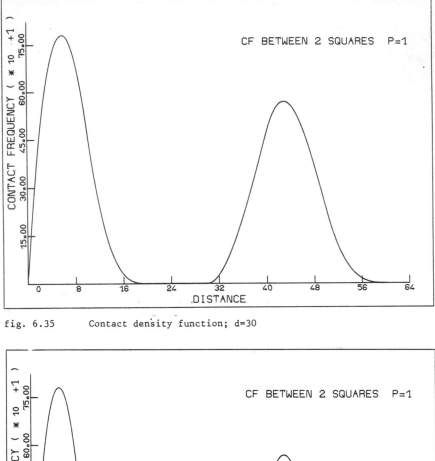

fig. 6.35   Contact density function; d=30

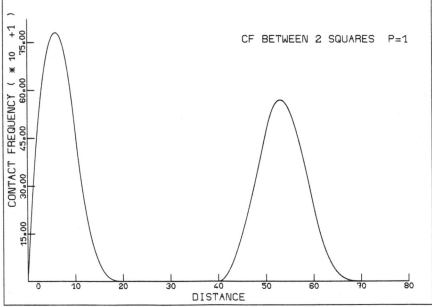

fig. 6.36   Contact density function; d=40

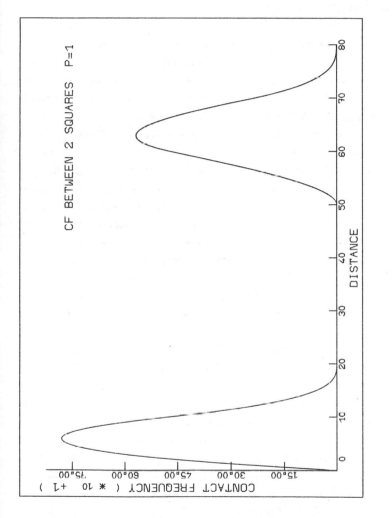

fig. 6.37   Contact density function: d=50

6.3 Conclusion

In the previous chapters a number of density functions and frequency distributions of distances are derived analytically; three types were selected:

1. distance distributions,
2. road-area distributions, and
3. contact distributions.

The distance distribution shows distances between points in a pregeographical space; these points are continuously distributed inside the defined set, and they are arranged according to their distance measure. The road area distribution pictures the share of the area covered with roads arranged according to the road-distance value. In order to measure that value, Minkowski distance measures for $p=1$, 2 and ∞ were used.

The distance density function is strongly related to the shape of the area. Looking at one point inside that set, the measure for the number of points at distance ℓ is maximum and remains maximum as long as ℓ is small enough (no points at distance ℓ are located outside the area); only the borders of the area can change this measure. When ℓ is increased and a number of points at distance ℓ from a point inside the set is located outside the area, the measure for the number of distances ℓ will decrease. Only the borders of the area determine the measure for the number of distances ℓ; the same holds for the road-area distribution. The density functions are continuously decreasing having their maximum value for the minimum distance, namely $\ell=0$; as ℓ increases, an increasing number of points inside the area shows a decreasing measure for the number of distances ℓ, and finally, when ℓ is large enough, the measure for the number of distances for each point inside the area will become zero; in that case the density function becomes zero too.

The contact distribution, often called distance distribution in the literature, is closely connected to our distance distribution; the main difference between them is that points inside the set are considered to have a non-zero area measure which means that the number of distances starting in one point is measured in a different way. The number of distances ℓ one can observe starting in a point is not only depending on the location of the borders (see the distance distribution) but also on the value of ℓ itself.

This number was determined by the circumference of a circle or square, containing points at distance ℓ (for p=2 a circle with radius ℓ, p=1 a square ($\ell\sqrt{2}$ x $\ell\sqrt{2}$)); as long as ℓ is small enough, so that the circumference is completely located inside the set, the number of distances depends only on ℓ itself and is increasing as ℓ increases; when the circumference is partly located outside the set this will have a negative effect on the number of distances which become finally zero when all points at distance ℓ are located outside the set.

To derive a distribution of distances, starting point was the pre-geographical space continuously filled with points; a set of points had to be defined and also measures for the number of distances and the number of points (see also the fundamental papers of Beguin and Thisse (1979) and Huriot and Thisse (1984)). The shape of the distance density function and the road-area density function were plotted to study the influence of the change of shape on the function curve; as the rectangle becomes more elongated the function becomes more flat. This kind of functions was also presented in Kuiper and Paelinck (1982), ten Raa (1983) and Paelinck (1983).

When instead of a two-dimensional space a one-dimensional space is used, all distributions become exactly the same.

We derived analytically density functions in a circle, a rectangle and a square and also in two seperate squares, using different distance measures; with our calculation method one can derive density functions in other well-defined shapes as well, for example triangles or shapes mentioned in Taylor (1971).

In the literature mostly contact distributions are mentioned, often in circles with Euclidean distances, although there are some more general publications; good examples are Thanh (1962), who derived contact distributions in a circle, a triangle and a square using Euclidean distances, de Smith (1977) who describes existing literature on contact distributions, namely in a circle and a rectangle, and Christofides (1971) who derived expected distances in different shapes and also used Manhattan distances.

General papers on distributions of distances between points in convex domains are Geciauskas (1976), Hammersley (1950), Vangular, Alagar (1976), Lord (1954), and ten Raa (1983). Euclidean distances in circles are reported by Barton, David and Fix (1963), who studied chromosome patterns in cells and by David and Fix (1964) who derived several moments of the distribution of distances inside the circle. Fairthorne (1964) shows distances between random points in two concentric circles, and Gilbert (1977) and Getis (1982) show some expected distances in a circle and a square. Horrowitz (1965) derived a model for the probability of random paths across elementary geometrical shapes.

In order to get a good impression of the shape of several density functions a lot of figures are shown in the previous chapters, especially the influence of the dimensions of the shape of the area (e.g. the rectangle) on the density function becomes more clear. A special case is the contact distribution between two separate equal squares; a lot of plots were made to show how the distribution changes as the squares move away. There are a few shapes, especially when the squares are close, which are much the same as the contact freqency distribution that can be observed in several countries (chapter 9).

The contact frequency distribution is also calculated for discrete points in space. Only p=1 and p=∞ are considered here (because they are easier to handle analytically) in squares and rectangles; it is shown that this distribution approaches the continuous one as the number of points increases. All distributions are analytically derived using a method that is very appropriate for well-defined shapes. The first moments of a lot of distributions are computed and for nearly all distributions the relative density function is presented.

Summing up the results of the first (six) chapters of this book the most important contributions are:
- the definition of three types of distributions and the explanation of the relation between them,
- the use of different distance measures for the calculation of the density functions,
- the use of different shapes in which distributions are calculated,
- the use of both continuously distributed and discrete distributed points inside the shapes,

- the analytical derivation of both absolute and relative density functions and in most cases the first moments.

Comparing this with results mentioned in literature it is strik-
ing that most studies describe one special type of distributions, the
contact distribution, use one special distance measure, the Euclidean
distance measure, and mostly in one shape, the circle, in which points
are continuously distributed. An exception is the paper of Thanh (1962)
who studied contact distributions using Euclidean distances in a circle,
a triangle and a square.

In the next chapters it will be tried to bridge the gap between
observed frequency distributions of distances and analytically calculated distributions. First, one of the distributions found in the previous chapters is directly compared with a number of frequency distributions of distances of European countries (chapter 8); since this is
one big jump, chapter 9 and 10 will insert two small jumps. An observed
frequency distribution of distances in a country is determined by the
shape of that country and by the selected sample of cities; first the
shape of the countries will be analysed using the analytically derived
density functions (chapter 9) and after that we will focuss on the
sample of cities in the countries and try to estimate p norms using frequency distributions of distances in each country. In chapter 7 these
ideas are introduced more precisely.

7 Comparing calculated and observed distributions of distances

7.1 Introduction

Distributions of distances considered here are always measured in a finite set; this is one of the reasons for the peculiarity of those distributions in geography: distances between points are restricted by the size and the shape of the region in which they are located: "In fact any areal shape will have associated with it a frequency distribution of distances between all points within its bounderies." (Taylor, 1971).

Distributions of distances in countries can be observed by collecting all distances between a set of cities in that country. Cities are represented by points, so distances are measured between a set of points located in a random shaped area; we are dealing with network distances since the distance between two cities is measured over a (road) network. If the observed distances are grouped according to their value, a distribution of distances is found; the question what type of distribution is found, has to be answered first.

In the previous chapters 3 types of distributions of distances are defined. Looking at the definition one has to conclude that the observed distribution has to be a contact distribution. A contact density function is found by considering each point in the defined set and counting all points, located inside the set at distance ℓ; the distance density function is found by dividing the number of points at distance ℓ located inside the set by the total number of points at distance ℓ. So in case of a distance distribution (the same holds for the road area distribution) also a number of points located outside the defined set, depending on the distance measure, is of interest. Since the frequency distribution of distances in a country is only determined by looking at cities inside the country and by collecting the distances in a way comparable with the construction of a contact distribution, the observed distribution has to be a contact distribution.

The observed contact frequency distribution could be considered as a sample out of a analytically derived contact density function. This last distribution is always related to relatively regular shapes and determined by a limited number of parameters. Countries that are very

compactly shaped, could be close to regular shapes as squares or
circles, whereas countries, which are stretched out will be close to a
long rectangle.

7.2. Comparing observed and analytically calculated contact distributions

      One can observe a contact frequency distribution by deriving a
distance table from a map: the distances are arranged according to their
value and after defining classes of distances, a histogram is found. For
a number of reasons this observed distribution will diverge from theoretical analytically derived density functions; the main reasons are:

1. The distances between cities on a map are measured along a (road)net-
   work, whereas the analytically calculated distributions are using
   uniform distance measures (for instance Euclidean or Manhattan distances).
2. The points, representing cities on a map, are distributed over the
   region in a random way, whereas the point pattern in the theoretical
   distributions is very regular; we worked in a pregeographical space
   with points continuously distributed or using sets with a very regular discrete point pattern.
3. The shape of existing regions is random, whereas in order to calculate theoretical contact distributions well-defined regular shapes
   are used.
4. Observed distance frequency distributions always show the distances
   between a (random) sample of cities, whereas the analytically calculated distributions concern all places in the area, or all points of
   a regular pattern.

      Concluding, one may say that the observed contact frequency dis-
tribution is determined by a number of factors that are fairly random
(the road network, the size and shape of the region, the actual distance
measure, the point pattern); therefore in comparing the analytically
calculated contact distribution and the observed distribution, one can
expect to meet several problems (in chapter 8 both distributions are
compared). If it is possible to find theoretical distributions that fit

with observed distributions in an acceptable way, one can represent a random shaped region by a well-defined mathematical shape of known dimensions; only p-distance measures p=1 and p=2 are used here, as only for these measures distributions are analytically derived. Before contact distributions can be compared, a choice has to be made about the shape of the set belonging to the theoretical distribution. It has to be a simple flexible shape as close as possible to any shape of a country.

We have decided to try contact distributions with a <u>rectangular shape</u> (a,b; b<a). Advantages of a rectangle are that only 2 parameters need to be estimated, that the shape is relatively flexible (from compact to elongated), and that the contact distribution could be derived easily (see chapter 5).

Although the rectangle is a relatively flexible shape, the real shape of countries is still much more irregular. We will not find the best approximation of the real shape but we will find a rectangular shape that is related as well as possible to the set of cities which are in the sample. On maps, network distances are measured, being defined as the minimum length of a route between two points; when the network is dense enough one can expect the network distance to have values that could be found by calculating the distances between the same points using a distance measure, so one should use a value for p between 1 and 2. Only for p=1 and p=2 norms contact distributions were analytically derived, therefore 2 different rectangles will be found.

Consider two points O and A on a network; the network distance is OA, A is situated somewhere in the shaded area (fig 7.1). When the value of OA is considered to be a Manhattan distance, one would find points like A_1, located on the square (a√2 x a√2) and when Euclidean distances are used, points like A_2 would be found, located on the circle (a).

Points A_1 are in general closer to 0 than points A_2; so the rectangle related to p=2 that one finds after comparing the distributions, will always be larger than the one that is found using p=1 norms.

In figure 7.2 the comparisation of distributions is schematically shown.

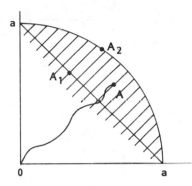

fig. 7.1. Network distances and p-norms

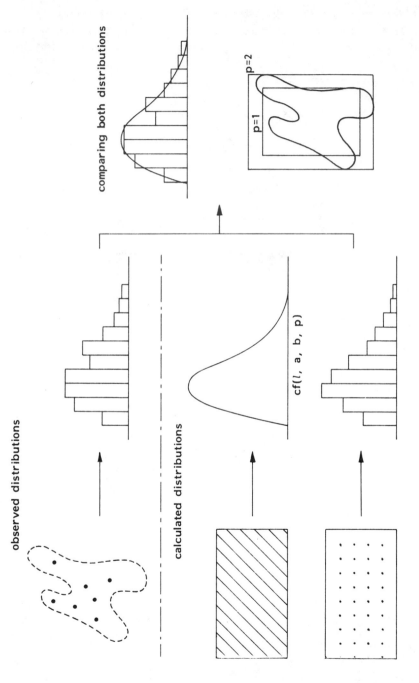

fig. 7.2.

In order to estimate a and b a maximum likelihood method is used.

Let $cf_{p=1}(\ell;a,b)$ — the relative contact density function of a rectangle

(a x b, b≤a), p=1,

$\hat{c}f(\ell)$ — the observed contact frequency distribution of a region

N — the number of observed classes of contact distances,

ℓ_i — the observed number of contacts in class i; i=1, ...,

N,

m — the size of the class-interval,

n — the number of observations (contacts),

$$\text{so} \quad \sum_{i=1}^{N} \ell_i = n.$$

The minimum contact distance to be observed is 0, the maximum Nm.

$$\text{We have} \quad \int_{1=0}^{a+b} cf_{p=1}(\ell;a,b)d\ell=1$$

Let $\hat{c}f(\ell)_i$ be — the observed relative contact frequency in the ith
class (the observed probability of finding a distance
in the ith class),

$$\overset{..}{c}f(\ell)_i \triangleq \frac{\ell_i}{\Sigma\ell_i} \quad \text{and} \quad \sum_{i=1}^{N} \overset{..}{c}f(\ell)_i = 1.$$

Each observed frequency $\hat{c}f(\ell)_i$ should be compared with a part of the
contact density function of a rectangle to be calculated as:

$$\int_{\ell=(i-1)m}^{\ell=im} cf_{p=1}(\ell;a,b)d\ell; \quad \text{one can also use a good approximation, namely}$$

$mcf_{p=1}(im-\tfrac{1}{2}m;a,b)$ when the number of classes is large.

The aim now is: find a and b in such a way that function L is

minimum;

$$\text{so min } L \triangleq \sum_{i=1}^{N} (mcf_{p=1}(im-\tfrac{1}{2}m;a,b)-\hat{c}f(\ell)_i)^2 \qquad (7.1)$$

An alternative L^* could be minimised, where L^* uses a weighted sum. In the sample the number of extreme values is very small and therefore in the extreme parts of the range of possible distances, the comparisation of the observed and the theoretical values could be less accurate. The weighted sum L^* takes account of this; the comparison in the part of the distribution with the highest frequencies is considered as most important so the weight has to be given a high relative value; where we can expect a small number of distances the weight will be small.

L^* is now defined as $L^* \stackrel{\Delta}{=} \hat{cf}(\ell)_i L; \quad 0 < \hat{cf}(\ell)_i < 1.$ (7.2)

When L or L^* is minimised the estimates a^* and b^* can be found; $cf(\ell;a^*,b^*)$ being the contact density function that is "as close as possible" to $\hat{cf}(\ell)$.

The problem of minimising non-linear functions, for which no analytical solution-method can be applied, can be solved by using e.g. iterative methods like the classical Newton-Raphson ar Gauss-Seidel methods. We used a quasi-Newton method, the variable metric method suggested by den Broeder (1980).

7.3 Shape Analysis

Few geographical areas of interest have the simple regular shapes that allow analytical derivation of distributions of distances; in geography one observes all possible distances between points such as distance tables from maps of the lengths of journeys within cities or the distances between the original homes of marriage partners (Thanh, 1962). As has been shown in the first chapters the distribution of distances is influenced by the shape of the area in which the points are located. So when one wishes to test observed distances against some standard distribution, one should always take into account the constraints imposed by the shape of the area.

An early example of a theoretical model that generates patterns which consist exclusively of straight lines, was developed by Horowitz (1965); in his paper the distribution of the lenghts of straight-line paths across fundamental geometric shapes was derived; the mathematical expressions of the Horowitz model for a circle, a square and a rectangle are also mentioned in Getis and Boots (1978); they give an example of pedestrian paths across a circular shopping plaza. The observed distribution of the path lengths across the plaza of 100 resp. 1000 pedestrians was compared by the distribution predicted with the Horowitz model and a significance test was constructed (see also Unwin, 1981). In our models points are not only located on the perimeter of geometrical space but dispersed over the area and distances are measured between all pairs; so this models could have larger applicability in geography.

In chapter 8 analytically calculated density functions are directly compared with observed frequency distributions of countries; dimensions of the rectangle were estimated and goodness of fit tests performed.

The observed frequency distribution is determined by the set of cities in the distance table. An infinite number of shapes can be constructed in order to locate this set; the real shape of the country is one of these. The relation between the set of cities and the real shape of the country depends mainly on the number of cities and their location inside the set; when the number of cities is increasing this relation will become clearer. Dimensions of the real shape can be better estimated as the distribution of cities in the country is closer to a uniform distribution and as the road network would be equally dense over the country so that network distances could be accurately approximated by a p-norm ($1 < p < 2$).

If one is interested in finding a rectangle as close as possible to the dimensions of the real shape, a method can be used that does not have the disadvantages just mentioned. This method, demonstrated in chapter 9 (Shape Analysis), is independent of the random set of cities in the country. The random shape of the country is covered by a grid of cells of equal size; each cell is represented by a point having value 1 if the cell is located inside the shape, otherwise it gets value 0. In this way each shape can be represented by a boolean matrix (Taylor, 1971); considering each point value 1 separately, one can calculate all contact distances to the other points of value 1, using known p norms ($p=1$, $p=2$). In this way a contact frequency distribution can be constructed which is strongly related to the shape of the area. If the number of cells increases, the shape will be approximated more accurately;

with the aid of a computer the contact frequency distribution can be
easily calculated. This "computer contact distribution" represents the
random shape, and will be compared with the contact density function of
a rectangle (a,b) (fig. 7.4). In this way one can expect better estimations of the dimensions of the rectangle that fits best the random
shape; results are presented in chapter 9.

7.4 Network analysis

In chapter 8 a contact density function of a rectangle was compared with an observed contact frequency distribution of a set of cities
in a country; in chapter 9 the set of cities is replaced by a set of
discrete points, uniformly distributed over the country. In chapter 10
(Network Analysis) the set of cities is analysed, especially the observed network distances between the cities, without looking at the
shape of the country; so no estimations of a rectangle will be made. The
most important factors that determine the observed frequency distribution are the number of cities and their locations and the road network. As mentioned before, network distances could be compared with p-
norms (one can expect $1<p\leqslant2$); in chapter 10 this p-norm will be estimated.

Theoretical contact density functions that are derived, are related to well-defined areas (circle, rectangle), point patterns (uniform) and distance measures (p=1 and p=2); we will now focus on a (random) set of points and a road network: if it is possible to construct
contact frequency distributions of a set of points closely related to an
observed set of cities, using not only p=1 or p=2 but different p-norms,
one could compare this frequency distributions with the observed one and
find the frequency distribution, closest to the observed one. The p-norm
of this theoretical frequency distribution is considered to be the best
estimate of the distance measure related to network distances in the
country; in this way a distance function could be found which best approximates the association between a set of cities and a set of distances.

An extra problem that arises in comparing actual networks and p-
norms is the orientation of the network. Having 2 points, so 2 pairs of

coordinates, and using Euclidean distances, it is irrelevant how the axes are orientated, but for all other p-norms it is important (fig. 7.3).

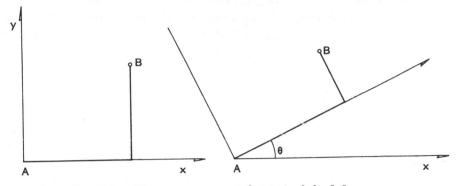

fig. 7.3. Distance measured for p=1; 0=0, θ=θ

The general expression for the distance between two points $A(x_1,x_2)$ and $B(y_1,y_2)$ is:

$$d_{AB} = \{ \left| (x_1\cos\theta+y_1\sin\theta)-(x_2\cos\theta+y_2\sin\theta) \right|^p +$$
$$\left| (-x_1\sin\theta+y_1\cos\theta)-(-x_2\sin\theta+y_2\cos\theta) \right|^p \}^{\frac{1}{p}} \qquad (7.3)$$

This means one has to estimate θ and p simultaneously, both the orientation (θ) and the p-norm that fits best should be estimated.

Theoretical contact frequency distributions between points related as close as possible to the observed set of cities are found by covering the country by a grid of cells. Each cell containing a city of the observed set gets value 1, otherwise 0; in this way a set of cities can be represented by a boolean matrix. Using (7.3) distances between points value 1 can be calculated and a frequency distribution of distances can be constructed when p and θ are known. For each country that is analysed a boolean matrix is constructed and a number of frequency distributions for different (p,θ) combinations are calculated and compared with the observed contact frequency distribution (fig. 7.5). The calculated distribution closest to the observed network distance distri-

bution determines the p and Θ values that fits best the (road) network
distances of the country. A problem is the choice of the number of (p,Θ)
combinations one has to investigate; we used a scanning method, assuming
1.0<p<2.0 and 0<Θ<90°. First different values of p, namely p=1.0, p=1.1.
..., p=1.9, p=2.0 were considered and each value of p was combined with
9 different values of Θ, namely Θ=0°, 10°, 20°, ..., 80° (Θ=0° and Θ=90°
give equal results); in this way 11 x 9 = 99 (p,Θ) combinations could be
made and for each combination a contact frequency distribution was constructed, each distribution being compared with the observed one (using
a minimum distance method) and the best ones were appointed. After those
computations an impression was gained about the area with the best p,Θ
combination; in order to find more accurate estimations several new p,Θ
combinations were chosen, close to the best ones, and explored in the
same way. The minimum distance method and the results are mentioned in
chapter 10.

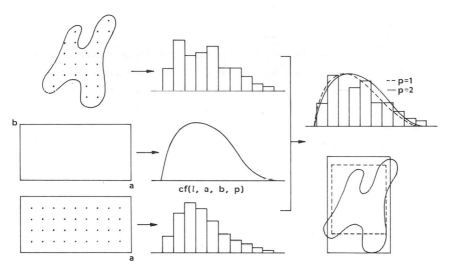

fig. 7.4. Shape analysis

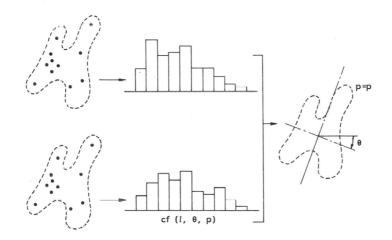

fig. 7.5. Estimation of p and θ

7.5 Goodness of fit tests

According to 7.3 observed contact frequency distributions should be compared with analytically determined contact density functions of a rectangle; the first problem is to estimate the dimensions of the rectangle, a and b: the theoretical distribution of a rectangle that fits best the observed, determines those values for a and b. When they are estimated it is necessary to test the goodness-of-fit between the "rectangle" distribution and the observed one.

There are a number of tests available; we shall confine ourselves to the chi-square test for goodness of fit and the Kolmogorov-Smirnov test. The first test is appropriate when the null-hypothesis specifies the distribution apart from certain unknown parameters; estimation of these parameters is then required both for the test and for subsequent use of the distribution if the null hypothesis is accepted (see Green and Margerison, 1978, chapter 10).

Our null hypothesis H_0 is : the density function of the contacts between cities in a country is $cf_{p=1,2}(\ell;a,b)$, where $cf(\ell)$ is known and a and b are unknown; the alternative hypothesis H_1 asserts that $cf_p(\ell;a,b)$ is not the density function of the observed contacts in a country. H_1 is a quite general alternative, there being an infinite number of density functions that are not the same as $cf(\ell;a,b)$.

7.5.1. The chi-square test

The occurence of one of the sets of possible values of the observations of distances in a country constitutes an event. Hence from the data, we obtain a set of observed frequencies or counts of the events. The expected frequencies of the events under H_0 should be calculated; by expected frequencies the total number of data is ment, N say, multiplied by the estimated probability of the events, estimated because a and b are not known.

Now the next theorem is used: (see Mood, Graybill, and Boes, 1974, pp, 446)

Let the possible outcomes of a certain random experiment be decomposed into k+1 mutually exclusive sets $A_1, \ldots, A_{k+1}$. Define $p_j = p(A_j)$,
$j=1, \ldots k+1$, and assume $p_j = P_j(\Theta_1, \ldots, \Theta_r)$, $j=1, \ldots, k+1$. In n independent repetitions of the random experiment, let N_j denote the number
of outcomes belonging to the set $A_j, j=1, \ldots, k+1$ so that

$\sum\limits_{j+1}^{k+1} N_j = n$. Let $\hat{\Theta}_1, \ldots, \hat{\Theta}_r$ be BAN estimators of $\Theta_1, \ldots, \Theta_r$ based on

$N_1, \ldots, N_k$. Then under certain general regularity conditions on the
P_j's

$$Q_k' = \sum_{j=1}^{k+1} \frac{(N_j - n\hat{P}_j)^2}{n\hat{P}_j} \text{ has as limiting distribution the chi-square}$$

distribution with k-r degrees of freedom, where

$$\hat{P}_j = P_j(\hat{\Theta}_1, \ldots, \hat{\Theta}_r), \quad j=1, \ldots, k+1.$$

The theorem can be used to obtain a goodness-of-fit test. Suppose
that one wishes to test that a random sample of n observations $\ell_1^r, \ldots, \ell_n^r$,
each representing a contact distance observed in a region
come from a density $cf(\ell; a, b)$, where a and b are unknown parameters, but
the function $cf(\ell)$ is known. The null hypothesis is the composite hypothesis H_0: ℓ_j^r has density $cf(\ell_j^r; a, b)$ for some a and b. The null hypothesis states that the random sample comes from a parametric family of
densities that is specified by $cf(\ell; a, b)$. If the range of the random
variable ℓ_j^r is decomposed into N subsets, and if ℓ_i is the absolute
number of ℓ_j^r falling in the ith class (subset), then according to the
theorem,

$$Q_{N-1} = \frac{\sum\limits_{i=1}^{N} (\ell_i - nmcf(im - \frac{1}{2}m; a^*, b^*))^2}{nmcf(im - \frac{1}{2}m; a^*, b^*)} \text{ is distributed as chi-square with N-1-2}$$

degrees of freedom (there are 2 unknown parameters) if n is large and H_0 is true. Hence a test of H_0 can be obtained by rejecting H_0 if and only if the statistic Q_{N-1} is large, that is, reject H_0 if and only if Q_{N-1} exceeds $\chi^2_{1-\alpha}(N-3)$, where $\chi^2_{1-\alpha}(N-3)$ is the $(1-\alpha)$ the quantile of the chi-square distribution with $k-2$ degrees of freedom. In applying this test, it is possible to conclude if the observations fit, or are consistent with, the assumption that they are observations from a density $cf(\ell;a,b)$.

7.5.2. The Kolmogorov-Smirnov test

The chi-square test was applied to investigate how well the frequency distribution of observed contact distances fits an analytically calculated contact frequency distribution on a rectangle.

An alternative test is the Kolmogorov-Smirnov test, which is based on the principle that one expects the frequency distribution of a sample to be similar to the density function under H_0. The test takes advantage of situations in which there can be some logical ordering of intervals so that the profiles of the frequency distributions can be compared. Unlike the chi-square test, there is no limitation on the number of observations or the size of each interval; furthermore the statistic may be calculated very easily. It does not, however, indicate the individual sources of variation as clearly as the chi-square statistic, but it is much more useful for small samples because is does not have a minimum frequency restriction for each interval.

We will use the next theorem: (see Mood, Graybill, and Boes, 1974, pp. 508)

Let $X_1,\ldots,X_n,\ldots$ be independent identically distributed random variables having common continuous cumulative distribution function $F_X(\cdot)=F(\cdot)$. Define

$$D_n=d_n(X_1,\ldots,X_n)=\sup_{-\infty<x<\infty}\left|F_n(x)-F(x)\right|,$$

where $F_n(x)$ is the sample distribution function. Then

$$\lim_{n\to\infty} F_{\sqrt{n}D_n}(x) = \lim_{n\to\infty} P(\sqrt{n}D_n \leqslant x)$$

$$= \left[1-2\sum_{j=1}^{\infty}(-1)^{j-1}e^{-2j^2x^2}\right] I_{(0,\infty)}(x) = H(x).$$

The cumulative distribution function ($\lim P(\sqrt{n}D_n \leqslant x)$) does not depend on the distribution function from which the sample was drawn, that is the distribution of $\sqrt{n}D_n$ is distribution-free.

So one wishes to test that the distribution that is being sampled from, is some specified continuous distribution, i.e. test H_0: $x_i \sim F_0(.)$, where $F_0(.)$ is some completely specified continuous cumulative density function. If H_0 is true, $K_n = k_n(X_1,\ldots,X_n) = \sqrt{n} \sup_{-\infty < x < \infty} |F_n(x) - F_0(x)|$ is approximately distributed as $H(.)$ (see theorem); if H_0 is false, then $F_n(.)$ will tend to be far from $F_0(.)$ and $\sup_{-\infty < x < \infty} |F_n(x) - F_0(x)|$ will tend to be large. So one has to reject H_0 if and only if $k_n > k_{1-\alpha}$ where $H(k_{1-\alpha}) = 1-\alpha$. ($P(K_n > k_{1-\alpha}) \approx \alpha$)). $H(.)$ has been labelled; this test is called the Kolmogorov-Smirnov goodness-of-fit test.

The method of construction of the test-statistic can be indicated as follows: first, both sets of data, that is the observed distribution and the analytically determined distribution, are ordered in an internally logical sequence; secondly, each frequency is expressed as a proportion of N; thirdly, the proportions are cumulated; forthly, the absolute values of the differences between the cumulated proportions for each event (class) are calculated. The largest of these differences is designated D, the test-statistic; the theoretical distribution of all possible D's calculated for all sample sizes is known, and so the critical limits of D at the 95 and 99 per cent confidence limits can be determined.

This Kolgomorov-Smirnov goodness-of-fit test assumes that the null hypothesis is simple, that is, the null hypothesis completely specifies (no unknown parameters) the distribution of the population. One might inquire as to whether such a goodness-of-fit testing procedure can be extended to a composite null hypothesis which states that the distribution of the population belongs to some parametric family of distri-

butions, say $CF(.;a,b)$. For such a null hypothesis $\sup\limits_{\ell} \left| CF_n(\ell)-CF(\ell;a,b) \right|$
is <u>no</u> longer a statistic since it depends on the unknown parameters a
and b. An obvious way of removing the dependence on a and b is to re-
place a and b by estimators a^*,b^*; the test-statistic then becomes
$\sup\limits_{\ell} \left| CF_n(\ell)-CF(\ell;a^*,b^*) \right|$. The distribution of such a test-statistic is
<u>not known</u> and depends on the hypothesised parametric family.

So in this case, it is not possible to apply the Kolmogorov-
Smirnov goodness-of-fit test.
(In a number of cases we still calculate $\sup\limits_{\ell} \left| CF(\ell)-CF(\ell;a^*,b^*) \right|$ without
drawing conclusions; but just in order to compare this number for dif-
ferent countries.)

In chapter 8, where analytically derived contact density functions, depending on papameters a and b, are compared with observed contact frequency distributions with (road) network distances, the chi-
square test can be applied. In chapter 9 (Shape Analysis) the same kind
of theoretical distributions are compared with constructed contact frequency distributions containing the contact distances between all cells
of a grid that covers a country; in this case also the chi-square test
can be applied, whereas the Kolmogorov-Smirnov test, because of the
existence of unknown parameters in the theoretical distribution, is not
applicable. In chapter 10 (Network Analysis) we compare observed contact
frequency distributions containing network distances between cities with
constructed contact frequency distributions of distances measured between a selected number of cells of a grid that covers the country; in
this case there is no theoretical contact distribution, but the cumulated frequencies of both distributions can be computed, so the
Kolmogorov-Smirnov test is applicable in this case.

8 Results of comparison of calculated and observed contact distributions

8.1. Introduction

Contact frequency distributions observed in a number of European countries will be directly compared with analytically calculated density functions. As mentioned before, the most significant causes of differences between both distributions concern: - distance measures,

- shapes,

- point patterns.

In this chapter we will derive a theoretical contact distribution that best fits the observed, many random elements containing, contact distribution.

In order to bridge this big gap in a meaningful way, the most important differences between both distributions will be first examined more closely.

8.2 Road networks

One can distinguish undifferentiated and differentiated space (Paelinck and Nijkamp, (1975), p.13). Undifferentiated space is an abstract geometric space, in which co-ordinates, distances and densities are dominating concepts; the space is often considered as continuous and distances can be measured both between zero-area consuming or area-consuming points. Differentiated space is provided with projections of geographical, social, cultural, economic, and physical history; this leads to transportation networks, concentrations of industries and cities, etc. Here a discrete approach of space is mostly used: differentiated space represents the real world with less regular and ideal structures than the abstract structures of undifferentiated space in which contact distributions can be calculated. One can describe differentiated space using graph-theory by defining points representing cities or economic concentrations, and links between those points representing roads or railways; the distances between points are measured over those networks while in undifferentiated space distances are measured geometrically using, for instance, a Minkowski distance measure for different p-norms.

Some characteristics of the network, its size and shape, its connectivity and its hierarchy, will cause considerable differences to some of the results; as an example four types of road-networks are presented in fig. 8.1 (Rodriguez-Bachiller, 1983).

Type a: this network is very dense, very irregular and highly connected: one can travel between any two points almost along a straight line; this is typical for old town centres. One can imagine the Euclidean distance measure (p=2) to be a fairly good approximation for the distance between two points on this network.

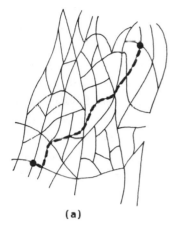

(a)

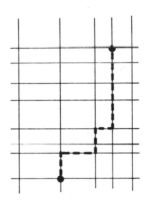

(b)

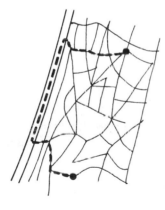

(c)

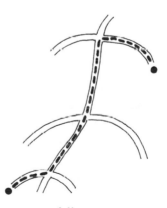

(d)

fig. 8.1. Some characteristic road-networks

Type b: the network consists of a rectangular non-hierarchical grid of
medium connectivity; this is a typical example of nineteenth-
and early twentieth-century town expansion; in this extreme case
too it is possible to approximate the distance between two
points by using a p-distance measure; this time a Manhattan one
(p=1).

Type c: this network contains elements of the previous two, but an element of hierarchy has been introduced, as represented by a section of an urban motorway (typical postwar period). A mathematical function that would represent distances between points in
this kind of networks is hard to find.

Type d: in this case the network is very simple, of very low connectivity and very hierarchical; examples can be found in rural
areas. When distances between cities in a country are examined
one can expect a network like this. A mathematical function
which can represent distances in this network will be defined
"somewhere" between a Euclidean and a Manhattan distance measure; in this case one can think of a distance measured along a
curved road between two points, the influence of the curvature
increasing as the points are closer to each other.

The problem is how to find a mathematical function that produces
a good estimate for the actual road-distance between two points; it
seems important in this respect to differentiate between small regions
and big countries.

Gainsburgh and Hansen (1974) suggest that it is not uncommon that
the actual road-network data are unreliable; they present a method to
check those data. The geographical coordinates of the given points in
the network should be read and the Euclidean distances d_{ij}^1 between i and
j computed; next one has to check whether this distance lies in the interval $[(1+k_1)d_{ij}^1, (1+k_2)d_{ij}^1]$, where k_1 and k_2 are constants, the values
to be given to k_1 and k_2 depending on the type of network considered.
When the network is comparable with type b, the values $k_1=0$, $k_2=\sqrt{2}$ are
adequate; when inter-city distances are computed on a flat area, using
the values $k_1=0$ and $k_2=0.3$ would be appropriate, and finally when inter-
city distances are computed on a hilly-area the values $k_1=0.1$ and $k_2=0.5$
may be used.

A simple way of examining the difference between the observed length-measure of a path between two points (O) and the Euclidean distance between those points (E) is to compute a constant q where O=qE (Nordbeck, 1965). The real distance O is assumed to lie within $E<O<E\sqrt{2}$; studies within the town of Trollhattan, Sweden, showed values for the constant q between 1.10 and 1.43 with extreme values over the shorter distances. Timbers (1967) investigated variations in this ratio of the road distance to the Euclidean distance for journeys within the United Kingdom; on the whole the average q for trips between 780 pairs of towns was found to be 1.17. Journeys within towns gave a somewhat higher value; one noticeable trend was for q to decrease with increasing distance between the trip terminals.

Love and Morris (1972, 1979) studied intercity road distances and looked for mathematical functions that best fitted a road network in Wisconsin (US) and the whole United States. They fitted 7 different functions to road distances; functions that appeared to be relatively accurate estimators of actual road distances were:

$$d_1(q,r) = k\left[\sum_{i=1}^{2} |q_i - r_i|^p\right]^{\frac{1}{p}} \quad \text{and}$$

$$d_2(q,r) = k\left[\sum_{i=1}^{2} |q_i - r_i|^p\right]^{\frac{1}{s}} , \quad \text{where k, p, and s are parameters,}$$

and q and r are points in 2-dimensional space. The parameter values that gave the best fit were for Wisconsin k=1.11, p=1.69 and for the U.S. k=1.15, p=1.78 for $d_1(q,r)$, and for Wisconsin k=1.16, p=1.60, s=1.62 and for the U.S. k=1.10, p=1.74 and s=1.73 for $d_2(q,r)$.

The values for p and s seem to be very close; as expected the p-norm for the U.S. is larger than for Wisconsin: distance-measures are closer to the Euclidean distance measure (p=2) as the size of the observed region increases (assuming the network to be highly connected).

8.3 Shapes of countries

Obviously an observed contact frequency distribution is, at least partly, determined by the shape of the corresponding area. Luu-Mau-Thanh and Sutter (1962) studied marriage distances in Finistère, a French department; they concluded that the observed distances are conditioned to some extent by the shape of the department.

In previous chapters a number of examples shows how analytically derived density functions change as the shape of the area changes; for example in case one considers a rectangular shape as it becomes longer, the range of possible distances will increase and the function becomes more spread out and flatter, so the amount of variation increases, positive skewness increases and the degree of concentration consistently declines.

"Shape is an important property since it is heavily involved in much geographical theory." (Bunge,p. 70, 1966); it is however difficult to "measure" shape, as Strabo argues:
"It is not easy to describe the whole of Italy under any one geometrical figure. Some say that it is a promontory of triangular form.... But a triangle, properly so called, is a rectilinear figure, whereas in this instance both the base and the sides are curved.... Thus the figure may be said to be rather quadrilateral than trilateral.... It is better to confess that you cannot define exactly ungeometrical figures."[2]

There exists a method of "measuring" shape based on two theorems.
Theorem 1: any simple connected shape can be matched by a polygon of any number of sides whose sides are of equal but variable length.
All vertices of the polygon can be made to fall on the boundary of the shape; by increasing the number of sides of the polygon the shape can be more nearly matched (fig. 8.2). In the limit, where an infinite number of sides is used, the polygon is identical with the shape; however, a limited number of sides is required to approximate most shapes satisfactorily.

-----

2) Quated by C. van Paassen, The classical tradition of geography, J.B. Wolters, Groningen, 1957.

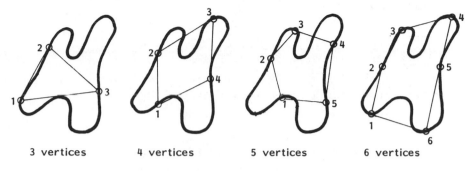

fig. 8.2.   Polygons and shapes

Theorem 2: If the distances between all vertices 'lag-one' are summed,
lag-two are summed, etc., until all unique sums are
determined; and if the distances between all vertices 'lag-
one' are squared and then summed, 'lag-two' are squared and
summed, etc., until all unique squared sums are determined,
then each shape will show a one-to-one correspondence with
one of these sets of sums. Distances are measured between all
vertices of an equilateral polygon; the vertices, situated on
the circumference of the shape could be clockwise numbered,
and be connected, so first 1 is connected to 2, 2 to 3, etc.
All distances are measured; after that vertices are connected
were next immediate vertex is skipped (lag-one) and distances
are measured, further every two immediate vertices are
skipped (lag-two) etc. The process of 'lagging' continues
until all previously described sums reappear (see also Blair
and Biss, 1967).

Every shape will have a one-to-one correspondence with a unique
set of sums; so for every shaped polygon there exists just one set of
sums, and for every set of sums there exists just one shape.

Example (Bunge, 1966)

	S_1	S_2	S_3	S_4^2	S_2^2	S_3^2
---12.1	18.3	16.4	24.0	24.0	24.0	
---11.8	18.0	15.9	24.0	24.0	24.0	
---10.9	17.3	15.7	24.0	24.0	24.0	
---10.2	16.6	15.2	24.0	24.0	24.0	

In this way each shape can be represented by a set of numbers; if the shape is not simply connected, i.e. if there are holes in it, this measure will not work satisfactory.

Many attemps are made to describe shape in a more or less simple way; shape characteristics have led to a considerable literature and a wide range of ratios have been derived. (see table 8.1 from Haggett and Chorley, 1969, p.70).

Table 8.1. Alternative ratios for the comparison of the shape of closed figures

---

Formula	Title	Origin
1. $\dfrac{A}{L^2}$	form ratio	Horton (1932)
2. $\dfrac{A}{\pi(\frac{P}{2\pi})^2}$	circularity ratio	Miller (1956)
3. $\dfrac{2\sqrt{\frac{A}{\pi}}}{L}$	elongation ratio	Schumm (1956)
4. $\dfrac{\frac{L}{2}}{\pi(\frac{L}{2})}A$	elliptically ratio	Stoddart (1965)
5. $\sum\limits_{i=1}^{n} \{100\dfrac{R_i}{\sum\limits_{i=1}^{n} R_i} - \dfrac{100}{n}\}$	radial-line ratio	Boyd and Clark (1964)
6. $\dfrac{A}{\sqrt{2\pi_a}\int R^2 dxdy}$	compactness index	Blair and Biss (1967)

---

variables A area (square km)
         P perimeter (km)
         L major axis (km)
         B minor axis (km)
         R_i radial axis from gravity centre to perimeter (km)
         a$\bar{R}$ radial axis from gravity centre to small area, (km)

Haggett developed a simple shape index S given by $S = \dfrac{1.27A}{\ell^2}$, where
A is the area of the country (km^2) and ℓ is the axis of the country
drawn as a straight line connecting the two most distant points within
the perimeter.

The shape of an area can be systematically treated by using
Bunge's polygons; however, this treatment requires many parameters to
define each shape and it will be difficult to incorporate this in a generalised form without great complication in the calculations involved.

8.3.1 A compactness index

The need to express quantitatively the shape of a figure has been
widely felt in many scientific areas; by "shape" we mean a set of properties possessed by a closed figure in two dimensions, which has a
planar representation and which possesses precise bounderies (Bachi and
Samuel-Cahn, 1976).

Any measurement of shape should be required to be the same for
geometrically similar shapes; it should be possible to calculate it in-
dependently of size and of orientation. One of the important properties
of shape is its compactness; compactness may be considered intuitively
as the extent to which an area is grouped or packed around its central
point (Blair and Biss, 1967). In stead of describing a shape as compact
or non-compact one wishes to measure this compactness; this measure (index) has to be applicable to all possible shapes and should be given as
a ratio and not refer to any measurable units such as km^2. When a shape
is more compact the index should be higher and when it is more elongated
it should be lower.

For the measurement of compactness all points of the shape are of
interest and not only a few extreme points: the numerical measure of

shape should correspond to the visual impression of the actual property
to be measured.

This is done by comparing the contact density function measured
between <u>all</u> points inside the shape and the contact frequency distribution related to contact distances between all points situated in a
rectangular shape. The rectangle that fits best, is then regarded as an
approximation of the shape of the country.

In Blair and Biss (1967) a number of shape measures, especially
measures of compactness, are described and evaluated; some of their comments on these indices are:
- the index is mainly dependent on the perimeter of the shape to be measured and can only be a crude approximation of the actual shape;
- the measure is overdependent on two or three extreme points;
- the orientation of the shape affects the index;
- a large number of parameters are required to describe the shape;
- the use of the index is restricted to simply connected shapes;
- the index is very limited in physical interpretation and practical
  meaning;
- the index is tedious to calculate especially for irregular shapes.

In the literature no agreement exists as to the proper way in
which to measure shape (see also Griffith, 1980).

As has been shown we try to approximate the shape of countries by
rectangular shapes with dimensions a and b (a<b); in this way a rectangle is found that represents as well as possible all spatial properties of the shape (especially the sample of the most important cities in
it) that has to be expressed quantitatively. The dimensions of the rectangle give an impression of the extent to which an area is grouped
around central points.

As a measure of compactness of a country (a region) we therefore
propose $\frac{b}{a}$; where b and a are the dimensions of the rectangle that best
approximates the shape.

Each shape has related to it a unique contact distribution; this
distribution can be determined more precisely as more points inside the
shape are considered. In chapter 9 a number of contact frequency distributions of countries is calculated and also measures of compactness of
the relevant countries.

Blair and Biss calculated a compactness index for a number of countries (Blair and Biss, 1967, p.12); they conclude that all countries have indices less than the square, the measure of compactness of the square in their method of calculation equalling .977.

Our method implies that the measure of compactness of a square equals 1. Countries with shapes close to a square have a high index while countries which are very elongated have a low index, an intuitively clear result.

Much attention should be paid to deriving the contact distribution of the shape and connected with this, the estimation of a and b. The accuracy of the calculation of this compactness index depends on the accuracy of the estimations.

Of course an inaccuracy is introduced by comparing a random shape with a rectangle. Still when countries are compared the rectangle found gives a good impression of the differences of compactness, an impression that fits well the intuitive feeling, a further advantage of the rectangle being its very simple shape.

The estimations of a and b are made using a contact frequency function that has to be calculated with known p-norms; one finds different dimensions of the rectangle using different p-norms. Dimensions were estimated both for p=1 and p=2 so an interval of the compactness index can be calculated.

8.4 Observed contact frequency distributions; histograms

In order to test the null-hypothesis a number of countries in Europe are chosen and the distances between cities in each country are registered. As an example the distance table of Switzerland, containing distances between 39 cities in that country, is shown below.

table 8.2 Distance table of Switzerland (39 cities).

The minimum distance value one observes in this table is 13 km, the maximum value 468 km. The data should be presented in such a way that they are easy to interpret; we used histograms to accomplish this. First a number of classes are to be defind, each observation belonging to a class; after determining the class width, the frequencies of occurrence of the data in the classes is counted. The occurrence of one of the sets of possible values of the observations a class constitutes an event; the frequency of each event is compared with the expected frequency under H_0, being the distribution function of contacts between cities in a country specified by an analytically derived contact distribution on a rectangle. Before presenting the results of these tests, we first focus on the construction of histograms and show some examples.

A histogram is constructed by grouping the data into a number of classes and counting the number of variates in each class. In grouping data of course soms information is lost; on the other hand by grouping the data the information (of the figures) is easier to interpret and aids comparison with other distributions; in this way the complexity of the information may be reduced, as individual values are generalised. One has to look for a balance between generalisation and the information retained.

A problem in this respect is, how to determine the size of a class interval; at least the class interval of a distribution should remain constant and the whole range of observations should be covered.

There exist a few objective guidelines, of which some examples are:

- $k = 1 + 3.3 \log_{10} n$ k number of classes, n number of variates; this was suggested by Huntsberger (1961);
- $k < 5 \log_{10} n$ suggested by Brooks and Carruthers (1953);
- $k = \sqrt{n}$ suggested by Norcliffe (1977);
- $6 < k < 16$ suggested by Croxton and Cowden (1948);

Clearly there can be no "correct" number of classes, so that a compromise should be established between very few classes, showing a relatively small part of the frequency distribution and too many classes, giving a too detailed view.

Evans (1977) suggests that dominantly unimodal distributions require class intervals related to the standard deviation of the data, and skewed distributions require class intervals which fall into geometric progression, the ratio of which increases as skewness increases; of course this requires some a priori information of the overall shape of the distribution before the class intervals are selected.

When one wishes to compare two samples with different numbers of variates it is necessary to standardise the frequencies; which e.g. may be converted into percentages of the total sample for each class. Using the chi-square goodness-of-fit test none of the $mcf(im-\frac{1}{2}m;a^*,b^*)$ (this is the probability a distance falls in class i) could be zero, the statistic χ^2 not being defined in that case; therefore the class intervals must be chosen so that none of them has zero probability. Moreover, if any $mcf(im-\frac{1}{2}m;a^*,b^*)$ is very small, a single observation falling wihtin the corresponding class would give rise to a very large term in the sum defining χ^2; class intervals must then be chosen so that their probabilities are not too small; sometimes it is recommended that the expected frequencies of the class intervals should be at least five, but it has been found that this is a bit conservative: one or two class intervals with expected frequencies near 1 can be tolerated.

This guideline borrowed from the chi-squared test, was used frequently. There were some problems because of the shape of contact density functions; the latter shows positive skewness especially when the rectangle is very elongated, this meaning that the distribution has to its the right a long tail with relatively very few observations; sometimes we had trouble with "one or two class intervals with expected frequencies near to 1".

As an example the observed contact distribution of Switzerland and the expected distributions (presented as a histogram) of rectangles "as close as possible" to the observed distribution are presented (fig 8.3).

For a number of countries in Europe distance tables were collected; the number of cities differs per country and also the range of distances. In order to examine the sensitivity of the class width, in one country (Ireland) two different interval widths were chosen frome the same distance table. Also the sensitivity with respect to the order of the distance matrix was examined. In two countries, the Netherlands and the FRG, different distance tables were collected; for the Netherlands one containing 24 cities and one containing 39 cities and

for the FRG one containing 25 cities and one 35 cities. In one country
(GDR) it was possible to obtain two samples of the same size (36 cities), containing different distance values, namely one where the distances were measured over the road network and another one where railway
distances were measured. The Greek distance matrix contains both road
network distances and distances by ferry boat; we also collected one
other distance table for Greece, only containing road network distances;
To summarise, 22 contact frequency distributions of countries in Europe
were collected (table 8.3). These countries, with the number of cities
and class width, are:

Table 8.3

Country	Nr. of cities	class width
1. The Netherlands 1	24	10 km
2. The Netherlands 2	39	10 km
3. The Netherlands 3	28	10 km
4. Belgium	40	10 km
5. France	50	50 km
6. FRG 1	25	50 km
7. FRG 2	35	50 km
8. Italy 1	16 x 73 table	100 km
9. Italy 2	29	100 km
10. Spain	46	45 km
11. Greece 1	53	50 km
12. Greece 2	49	50 km
13. Switzerland	39	10 km
14. Turkey	67	100 km
15. Czecho-Slovakia	30	50 km
16. GDR 1	36	20 km road network
17. GDR 2	36	20 km railway network
18. Great Britain	44	50 miles
19. Ireland 1	55	10 km
20. Ireland 2	55	20 km
21. Denmark	33	20 km
22. Sweden	12 x 43 table	100 km the distance matrix was not square

In section 8.5 histograms for a number of countries are shown.

8.5. Results

8.5.1. Introduction

In this section results are presented of a comparison of observed contact frequency distributions in a number of countries and calculated contact density functions on rectangles. There are several methods available for comparing distributions; one can use graphical methods and descriptive statistics or/and statistical tests (Gardiner and Gardiner (1979) and Rogers (1974)).

The contact density function of a rectangle is known but for the dimensions a and b. These parameters should be estimated in such a way that the observed and calculated distributions are as close as possible; this is done by using a maximum likelihood method, and the VARM method (Den Broeder (1980)) to estimate the values of a and b. The use of the chi-square goodness-of-fit test is justified only if efficient estimates are used.

8.5.2. Statistical tests; results.

First the statistical test results are presented and afterwards there is a graphical presentation (8.5.3.).

Next table shows:
- the estimates for a^* and b^* under two distance measures (p=1, p=2),
- the chi-square values; these are computed by summing for each distance interval i defined:

$$\chi^2 = \sum_i \frac{(\text{absolute observed value} - \text{expected value})^2}{\text{expected value}} ,$$

the observed value being found via a distance table and showing the number of distances observed in interval i; the expected value is computed via:

$\frac{1}{2}n(n-1)$ m cf $(im-\frac{1}{2}m;a^*,b^*)$ where m cf$(im-\frac{1}{2}m;a^*,b^*)$ is the probability a distance appears in interval i, and $\frac{1}{2}n(n-1)$ the number of distances observed (n being the number of cities).

Although is is not possible to draw conclusions of the Kolmogorov-Smirnov test statistic (see 7.5.2), the value

$$K/S = \sup_{\ell} \left| CF_n(\ell) - CF(\ell; a^*, b^*) \right|$$ is calculated, in order to get an

impression of how close both distributions are.

Table 8.4. Estimates and test results (significant results are underlined)

Country	Number of observations	p=1 (Manhattan) a* (km)	b* (km)	χ²	K/S	p=2 (Euclidean) a* (km)	b* (km)	χ²	K/S
Belgium	18	240	132	28.40	.0219	302	163	27.04	.0178
Czecho-Slovakia	17	614	266	37.08	.322	614	266	34.48	.1533
Denmark	27	458	203	20.58	.0207	524	319	20.05	.0360
France	28	798	798	31.71	.0159	1102	899	23.32	.0180
F.R.G. 1 (35 cities)	22	814	518	11.90	.0134	1045	633	9.74	.0125
F.R.G. 2 (25 cities)	22	684	684	18.54	.0448	962	750	17.29	.0476
GDR (roads)	33	537	206	21.96	.0145	625	281	18.95	.0106
GDR (railways)	33	534	176	17.06	.0113	621	254	18.52	.0106
Great Britain	18	598	235	30.06	.0211	732	304	21.50	.0149
		(miles)	(miles)			(miles)	(miles)		
Greece (total, 53 cities)	26	993	282	32.45	.0131	1141	431	23.05	.0137
Greece (49 cities)	25	945	285	20.87	.0143	1093	412	13.28	.0085
Ireland 1 (55 cities)	37	216	214	22.69	.0121	311	230	31.09	.0127
Ireland 2 (55 cities)	19	216	215	14.57	.0094	313	230	20.28	.0106
Italy 1 (16x73 table)	19	1429	271	365.4	.0795	1617	410	86.99	.0636
Italy 2 (29 cities)	14	1289	222	45.31	.0246	1435	321	6.31	.0143
The Netherlands (39 cities)	42	224	224	27.20	.0179	321	242	32.94	.0161
The Netherlands (28 cities)	37	235	161	21.16	.0225	296	199	22.36	.0317
The Netherlands (24 cities)	37	259	123	26.61	.0277	308	167	27.68	.0314
Spain	29	930	711	34.22	.0170	1220	839	27.55	.0208
Sweden	19	1417	200	81.32	.0798	1464	406	106.60	.0820
Switzerland	24	311	213	20.09	.0105	389	269	21.34	.0126
Turkey	22	1537	864	21.71	.0136	1930	1066	22.59	.0146

8.5.3. Discussion

Estimates and test results for 22 samples in European countries are presented in table 8.4. Looking at the chi-square values and supposing one is working at a 95 % level of significance, 16 out of 22 samples show significant results in case Manhattan distances are considered, and 18 out of 22 samples show significant results when Euclidean distances are used; that means most samples are consistent with the null hypothesis, which states that the observed data form a sample of a random variable of which the density function is specified by the contact density function on a rectangle of unknown dimensions, but with a known distance measure.

Sometimes more than one distance table was investigated for one country; as the number of towns in the sample increases, keeping the number of observed distance-classes (observations) constant, lower values of chi-square (so a better goodness-of-fit) were found (for example the FRG and the Netherlands). For Greece two different distance tables were investigated, first a large one, concerning the whole country including the islands, with distances measured over road networks and also including ferry boat distances and secondly one without towns on islands so only distances over networks are observed; the last distribution shows lower chi-square values. For Italy two different distance tables were observed, one concerning distances between 29 cities (showing significant results), the other concerns a rectangular distance table including distances between 16 cities in the northern part of Italy and 73 other Italian cities scattered all over the country; also for Sweden a rectangular distance table (12 x 43) was observed and here no significant result was found either. The theoretical contact distribution on a rectangle is supposed to originate with square distance tables.

Only one distance table was observed for Ireland; the distribution of distances was presented in two ways, one dealing with class width of 10 km, the other one 20 km; the estimated dimensions of the rectangle were equal for both distributions, but the chi-square value of the distribution with the smallest classwidth was higher (both results were significant). For the GDR two distance tables were investigated,

one containing road network distances, the other using railway network
distances measured between the same set of cities; both showed significant results and estimated dimensions of the rectangle did not differ
very much. Both Great-Britain and Italy 2 showed significant results only for Euclidean distances and for Czecho-Slovakia and Belgium no significant result was found.

Concluding one can say that the comparison of both contact distributions show a better goodness-of-fit as:

the number of cities in the sample is larger,

the cities are more uniformly distributed,

the road network has a more uniform density over the whole area.

The dimensions of the rectangle which are estimated are determined by the locations of the cities in the sample, so there is no direct relation to the shape and size of the country in which they are located. Of course, the locations of cities are limited by the frontiers
of the country and so are the observed distances, so there will be an
indirect relation between them. This relation will be the stronger as
the cities in the sample are more uniformly distributed over the country
and as the shape of the country is less distorted. In order to get a
global impression of the similarity of the actual size and shape of a
country and the dimensions of the rectangle related to the contact distribution, a number of countries and rectangles are presented in one
figure (fig. 8.15, ..., 8.20).

From this comparison one cannot draw conclusions concerning the
theoretical distance measure (p-value) related to the road network distance of the country, so it is not possible to conclude that road network distances in one country are closer to, for instance, Euclidean
distances than in the other one.

The whole set of network distances observed between a sample of
cities in a country is compared with just two theoretical distributions
using two different distance measures, p=1 and p=2; those are the only
relevant p-values for which we derived analytically the theoretical contact density function; of course for each p, $1 < p < 2$, there exist a
theoretical distribution of distances.

If countries were rectangularly shaped and if the analytical expression for contact distributions of a rectangle was known, a compari-

son as described here, would make it possible to draw conclusions about the p-value which is closest to the network distances of that country. Since none of those conditions is fulfilled we used another method for the estimate of this p-value, to be described in chapter 10.

8.5.4. A graphical presentation

In order to get an impression of the difference between the observed and the calculated distributions we also used a graphical method. One can present the calculated density function in a discrete way using the same interval width as the observed frequency distribution; this is done for Switzerland (for p=1 and p=2). The picture becomes clearer if both the calculated and the observed distributions are plotted in one figure, using a continuous presentation for the calculated distribution (this is also done for Switzerland; fig 8.3). Finally, for each country we plotted in one figure three distributions:
- the observed frequency distribution (histogram),
- the calculated density function for p=2 (dotted line),
- the calculated density function for p=1.

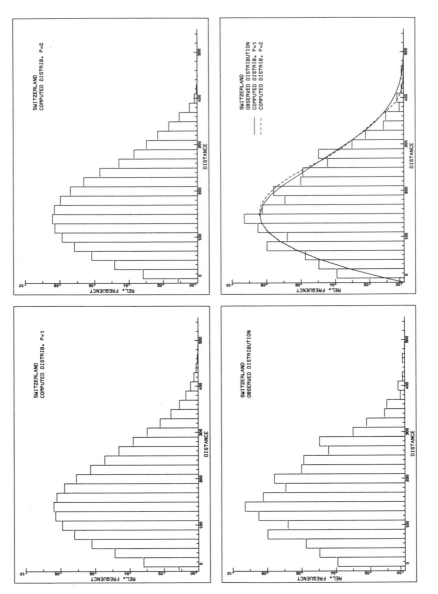

fig. 8.3   Contact Frequency distributions of Switserland

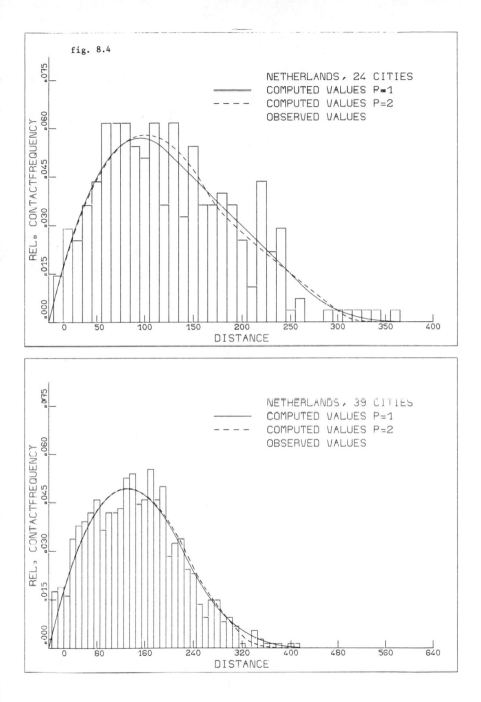

fig. 8.4

NETHERLANDS, 24 CITIES
COMPUTED VALUES P=1
COMPUTED VALUES P=2
OBSERVED VALUES

NETHERLANDS, 39 CITIES
COMPUTED VALUES P=1
COMPUTED VALUES P=2
OBSERVED VALUES

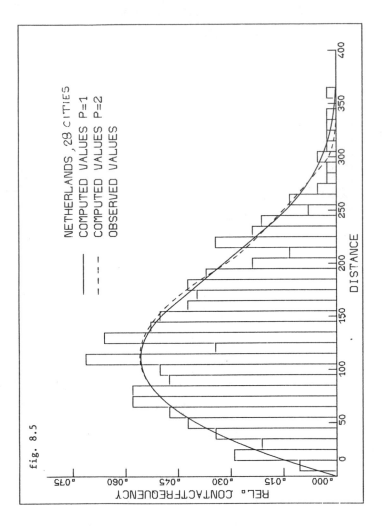

fig. 8.5

NETHERLANDS, 28 CITIES
COMPUTED VALUES P=1
COMPUTED VALUES P=2
OBSERVED VALUES

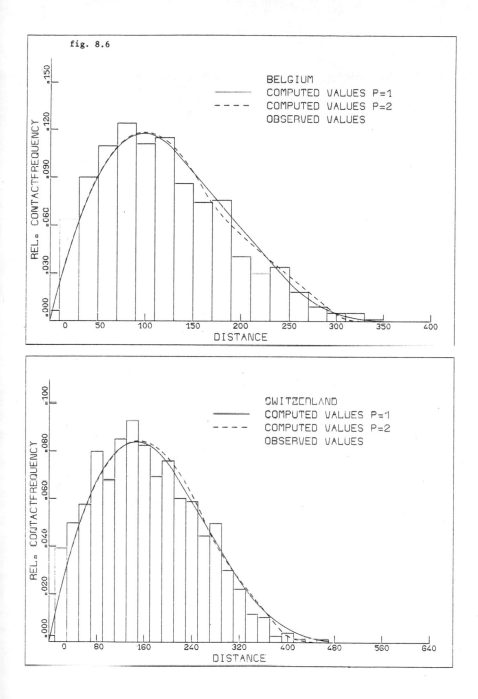

fig. 8.6

BELGIUM
COMPUTED VALUES P=1
COMPUTED VALUES P=2
OBSERVED VALUES

SWITZERLAND
COMPUTED VALUES P=1
COMPUTED VALUES P=2
OBSERVED VALUES

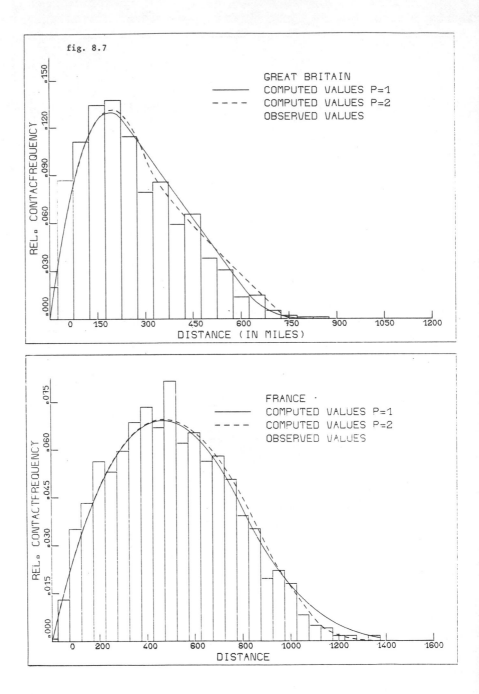

fig. 8.7

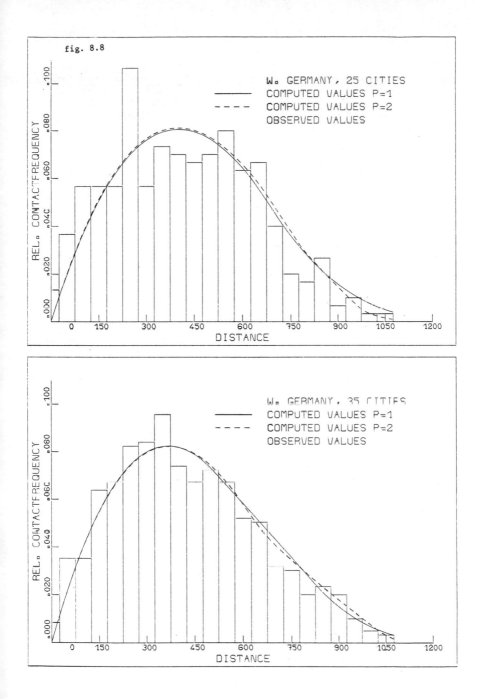

fig. 8.8

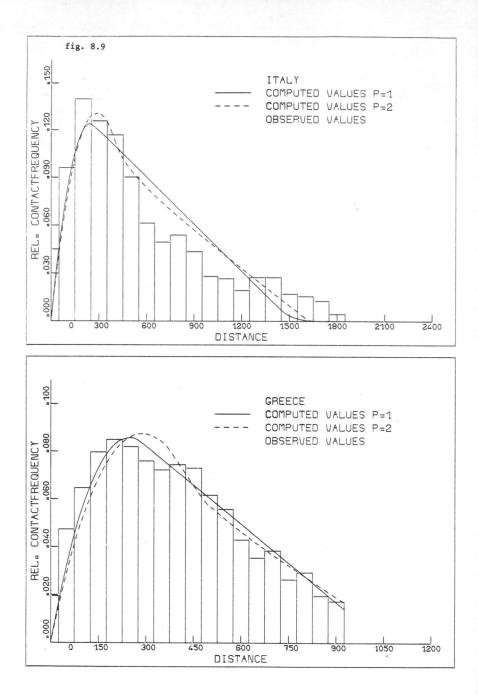

fig. 8.9

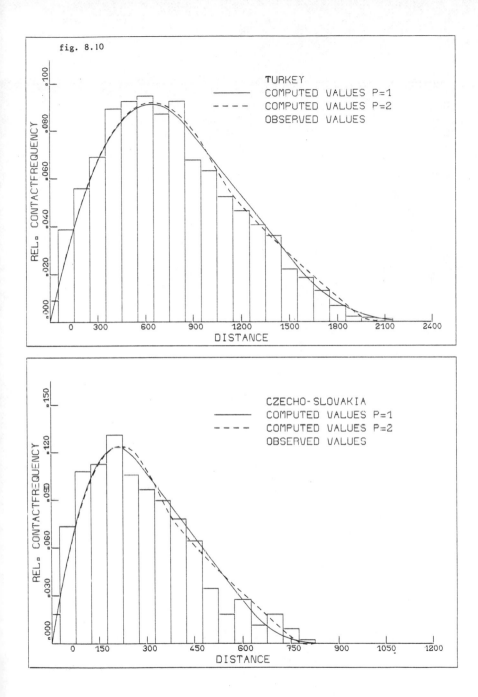

fig. 8.10

TURKEY
COMPUTED VALUES P=1
COMPUTED VALUES P=2
OBSERVED VALUES

CZECHO-SLOVAKIA
COMPUTED VALUES P=1
COMPUTED VALUES P=2
OBSERVED VALUES

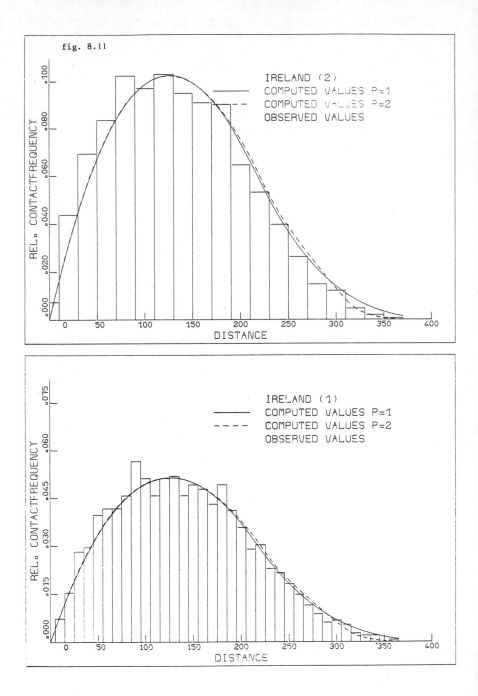

fig. 8.11

IRELAND (2)
COMPUTED VALUES P=1
COMPUTED VALUES P=2
OBSERVED VALUES

IRELAND (1)
COMPUTED VALUES P=1
COMPUTED VALUES P=2
OBSERVED VALUES

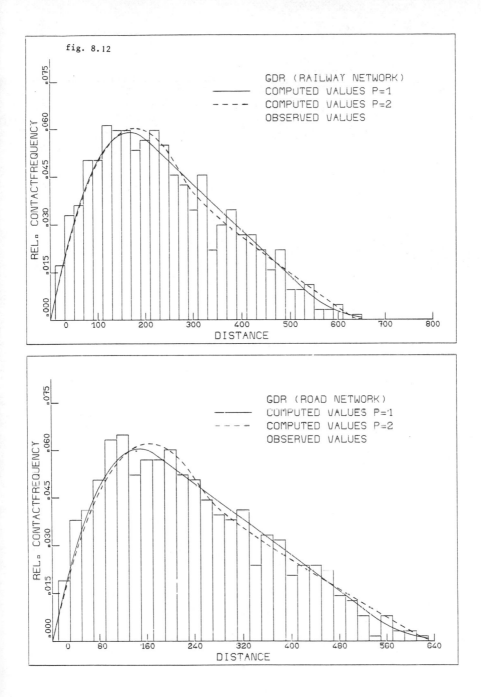

fig. 8.12

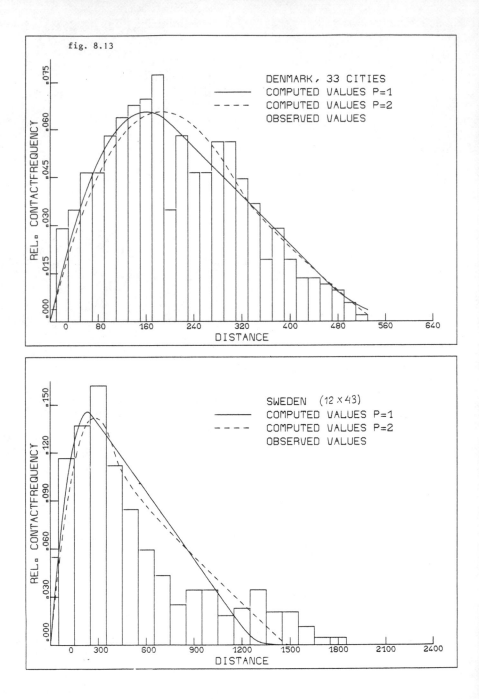

fig. 8.13

DENMARK, 33 CITIES
———— COMPUTED VALUES P=1
- - - - COMPUTED VALUES P=2
OBSERVED VALUES

SWEDEN (12×43)
———— COMPUTED VALUES P=1
- - - - COMPUTED VALUES P=2
OBSERVED VALUES

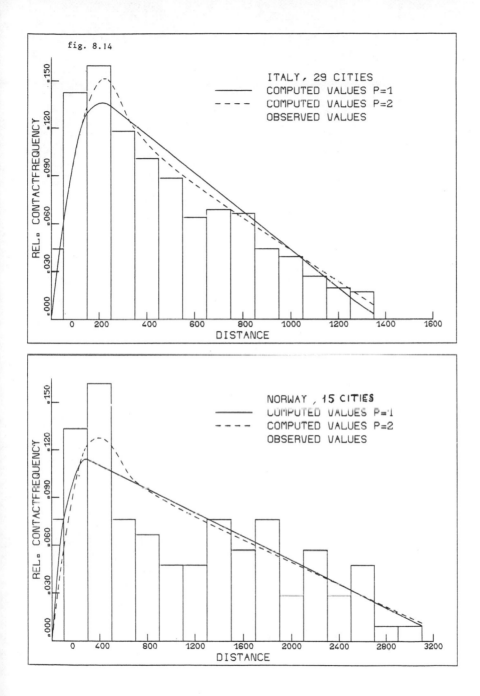

fig. 8.14

ITALY, 29 CITIES
COMPUTED VALUES P=1
COMPUTED VALUES P=2
OBSERVED VALUES

NORWAY , 15 CITIES
COMPUTED VALUES P=1
COMPUTED VALUES P=2
OBSERVED VALUES

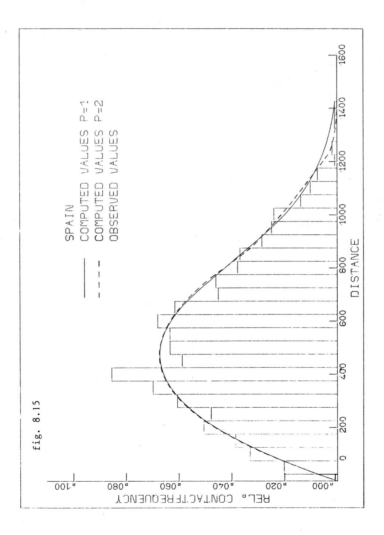

fig. 8.15

SPAIN
COMPUTED VALUES P=1
COMPUTED VALUES P=2
OBSERVED VALUES

REL. CONTACTFREQUENCY

DISTANCE

8.5.5. The comparison of surfaces

A question that arises is how well the real shape of a country is approximated by the estimated surface of the rectangle both in case p=1 and p=2.

One expects the real p-value of a road network to lie between 1 and 2. The surface of the rectangle found, using p=2 will overestimate the real surface, while p=1 would underestimate this value. One can expect the estimated surface related to p=1 to be $\frac{\frac{1}{2}\ell^2}{\frac{\pi}{4}\ell^2} = \frac{2}{\pi} = 0.636$ times (fig. 7.1)

the surface to p=2 (see also the last column of table 8.5).

On the maps of 6 countries the rectangles, estimated via the observed contact frequency distributions, both for p=1 and p=2, are drawn (p=2 is the dotted line). The orientation of the rectangle is not calculated here, only a set of observed distances in a country is compared with a theoretical contact density function, so the figures give not more than an impression of how well this rectangles cover the real shapes of the countries.

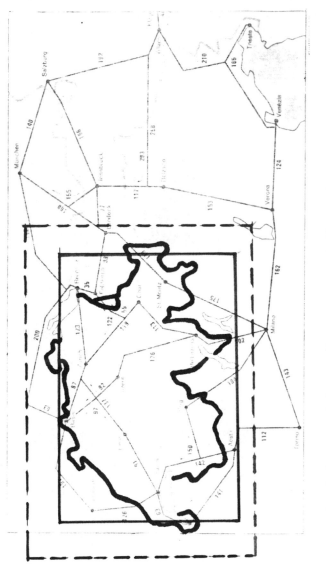

fig. 8.15 ———— Manhattan distances————Euclidean distances

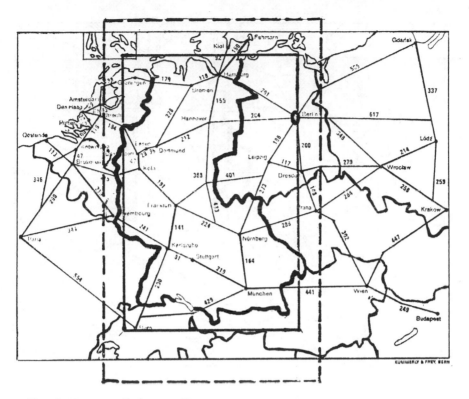

fig. 8.16   — Manhattan distances-------Euclidean distances

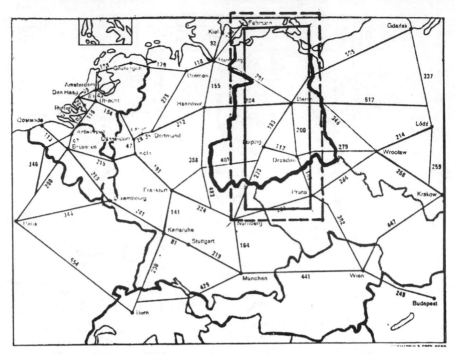

fig. 8.17 ——— Manhattan distances - - - - - - - Euclidean distances

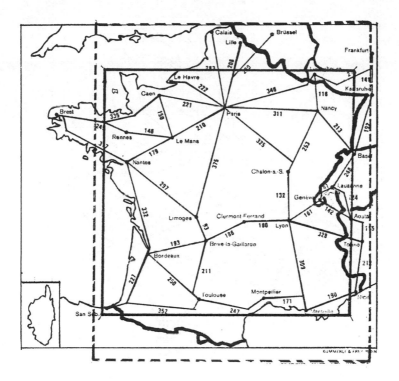

fig. 8.18 ———— Manhattan distances-------Euclidean distances

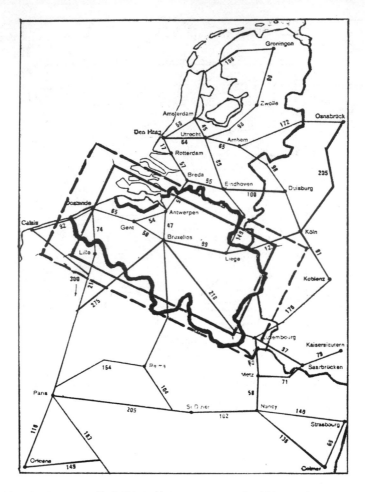

fig. 8.19 ———— Manhattan distances ------- Euclidean distances

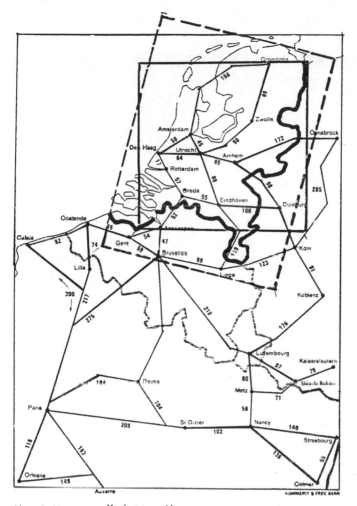

fig. 8.20 ———— Manhattan distances————Euclidean distances

Table 8.5. Surface of countries.

Country	nr. of cities in the set	nr. of observations	(1) surface (km²)	(2) est. surface p=1	(1)/(2)	(3) est. surface p=2	(1)/(3)	(2)/(3)
The Netherlands	24	37	40,844	31,945	1.278	51,777	0.788	0.616
The Netherlands	39	42	40,844	50,498	0.808	77,856	0.524	0.647
The Netherlands	28	37	40,844	37,892	1.077	59,149	0.690	0.640
Belgium	40	18	30,513	31,886	0.956	49,533	0.616	0.643
France	50	28	547,026	638,185	0.857	992,299	0.551	0.643
W. Germany	25	22	248,630	468,649	0.530	722,587	0.344	0.648
W. Germany	35	22	248,630	421,837	0.589	661,832	0.375	0.637
Italy	52	19	301,225	388,233	0.775	664,345	0.453	0.584
Italy	29	14	301,225	286,380	1.052	460,635	0.645	0.621
Spain	46	29	504,782	662,081	0.762	1,024,516	0.492	0.646
Greece	53	26	131,944	280,859	0.469	492,933	0.267	0.569
Switzerland	39	24	41,293	66,368	0.622	104,706	0.394	0.633
Turkey	67	22	780,576	1,328,060	0.587	2,059,330	0.379	0.644
Great Britain	43	18		141,091 (miles²)		220,319 (miles²)		0.630
Ireland	55	19	70,283	26,716	1.504	72,144	0.974	0.647
Ireland	55	37	70,283	46,515	1.510	71,832	0.978	0.647
Czecho-Slovakia		17	127,869	163,562	0.781	163,562	0.781	1.000
GDR (railway)	36	33	107,779	94,574	1.139	158,164	0.681	0.597
GDR (road)	36	35	107,779	109,003	0.988	175,790	0.613	0.620
Denmark	33	27	43,069	93,162	0.462	167,299	0.257	0.556
Sweden	[12 x 43]	29	449,964	284,001	1.584	595,813	0.755	0.476
Greece (cities)	49	19	131,944	270,071	0.488	451,080	0.292	0.598

8.5.6. Discussion

The relation between observed distances in a region and the shape
of that region has already been examined by Thanh (1962). Observed distances (more precisely the observed contact frequency distribution) are
compared with theoretical contact distances, which are a.o. determined
by the dimensions of a rectangle. In this way observed distances are related to two different shapes, the shape of the region in which they are
located, and the shape of a rectangle with estimated dimensions. In this
section it is shown how close both shapes are, by a graphical presentation (fig 8.15,...,8.20) and by figures presented in table 8.5.

The graphical presentation gives a rough impression; the largest
rectangle, related to Euclidean distances, almost always includes the
real shape of the country completely (exceptions are some extreme projections of countries, for instance Bretagne in France), and the smallest
rectangle, related to Manhattan distances, is always relatively close to
the real borderlines. When a country has a high compactness index the
relation between surfaces seems to be clearer (see Belgium and France).
Looking at special countries like the FRG where the city of Berlin is
completely seperated spatially from the rest, and countries which contain a lot of lakes or islands (Denmark), the surface of the estimated
rectangle will show a poor relation to the real surface of the country.

An important conclusion to be drawn from this comparison of surfaces, is the importance of the orientation of the rectangle (see
Belgium and The Netherlands). If network distances are compared with
theoretical contact distances the orientation of the rectangle has been
fixed; for reasons of simplicity, the theoretical contact distribution,
using p=a distance-measure, is analytically derived for one special
orientation Θ, $\Theta=0°$; however, except for p=2 distance-measure, each
value of Θ, $0° \leq \Theta \leq 90°$, determines another theoretical contact distribution. When one tries to find a rectangle as close as possible to the
real shape of the country in which network distances are measured, one
has to take into account the orientation of the rectangle. So theoretical contact distributions should be derived, that are determined by 4
parameters: a, b, p, and Θ.

We did not derive such complex distributions but tried another, probably simpler, method described in chapter 9 and 10. In table 8.5 ratios of observed and estimated surfaces are presented; a large variety of values was found (from .462 (Denmark) to 1.510 (Ireland) with Euclidean distances). Because of this large variety, caused by a number of reasons mentioned before, both the shape and the network distances are examined more closely and separately in chapter 9 and 10.

The relation between estimated surfaces of p=1 and p=2 is fairly constant for all countries and close to the expected value (= .636).

9 Results of the shape analysis

9.1. Introduction

In the previous chapter an absolute contact frequency distribution, representing the network distances between a set of cities in a country, was compared with a theoretical contact density function, representing the distances between all points inside a rectangle; the dimensions of the rectangle were estimated in such a way that both distributions were "as close as possible" (according to section 7.2). At the end of that chapter the rectangle found in this way, was compared with the real shape of the country; problems of this comparison are mentioned in 8.5.3; important disturbing factors are the dispersion of the cities throughout the country, the road network and the p-norm used in the theoretical distribution.

In this chapter only the shape of the country will be estimated and therefore the random set of cities and the random road network, both disturbing factors are eliminated here.

Now the country will be completely filled, in a regular way, with discrete points and between those points distances will be measured using well-known distance measures (p=1, p=2). Only rectangular shapes will be adapted to real shapes of countries.

9.2 The grid cell method

Any shape can be presented as a boolean matrix using a grid; if a cell is located inside the shape, it gets value 1, otherwise 0. The shape is more accurate approximated as the grid network becomes more dence. This method is also used by Taylor (1971), when he tries to analyse several shapes; he identifies five types of shapes: (1) compact; (2) elongated; (3) indented; (4) punctured; and (5) fragmented. A set of experiments has been carried out on thirteen different shapes (fig. 9.1) in order to see whether divergences from compactness can be identified from the distribution of distances within the shapes. In determining the contact distribution he uses an algorithm in which shapes are considered as arrays of zeros and ones. Taylor produces the contact frequency distribution by using an iterative loop; taking each cell in turn which does not have a zero recorded, the distance is calculated in units of grid cell side, to every other cell of value 1. Using this method one can get an impression of the contact frequency distribution related to any random shape; Taylor gives a few examples of countries, namely Argentina, Norway, Pakistan, and Somaliland (fig. 9.2)

In a way comparable to Taylor's method we derived contact frequency distributions for a number of European countries. In 9.3 the contact frequency distributions are graphically presented; contact distributions are used to analyse the shape of the corresponding countries, by comparing the distributions with theoretical contact distributions on rectangles.

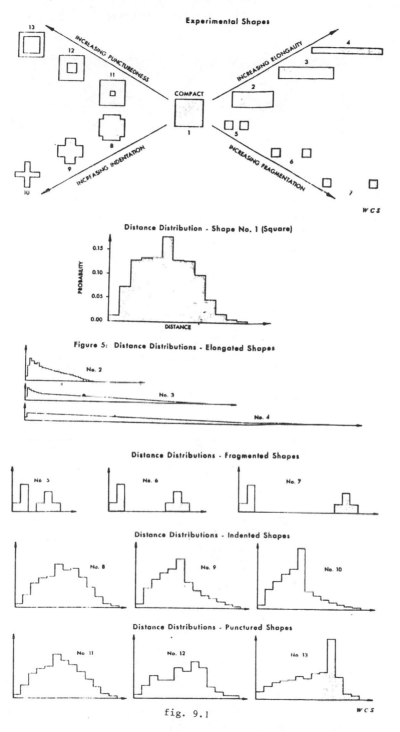

Experimental Shapes

Distance Distribution - Shape No. 1 (Square)

Figure 5: Distance Distributions - Elongated Shapes

Distance Distributions - Fragmented Shapes

Distance Distributions - Indented Shapes

Distance Distributions - Punctured Shapes

WCS

fig. 9.1

-237-

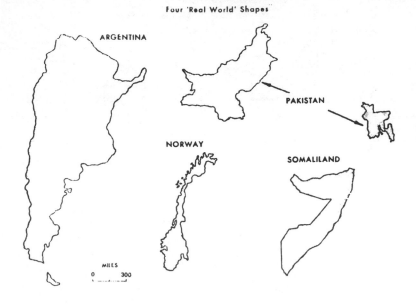

Four 'Real World' Shapes

ARGENTINA

PAKISTAN

NORWAY

SOMALILAND

MILES
0   300

Figure 10: Distance Distributions - 'Real World' Shapes

ARGENTINA

NORWAY

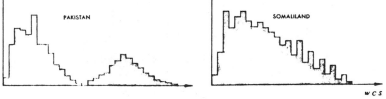

PAKISTAN

SOMALILAND

w c s

fig. 9.2

9.3. Results

9.3.1. A graphical presentation

An observed contact frequency distribution from a known space
filled with discrete points, is compared with a theoretical contact density function of a rectangle of unknown dimensions continuously filled
with points; 11 countries are covered by a cell grid; each cell is of
equal size (0.5 x 0.5 cm); if the same scale for different countries is
used, this means that big countries will be more accurate by approximated than small ones. The scale of the maps used to construct the
boolean matrices are:

The Netherlands	1 cm ~ 30 km	
Belgium	1 cm ~ 30 km	
Ireland	1 cm ~ 30 km	
France	1 cm ~ 30 km	
Spain	1 cm ~ 45 km	
FRG	1 cm ~ 45 km	
Great Britain	1 cm ~ 30 km	
GDR	1 cm ~ 45 km	
Czecho-Slovakia	1 cm ~ 45 km	
Switzerland	1 cm ~ 25 km	
Greece	1 cm ~ 40 km	

This means that for example both Belgium and France are covered
by cells of 15 x 15 km; France therefore has much more observations in
the contact frequency distribution.

The contact frequency distribution that can be observed is computed for both the p=1 and p=2 norm. The distances that are found in
case p=1 are always a multiple of half the scale size. The histograms
have a class width that equals half the appropriate scale (so 12.5, 15,
20 or 22.5 km). Because of these class width the histograms for p=1 show
a more regular pattern than those for p=2. When the class width would
diminish, the histogram pattern for p=2 would become more regular too
(see for example France, having a relative small class width).

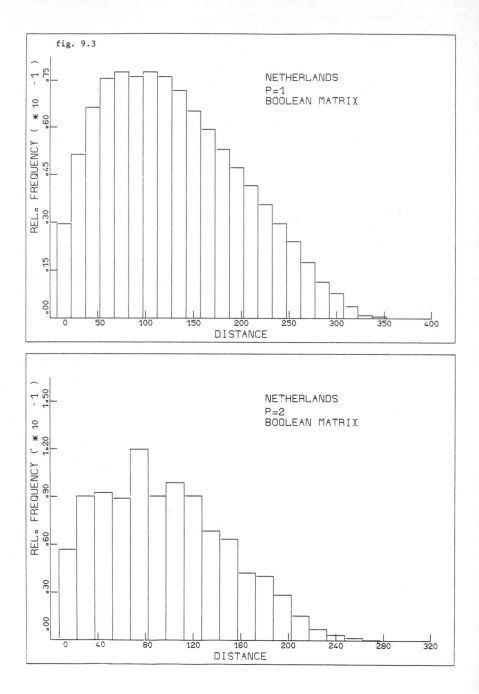

fig. 9.3

NETHERLANDS
P=1
BOOLEAN MATRIX

NETHERLANDS
P=2
BOOLEAN MATRIX

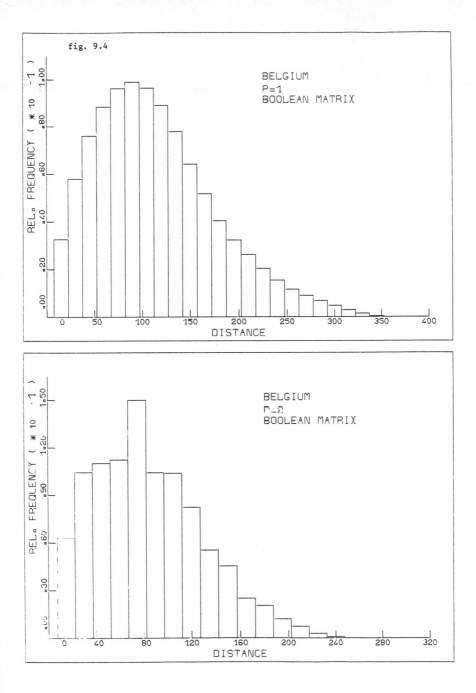

fig. 9.4

BELGIUM
P=1
BOOLEAN MATRIX

BELGIUM
P=2
BOOLEAN MATRIX

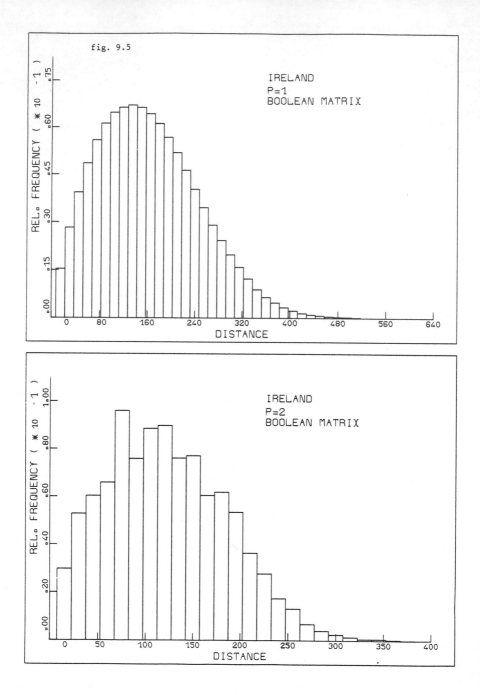

fig. 9.5

IRELAND
P=1
BOOLEAN MATRIX

IRELAND
P=2
BOOLEAN MATRIX

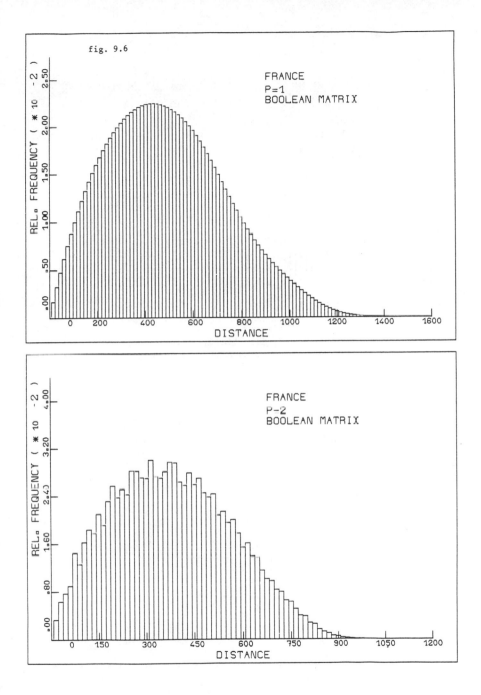

fig. 9.6

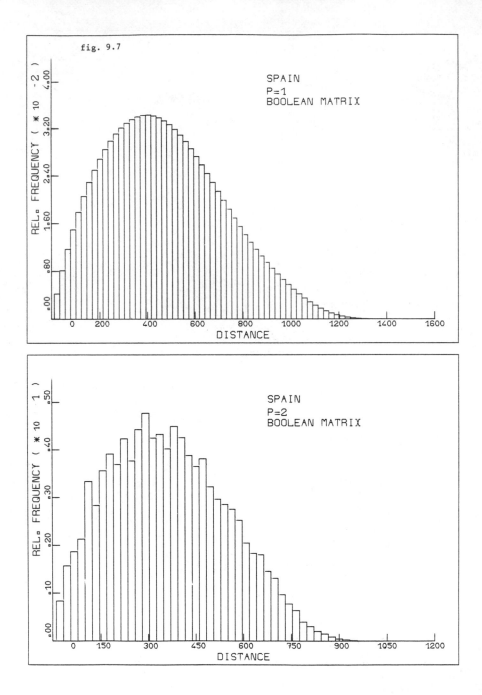

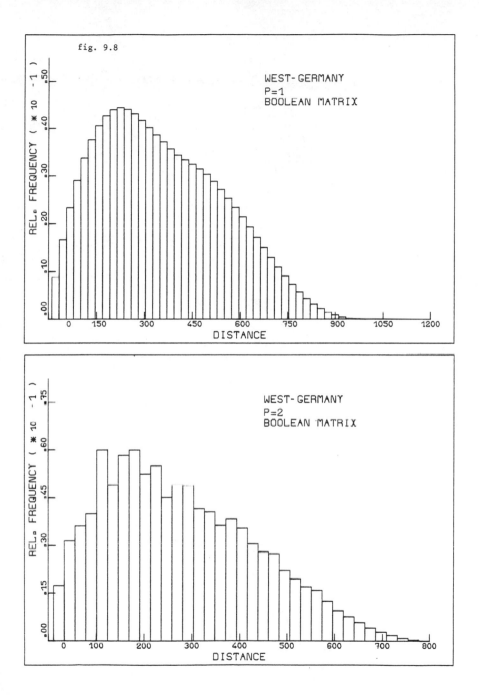

fig. 9.8

WEST-GERMANY
P=1
BOOLEAN MATRIX

WEST-GERMANY
P=2
BOOLEAN MATRIX

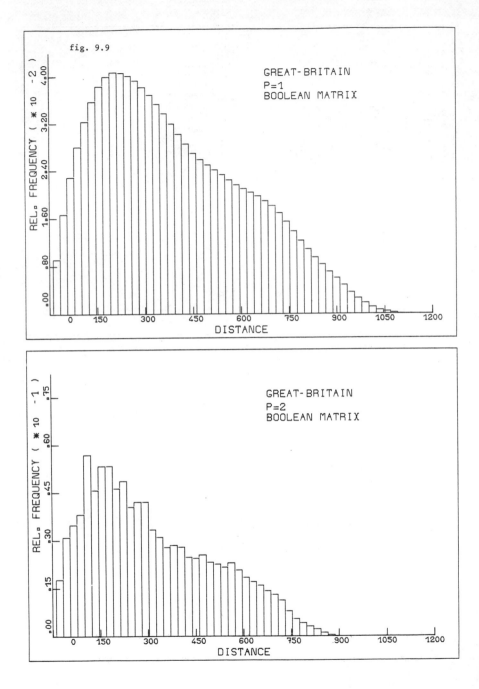

fig. 9.9

GREAT-BRITAIN
P=1
BOOLEAN MATRIX

GREAT-BRITAIN
P=2
BOOLEAN MATRIX

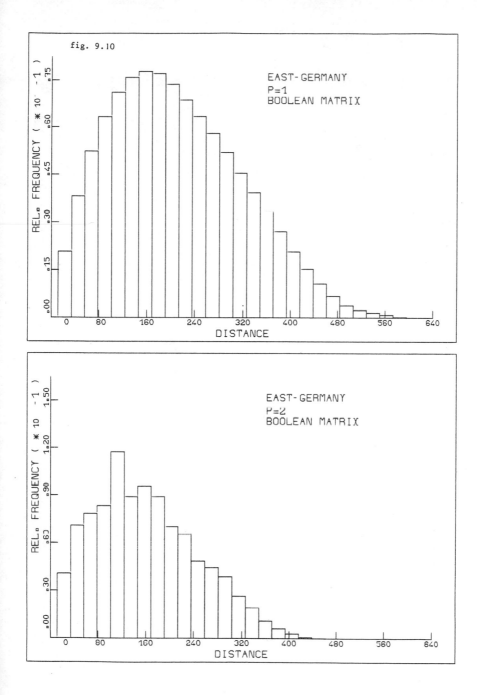

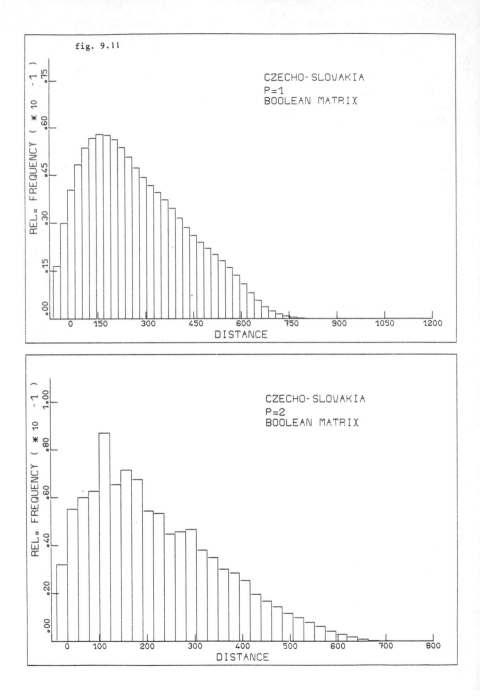

fig. 9.11

CZECHO-SLOVAKIA
P=1
BOOLEAN MATRIX

CZECHO-SLOVAKIA
P=2
BOOLEAN MATRIX

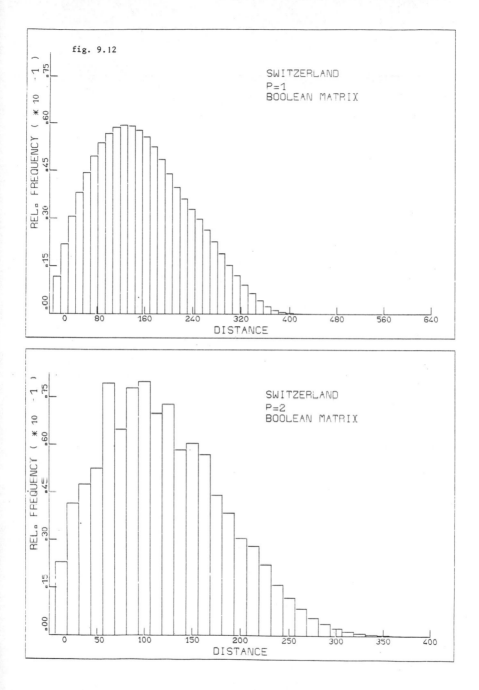

fig. 9.12

SWITZERLAND
P=1
BOOLEAN MATRIX

SWITZERLAND
P=2
BOOLEAN MATRIX

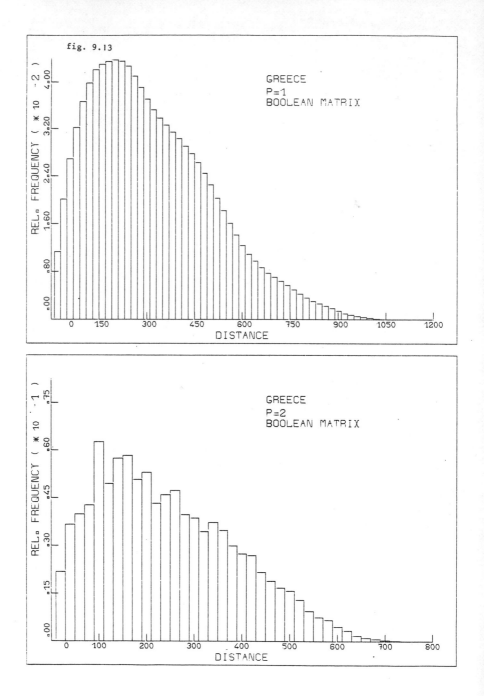

9.3.2. Discussion

In the previous section two-dimensional shapes of 11 European countries are described as one dimensional frequency distributions. Shapes can be analysed by analysing the distributions of distances related to them. A number of theoretical distributions of distances in familiar shapes as squares, rectangles and circles are analytically derived; the observed frequency distribution can be compared with a theoretical distribution in order to draw conclusions about the shape of the observed country. Looking only at the histograms a global impression of the shape of a country can be obtained; further computations concerning the comparison of observed and theoretical distributions could clear up this picture further (9.3.3).

When one glances one's eye at the histograms, three different types of shapes can be disinguished:

1. histograms of Belgium, France, Ireland and Spain,
2. histograms of the GDR, Czecho-Slovakia, the Netherlands and
   Switzerland,
3. histograms of Great Britain, Greece and the FRG.

The first group shows histograms that look very much like the distributions found on squares and on rectangles close to squares; the second group shows that typical linear decreasing part in the histogram, characteristic for theoretical density functions on elongated rectangles, and a look at the real shape of those countries (in both groups) confirms this impression. The last group shows in the histogram a typical hump; these hump-shaped distributions were also found in chapter 6, where the contact distribution for points located in two separate squares was derived: the shape of those countries has indeed some similarity with a shape that is close to two, not to far removed, separate parts, which can be observed in those countries, although the country remains connected.

9.3.3. Statistical results

The dimensions of a rectangle, continuously filled with points, are calculated in such a way, that the contact density function of this rectangle is as close as possible to the contact frequency distribution calculated from a boolean matrix that represents the shape of a country.

These contact distributions are determined for both p=1 and p=2 norms. In order to get an impression how close both distributions are a goodness-of-fit test is performed; a compactness index is also computed, being the quotient of the values of the dimension of the rectangle $\left(= \frac{b}{a} \right)$; furthermore the area of the calculated rectangle and the real area of the country are compared (table 9.1 and 9.2).

Table 9.1.   Manhattan distances (p=1)

Country	number of observations	a* (km)	b* (km)	$\frac{b^*}{a^*}$	a*b*	area of the country	χ^2	K/S
Belgium	24	225	158	.701	35,679	30,513	479.0	.0264
The Netherlands	24	280	128	.455	35,929	40,844	47.9	.0089
Ireland	35	285	217	.759	62,013	70,283	155.6	.0070
GDR	29	403	253	.628	102,003	107,779	47.0	.0078
Spain	65	848	607	.716	515,837	504,782	577.2	.0030
FRG	49	781	318	.406	248,312	248,150	453.9	.0096
Great Britain	54	943	261	.277	246,701	232,374	225.6	.0069
Czecho-Slovakia	38	639	210	.328	134,167	127,869	54.5	.0051
Greece	53	730	233	.320	170,612	131,944	4533.0	.0187
Switzerland	38	284	195	.688	55,638	41,293	282.3	.0083
France	100	747	747	.999	558,219	547,026	2486.0	.0050

Table 9.2.   Euclidean distances (p=2)

Country	number of observations	a* (km)	b* (km)	$\frac{b^*}{a^*}$	a*b*	area of the country	χ^2	K/S
Belgium	18	233	140	.602	32,951	30,513	598.8	.0166
The Netherlands	19	245	142	.582	34,932	40,844	95.1	.0175
Ireland	23	274	213	.777	58,624	70,283	492.3	.0107
GDR	21	403	232	.576	93,621	107,779	190.9	.0150
Spain	45	825	600	.727	495,926	504,782	2190.0	.0048
FRG	36	743	317	.426	235,831	248,150	1076.0	.0137
Great Britain	42	902	255	.282	230,196	232,374	910.9	.0103
Czecho-Slovakia	31	608	204	.336	124,656	127,869	1225.0	.0088
Greece	38	678	239	.352	162,065	131,944	662.3	.0173
Switzerland	30	284	181	.637	51,645	41,293	1583.0	.0140
France	71	821	658	.802	540,791	547,026	9172.0	.0043

9.3.4. Discussion

In chapter 8 the contact frequency distribution observed in a number of countries was considered to be a sample of the contact density function on a rectangle continuously filled with points. The estimated dimensions were based on an observed random set of points (cities) and not on the real shape of the country. If points (cities) were distributed in a very regular way over the whole country, the estimated rectangle would be more closely related to the shape of that country; this idea was tested in chapter 9. No random set of points was used and no network distances; the country was completely covered by a grid and only well-known distance measures were used. In this way a contact distribution should be found on a rectangle of which the dimensions are closely related to the real shape of the country.

When Euclidean distances are considered one always finds a smaller rectangle, because considering two points the Euclidean distance is smaller than the Manhattan distance. The interval of the estimated rectangular area, using p=1 and p=2 norm, is much smaller than was observed in chapter 8; these areas are closer to the real area of the country. Because only the grid cells, completely located inside the shape of the country were considered, an inaccuracy in the estimation of the real shape of the country is introduced; this is important especially in small countries (Belgium, Ireland and the Netherlands). The estimation of countries with very irregular shapes and relative much sea area differs much from the real area (Greece). In a number of big countries, of which the mentioned "border inaccuracies" are expected to be less important, we observe values of the real area between the estimated values for p=2 and p=1 (Spain, Great Britain, Czecho-Slovakia and France).

The compactness indices found using p=1 and p=2 are mostly close to each other; when the countries are classified according to their compactness index one would find almost the same sequence for p=1 and p=2. The figures show a wide variety from, .999 for France to .277 for Great Britain; very compact countries are France, Ireland and Spain and the most elongated countries appear to be Greece, Czecho-Slovakia and Great Britain.

Although the estimations of the dimensions of the rectangle are good, the value of χ^2, being a goodness-of-fit criterion, is high.

Of course the real shape of a country differs from a rectangle, so when the shape is accurately estimated by covering it with a dence grid, one will find a contact distribution that will differ from a contact distribution on a rectangle, and when significant goodness-of-fit results would be found, one could probably find non-significant results by increasing the number of cells (see also Wonnacott and Wonnacott, 1972, chapter 17). The countries most accurately estimated are the big countries (because cells of equal size are used), show relatively high values of χ^2 (see France, Spain and the FRG).

It is possible to find other values for χ^2 if the observed distribution would be compared with a distribution on a rectangle, containing the orientation (Θ) of the rectangle as an extra parameter (fig. 9.14).

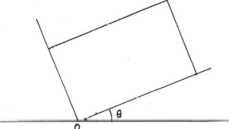

fig. 9.14. Rectangle with orientation Θ.

With the exception of Euclidean distances, the distance value between two points depends on the orientation of the axes.

Let us consider two points x and y in two-dimensional space and look at the Euclidean and Manhattan distance between those points in relation to the orientation of the axes (Θ) (fig. 9.15).

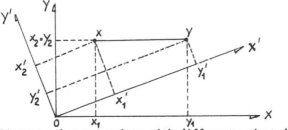

fig. 9.15. Distances between points with different oriented axes.

-255-

If Manhattan distances are considered

$$d(x,y)_{\Theta=\Theta^\circ} = \left| x_2'-y_2' \right| + \left| x_1'-y_1' \right| = d(x,y)_{\Theta=0^\circ} \, (\sin\Theta + \cos\Theta), \qquad (9.1)$$

where $d(x,y)_{\Theta=0^\circ}$ equals the Euclidean distance between x and y. One can have a closer look at this function, depending on the value of Θ:

$$\frac{\partial d(x,y)_{\Theta=\Theta^\circ}}{\partial\Theta} = d(x,y)_{\Theta=0^\circ} \, (\cos\Theta - \sin\Theta) \qquad (9.2)$$

The maximum value is: $d(x,y)_{\Theta=0^\circ} \, \sqrt{2}$ when $\Theta=45^\circ$, $\qquad (9.3)$

and $d(x,y)_{\Theta=0^\circ} = d(x,y)_{\Theta=90^\circ}$; $\qquad (9.4)$

the function varies around $\Theta=45^\circ$ in a symmetrical way.
The relation between the Euclidean distance and the average Manhattan distance between two points is found by:

$$\frac{d(x,y)_{\Theta=\Theta^\circ}}{d(x,y)_{\Theta=0^\circ}} = \frac{1}{\frac{\pi}{4}} \int_{\Theta=0^\circ}^{\Theta=45^\circ} \sin\Theta + \cos\Theta \; d\Theta = 1.273 \qquad (9.5)$$

This means when an area is considered with uniformly distributed points, the Manhattan distance will on the average be 1.273 times the Euclidean distance (Perreux, 1974 and Christofides et.al., 1971).

The contact distributions that are derived, are defined on rectangles without this extra parameter (i.e. always $\Theta=0^\circ$); it is however possible with the method described in this study to derive analytically the contact distribution on a rectangle (p=1) with the orientation Θ as an extra parameter; but the expressions become very complicated, and so another method is used: instead of turning the rectangle it is also possible to turn the shape of the country, in the following way: consider the shape of a country and draw a line through the country parallel to the equator; this line represents $\Theta=0^\circ$; the country now can be turned successively 10° with respect to the line parallel to the equator, until $\Theta=90^\circ$ ($\Theta=90^\circ$ yields the same rectangle as $\Theta=0^\circ$) (fig. 9.15). For each orientation (0°, 10°, 20°, ..., 90°) the shape is covered by a grid that is always equally oriented (parallel to the equator); each orientation yields a contact frequency distribution. In this way 9 values will finally be generated.

As an example, Belgium is considered more closely. If one looks at a map of this country, one expects better estimations of a rectangle (p=1) if the country would be turned about 50 degrees clockwise (or 40 degrees in the opposite direction). The results of a test are presented in table 9.3.

Table 9.3: Results for Belgium

Number of observations	Θ	a^*	b^*	$\dfrac{b^*}{a^*}$	$a^* b^*$	area of the country	χ^2	K/S
26	0°	225	158	.701	35,679	30,513	479.0	.0264
26	10°	242	146	.603	35,404		809.4	.0302
25	20°	231	146	.632	33,818		388.8	.0216
25	30°	233	146	.626	34,192		120.5	.0133
25	40°	231	146	.631	33,762		33.2	.0070
25	50°	223	155	.696	34,648		31.2	.0071
25	60°	220	157	.712	34,771		42.2	.0066
25	70°	220	156	.706	34,458		51.5	.0059
26	80°	231	152	.657	35,089		115.8	.0169

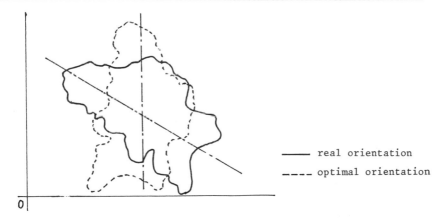

——— real orientation

‒ ‒ ‒ ‒ optimal orientation

fig. 9.16. Real and optimal orientation of Belgium.

The χ^2 value appears to be very sensitive for rotation of the rectangle. The lowest value for χ^2 was found for $\Theta=50°$: when Belgium is turned 50° clockwise, a contact distribution on a rectangle can be estimated which is as close as possible to the observed contact distribution on the real shape of Belgium (fig. 9.16). The estimations of the rectangles do not change very much when the orientation changes; when $\Theta=40°$ the estimated area is the closest to the real area. The optimal value of Θ will be somewhere between $\Theta=40°$ and $\Theta=50°$.

10 Network analysis

10.1. Introduction

In chapter 8 contact distances between points representing cities in several European countries were observed. The contact frequency distributions were compared with theoretical contact density functions derived for points continuously distributed in rectangles; the dimensions of the rectangle related to the theoretical contact distribution as close as possible to the observed distribution, were estimated.

In chapter 9, instead of using a distance table, a boolean matrix was used, representing the area of a country; starting with this boolean matrix a contact frequency distribution could be calculated, describing all contact distances, using well-known distance measures, between the relevant points in the matrix; this contact frequency distribution was compared with a theoretical contact density function on a rectangle; the dimensions of the rectangle were estimated and in this way the shape and the area of a country could be approximated by a rectangle.

In chapter 10 the shape and area of the country will be less important; starting, once again, with the distance table that represents the network distances between a set of cities, we now want to estimate a theoretical distance measure p for the observed network distances (see also Love and Morris, 1972, 1979).

The expression of theoretical contact density functions is only derived for special distance measures ($p=1$, 2, and ∞), for special shapes (rectangle, circle) and for special point patterns; however, the contact distributions one observes are related to random point patterns, random shapes and to network distances; the problem is how to calculate a contact distribution with a variable p-value as close as possible to the observed contact distribution, the one as close as possible to the observed generating the "best" p-value. Another important parameter that has to be estimated is the orientation of the axes in the metric space.

In section 10.2 a method will be described for the estimation of the p-valiue and the orientation of the axes; section 10.3 contains a description of the input data of the networks of 11 European countries and a graphical presentation; finally the results of the estimations are presented in 10.4 and a discussion in 10.5 concludes this chapter.

10.2. The estimation method

In this chapter estimates are made of theoretical distance parameter p and Θ that represent the actual road distances between points (cities) on a map. As has been shown in (7.3) the ℓ_p distance between 2 points $A(x_1,x_2)$ and $B(y_1,y_2)$ is:

$$d_1(A,B) = \left[\sum_{i=1}^{2} \left| A_i(\Theta) - B_i(\Theta) \right|^p \right]^{p^{-1}}$$

where
$$A_1(\Theta) = x_1\cos\Theta + x_2\sin\Theta \qquad B_1(\Theta) = y_1\cos\Theta + y_2\sin\Theta$$
$$A_2(\Theta) = -x_1\sin\Theta + x_2\cos\Theta \qquad B_2(\Theta) = -y_1\sin\Theta + y_2\cos\Theta$$

For a number of European countries the contact frequency distribution is shown in 8.5.4; these distributions contain network distances between a number of cities in the country. In order to find the values of p and Θ that represent those network distances, a contact distribution with a known p and Θ will be constructed as close as possible to the observed contact distribution. As has been mentioned there is no analytically contact distribution available containing the unknown parameters p and Θ, therefore the (theoretical) contact distribution is calculated in another way. The map of a country is covered by a grid and each cell that contains a city out of the sample gets value 1, all other cells get value 0; in this way a set of cities can be presented by a boolean matrix. The distance between each pair of ones can be calculated now, using the appropriate scale and the general expression for the distance measure; the contact frequency distribution that is calculated in this way depends on the values of p and Θ; each parameter set yields another contact frequency distribution.

In order to generate the "best" p and Θ values, the "distance" between two contact distributions is calculated, the observed frequency distribution of the distance table and a calculated frequency distribution determined by one p,Θ combination. By considering many different p,Θ combinations and the related distributions, it is possible to calculate many "distances" between contact distributions; finally the smallest "distance" determines the p,Θ combination which indicates the best estimation of p and Θ for the observed network (Matusita, 1965).

Supposing 1<p⩽2 and 0⩽Θ<90°, a scanning method is used to calculate the distributions; for each country we started to calculate 99 different contact distributions for

p = 1.0, 1.1, 1.2, ..., 2.0 and

Θ = 0°, 10°, 20°, ..., 80° (Θ=90° equals Θ=0°) and each of this distributions was compared with the observed distribution.

There are several methods available for obtaining point estimators of parameters; we mention — maximum likelihood,

- least squares,

- the Bayes method,

- the minimum distance method, and

- the minimum chi-square method

(Mood, Graybill and Boes, 1974).

Only if p and Θ, being the unknown parameters, are given a fixed value, is it possible to calculate the contact distribution.

10.2.1. The minimum distance method.

Suppose one has two distributions, an observed one and a another distribution depending on some unknown parameters λ_j, j=1, 2, ..., N. If both distributions are compared the one closest to the observed distribution gives the best estimates for the values of the λ's; the minimum distance method is described in Wolfowitz (1957).

As an example, let x_1, ..., x_n be a sample from a distribution given by the cumulative distribution function $F_x(x,\lambda) = F(x,\lambda)$ and let d(F,G) be a distance function that measures the distance between F and G; a distance function could be: $d(F,G) = \sup_x F(x) - G(x)$, which is

the largest vertical distance between F and G; the minimum distance estimate of λ is that $\hat{\lambda}$ among all possible λ's for which the distance is minimised (Mood, Graybill, Boes, 1974).

10.2.2. The minimum chi-square method

If the data are grouped into cells with expected frequency typified by λ_j and observed frequency by ℓ_j, then the function

$$\chi^2 = \sum_j \frac{(\ell_j - \lambda_j)^2}{\lambda_j} = \sum_j \frac{\ell_j^2}{\lambda_j} - n \quad \text{where} \quad n = \sum_j \lambda_j = \sum_j \ell_j$$

can be used as a measure of closeness of fit. The minimum chi-square method adapts this standpoint and attemps to determine λ_j such that chi-square is a minimum. It may be shown that for large samples the minimum chi-square estimator tends to the maximum likelihood estimator (Cramer, 1946; Kendall, 1966). In our case for each discrete set of p and Θ one can find a value for χ^2; the minimum value of all χ^2 determines the minimum chi-square estimator.

It is often difficult to locate that $\hat{\lambda}$ which minimises χ^2; hence the denomminator λ_j is sometimes changed to ℓ_j (if $\ell_j=0$ unity is used)

forming a modified $\chi'^2 = \dfrac{\sum(\ell_j - \lambda_j)^2}{\ell_j}$. The modified minimum-chi-square es-

timate of λ is then that $\hat{\lambda}$ which minimises the modified χ'^2 . This χ'^2 will not be the same as χ^2; however for large n the difference is of order $n^{-\frac{1}{2}}$ (Kendall, 1966).

On theoretical grounds there seems to be no reason to use minimum χ^2 instead of maximum likelihood. The method has practical value, however, when the maximum likelihood equations are difficult to solve. Here we used a method to find χ^2 or χ'^2 for some trial values of the parameters, and approximate the value which minimises χ^2 or χ'^2.

The method of least squares bears an analogy to the minimum chi-square method. Suppose there is an expression on a number of unknown parameters λ_1, λ_2, $\cdots$, λ_p and certain observed values x. This can be thrown into a form as $f(x_j; \lambda_1, \ldots, \lambda_p) = 0$, where f is a given function. If we have n values of x and n>p, it is not possible to solve the n resulting equations for the λ's. We then consider the "residuals" f $(x_j, \lambda_1, \ldots, \lambda_p)$, and the principle of least squares states that the values of $\lambda_1, \ldots, \lambda_p$ are to be chosen so that

$$\Sigma\{f(x_j, \lambda_1, \ldots, \lambda_p)\}^2 = \text{minimum}.$$

10.3 The observations; a graphical presentation

We started with a country containing a set of points, representing cities, on a map (for example Switzerland and Czecho-Slovakia, fig 10.1, and Great Britain fig. 10.2). The set of cities of 11 countries in Europe are observed and the theoretical p- and Θ-value for the network distances in these countries were estimated (in one country, the GDR, both the road network and the railway network distances were estimated). The observed contact frequency distribution of each country is compared with a number of calculated contact frequency distributions and the distance between each pair of distributions is computed using as a distance both the χ^2 value and the maximum vertical distance between the cumulative frequency distributions (described in 10.2). Two calculated contact frequency distributions   are plotted as histograms, using special values of p and Θ, namely p=1 and 2 and $\Theta=0°$; the histograms are shown in fig. 10.3, ..., 10.14.

fig. 10.1   SWITSERLAND 39 cities, scale 1:2,500 000

CZECHO-SLOVAKIA, 30 cities, scale 1:4,500 000

fig. 10.2   GREAT BRITAIN, 44 cities, scale 1:4,500 000

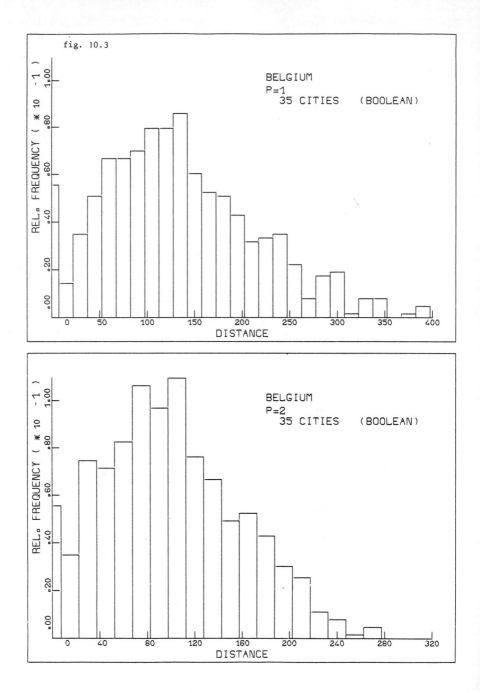

fig. 10.3

BELGIUM
P=1
    35 CITIES   (BOOLEAN)

BELGIUM
P=2
    35 CITIES   (BOOLEAN)

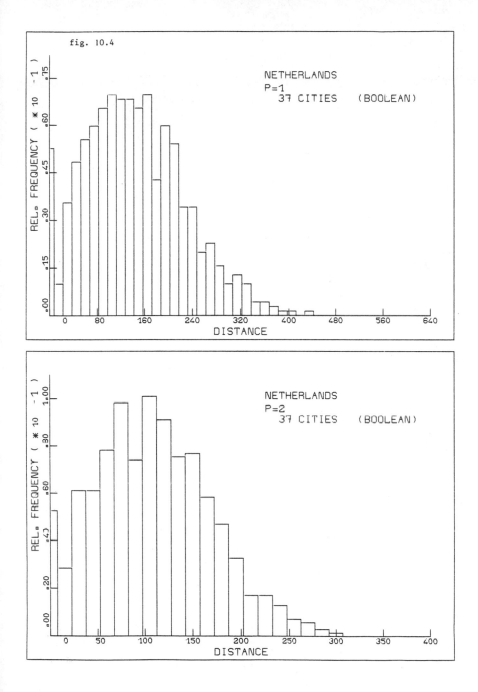

fig. 10.4

NETHERLANDS
P=1
    37 CITIES   (BOOLEAN)

NETHERLANDS
P=2
    37 CITIES   (BOOLEAN)

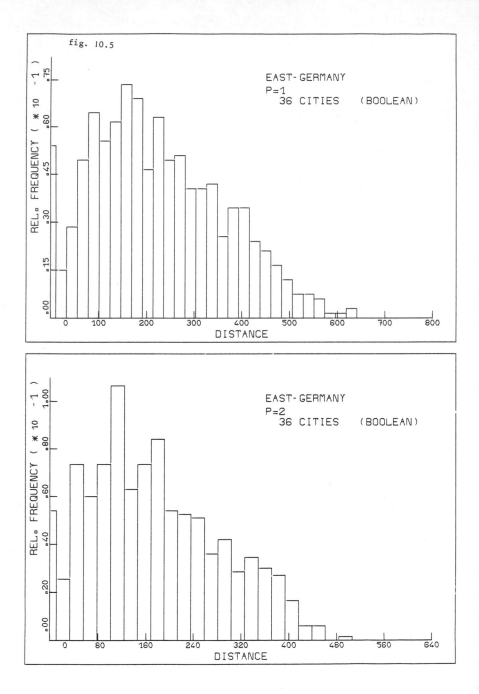

fig. 10.5

EAST-GERMANY
P=1
36 CITIES (BOOLEAN)

EAST-GERMANY
P=2
36 CITIES (BOOLEAN)

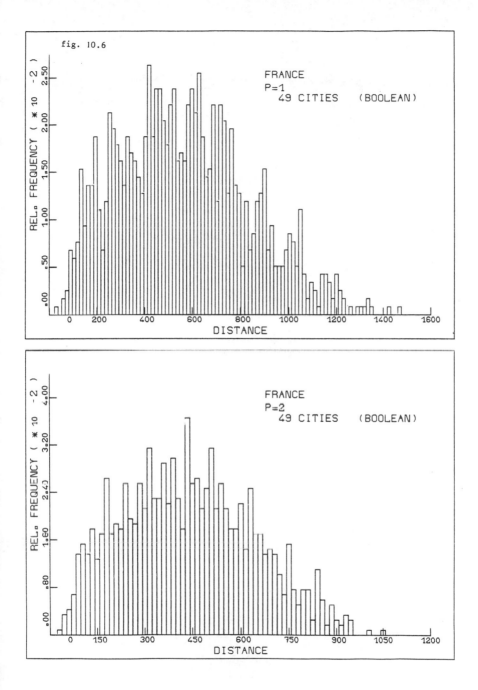

fig. 10.6

FRANCE
P=1
    49 CITIES   (BOOLEAN)

FRANCE
P=2
    49 CITIES   (BOOLEAN)

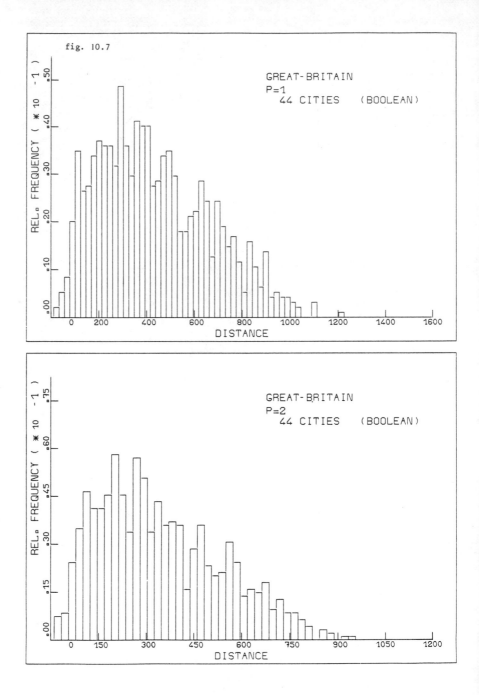

fig. 10.7

GREAT-BRITAIN
P=1
    44 CITIES   (BOOLEAN)

GREAT-BRITAIN
P=2
    44 CITIES   (BOOLEAN)

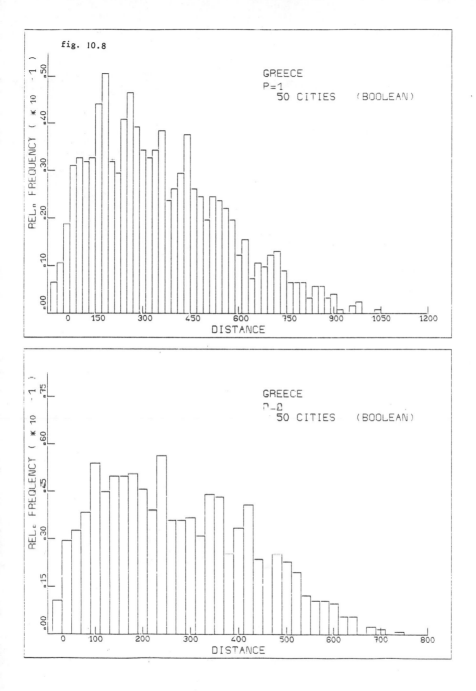

fig. 10.8

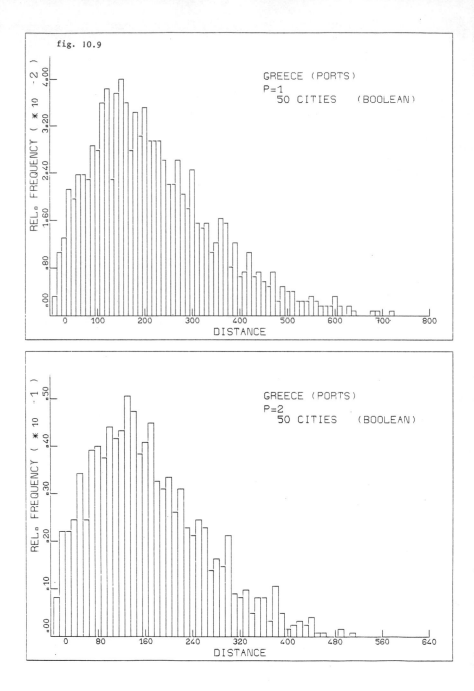

fig. 10.9

GREECE (PORTS)
P=1
50 CITIES (BOOLEAN)

GREECE (PORTS)
P=2
50 CITIES (BOOLEAN)

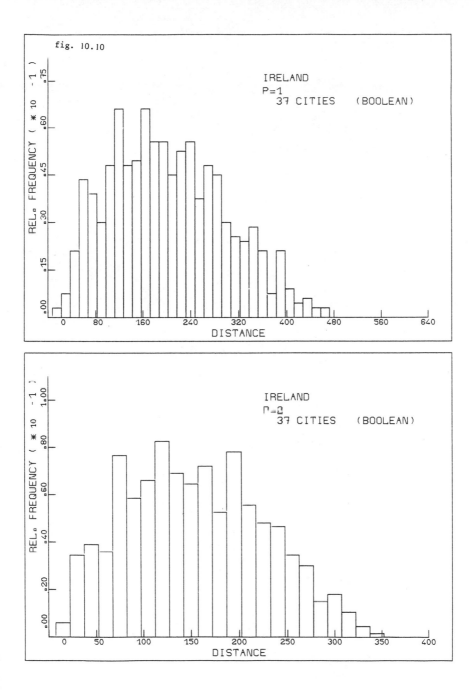

fig. 10.10

IRELAND
P=1
37 CITIES (BOOLEAN)

IRELAND
P=2
37 CITIES (BOOLEAN)

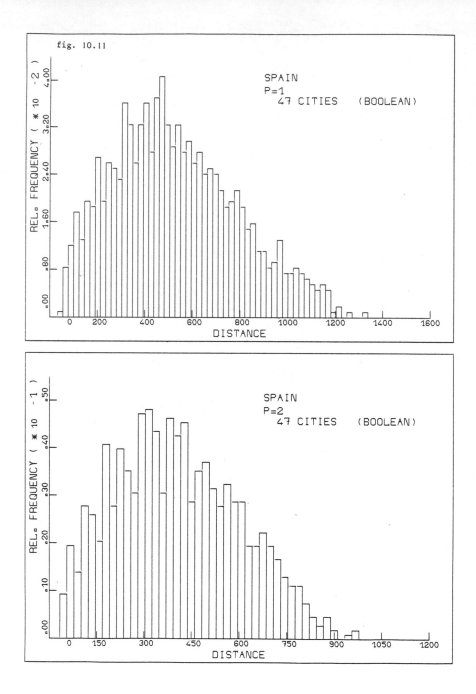

fig. 10.11

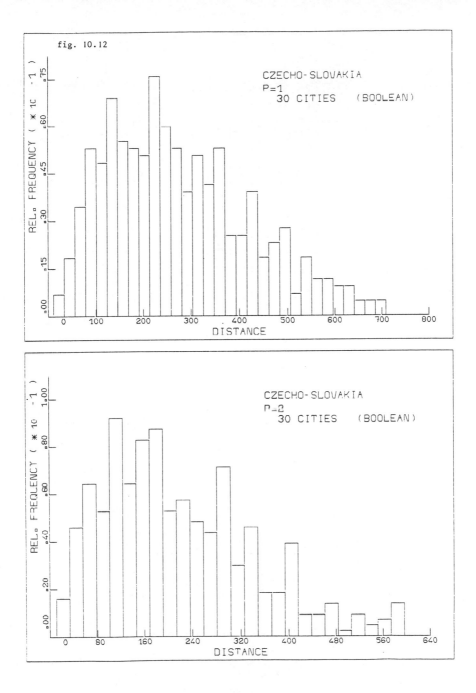

fig. 10.12

CZECHO-SLOVAKIA
P=1
30 CITIES   (BOOLEAN)

CZECHO-SLOVAKIA
P=2
30 CITIES   (BOOLEAN)

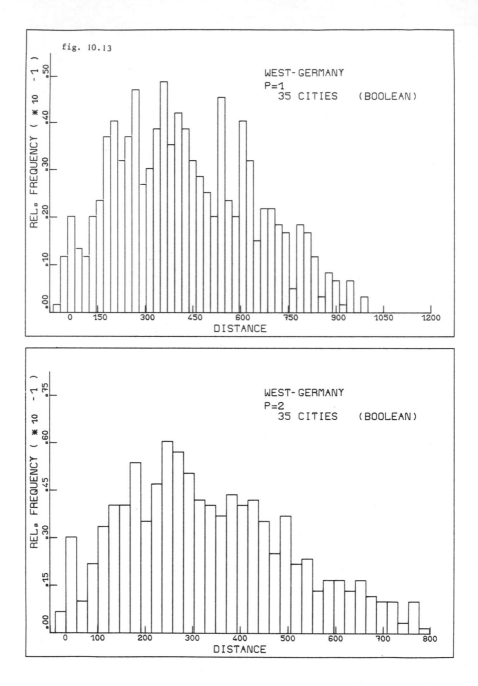

fig. 10.13

WEST-GERMANY
P=1
   35 CITIES   (BOOLEAN)

WEST-GERMANY
P=2
   35 CITIES   (BOOLEAN)

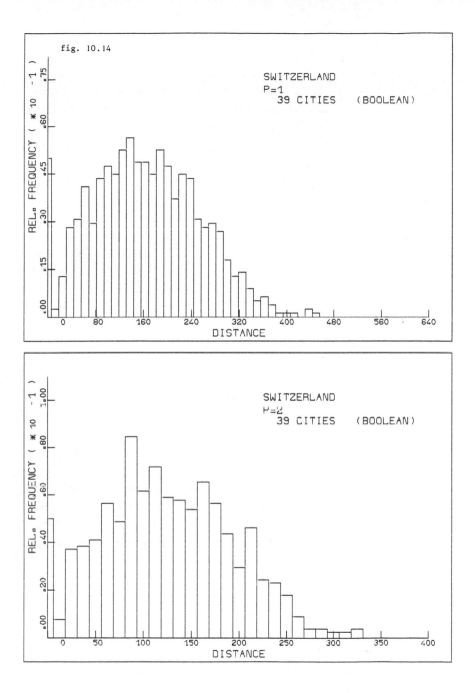

10.4. Test results

Estimates of p and Θ were made using the minimum distance criterium; two different distances were measured, the minimum χ^2 and the supremum of the vertical distance between the cumulative frequency distributions; 2 x 99 observations of χ^2 and the vertical distance were found. The minimum value of each criterium determines the contact frequency distribution closest to the observed frequency distribution and yields the estimates for p and Θ. Since two different criteria were used to measure the gap between both distributions one probably will find different values for the estimates.

In order to examine if both criteria point more or less in the same direction, looking for the best p- and Θ-value, table 10.1 is constructed. One expects when that the χ^2 values are close to their minimum, the vertical distance is not far from its minimum either, and vice versa. In table 10.1 the whole range of observed values of both criteria are presented, horizontally the χ^2 values and vertically the whole range of "vertical distance" values.

Considering the outcomes for one country, an observation in the table indicates the number of times a specified χ^2 value was found in combination with a specified "vertical distance" value. All observations, that is a result of comparison of an observed frequency distribution and a calculated frequency distribution, are presented in the table. When an observation is located on the diagonal of the table, both criteria give approximately the same result and therefore point in the same direction; if the observation is in the south-west triangle of the table it means that the χ^2 value is relatively closer to a minimum value than the vertical distance value (the observations for p=2 are independent of the orientation of the axes, therefore only one observation for p=2 is presented in the table).

Finally in tables 10.2 and 10.3 the estimates of p and Θ are presented. For each criterium in each country three estimates are shown, the best, second best and third best ones. In table 10.2 the results of a first, global scanning are presented. The results of these scanning pointed the area in which the best estimates would be found, whereafter it could be decided to concentrate the scanning more accurately in that area; in table 10.3 the results are presented.

Table 10.1. <u>Observations of the scanning procedure in 3 countries.</u>

1. <u>France</u>

vertical distance ↓	χ^2 → 99.56	119.79	140.01	160.24	180.46	200.68	220.91	241.13	261.36	281.58	
0 .01356	2*	2	3	5	0	1	1	0	0	0	14
.01937	0	2	2	1	2	1	2	1	0	0	11
.02518	0	0	4	2	0	1	2	0	0	0	9
.03100	0	4	2	2	2	1	1	0	0	1	13
.03681	0	0	3	2	3	2	1	1	0	0	12
.04263	1	0	4	1	0	1	0	1	0	0	8
.04844	0	0	1	2	3	0	4	0	0	1	11
.05425	0	0	2	1	5	1	1	0	0	0	10
.06007	0	1	0	2	3	1	1	0	1	0	9
.06588	0	0	0	0	1	1	0	0	0	0	2
	3	9	21	18	19	10	13	3	1	2	99

* this means 2 observations were found having vertical distance value between 0 and .01356 and a χ^2 value between 0 and 99.56.

2. <u>FRG</u>

vertical distance ↓	χ^2 → 52.20	68.98	85.77	102.55	119.34	136.12	152.90	169.69	186.47	203.26	
0 .02857	1	1	2	1	0	0	0	0	0	0	5
.03815	2	5	1	3	1	0	0	0	0	0	12
.04773	3	2	0	1	3	0	0	0	0	0	9
.05731	0	0	4	3	1	1	0	0	0	0	9
.06689	0	4	0	1	3	0	1	1	0	0	10
.07647	0	0	2	2	3	0	1	1	0	0	9
.08605	0	0	0	1	6	1	1	1	0	0	10
.09563	0	0	2	1	1	3	3	0	1	2	13
.10521	0	0	1	1	3	5	1	1	2	2	16
.11479	0	0	0	0	1	2	0	3	0	0	6
	6	12	12	14	22	12	7	7	3	4	99

3. <u>Great Britain</u>

vertical distance ↓	χ^2 → 80.77	99.73	118.69	137.65	156.61	175.58	194.54	213.50	232.46	251.42	
0											
.01942	2	2	1	0	1	0	0	0	0	0	6
.02776	1	4	1	1	1	0	0	0	0	0	8
.03610	0	3	3	2	0	0	0	0	0	0	8
.04443	0	3	4	1	1	0	0	0	0	0	9
.05277	2	0	7	1	0	0	0	0	0	0	10
.06110	2	1	0	1	0	4	1	0	0	0	9
.06944	1	1	5	3	3	2	3	2	0	1	20
.07778	0	3	1	4	3	2	1	0	0	0	15
.08611	0	0	0	1	3	2	3	1	0	0	10
.09445	0	0	0	0	0	1	0	1	2	1	4
	8	17	22	14	12	11	8	4	2	1	99

Table 10.2. **Estimates of p and Θ; global scanning.**

Country	degrees of freedom	min χ^2	$\hat{p}$	$\hat{\Theta}$	K-S	$\hat{p}$	$\hat{\Theta}$
Belgium	28	53.979	p=1.4	Θ=30°	.0121	p=1.3	Θ=80°
	28	54.180	p=1.3	Θ=10°	.0144	p=1.3	Θ=30°
	28	55.145	p=1.2	Θ=60°	.0175	p=1.3	Θ=70°
The Netherlands	31	39.001	p=1.1	Θ=10°	.0186	p=1.0	Θ=60°
	31	43.197	p=1.0	Θ=60°	.0231	p=1.0	Θ=40°
	31	55.098	p=1.0	Θ=80°	.0242	p=1.0	Θ=50°
FRG	51	52.195	p=1.1	Θ=10°	.0285	p=1.0	Θ= 0°
	51	70.194	p=1.1	Θ=60°	.0285	p=1.0	Θ=80°
	48	71.448	p=1.0	Θ=10°	.0330	p=1.0	Θ=50°
Spain	64	97.958	p=1.0	Θ=80°	.0360	p=1.0	Θ=20°
	64	101.59	p=1.0	Θ=10°	.0370	p=1.0	Θ= 0°
	64	109.71	p=1.0	Θ= 0°	.0388	p=1.0	Θ=30°
France	91	104.48	p=1.0	Θ=30°	.0104	p=1.1	Θ=20°
	91	126.50	p=1.1	Θ=50°	.0128	p=1.1	Θ=60°
	91	127.71	p=1.1	Θ=80°	.0129	p=1.1	Θ=50°
GDR (rail)	30	32.054	p=1.0	Θ= 0°	.0217	p=1.0	Θ= 0°
	33	32.365	p=1.0	Θ=80°	.0337	p=1.0	Θ=80°
	33	34.417	p=1.0	Θ=30°	.0361	p=1.0	Θ=70°
GDR (road)	33	25.388	p=1.1	Θ=70°	.0158	p=1.0	Θ=70°
	30	31.924	p=1.0	Θ= 0°	.0165	p=1.0	Θ=20°
	33	32.588	p=1.0	Θ=70°	.0180	p=1.0	Θ=10°
Czecho-Slovakia	37	45.325	p=1.1	Θ= 0°	.0489	p=1.0	Θ=40°
	37	48.757	p=1.1	Θ=10°	.0508	p=1.0	Θ=50°
	39	52.253	p=1.0	Θ=80°	.0519	p=1.0	Θ=30°

Switzerland	38	<u>31.484</u>	$\hat{p}=1.0$	$\hat{\Theta}=10°$	.0229	$\hat{p}=1.0$	$\hat{\Theta}=70°$
	38	<u>45.208</u>	$\hat{p}=1.0$	$\hat{\Theta}=30°$	.0242	$\hat{p}=1.0$	$\hat{\Theta}=60°$
	38	<u>47.711</u>	$\hat{p}=1.0$	$\hat{\Theta}=50°$	.0269	$\hat{p}=1.0$	$\hat{\Theta}=80°$
Ireland	40	1336.3	$\hat{p}=1.0$	$\hat{\Theta}=70°$	.0949	$\hat{p}=1.0$	$\hat{\Theta}=0°$
	40	1406.7	$\hat{p}=1.0$	$\hat{\Theta}=0°$	.1099	$\hat{p}=1.0$	$\hat{\Theta}=10°$
	40	1450.3	$\hat{p}=1.0$	$\hat{\Theta}=40°$	.1118	$\hat{p}=1.0$	$\hat{\Theta}=20°$
Greece	61	173.85	$\hat{p}=1.0$	$\hat{\Theta}=30°$	.0865	$\hat{p}=1.0$	$\hat{\Theta}=0°$
	61	196.68	$\hat{p}=1.0$	$\hat{\Theta}=70°$	.0930	$\hat{p}=1.0$	$\hat{\Theta}=20°$
	61	196.99	$\hat{p}=1.0$	$\hat{\Theta}=80°$	.0938	$\hat{p}=1.0$	$\hat{\Theta}=80°$
Great Britain	63	<u>80.770</u>	$\hat{p}=1.0$	$\hat{\Theta}=70°$	.0194	$\hat{p}=1.0$	$\hat{\Theta}=70°$
	63	91.479	$\hat{p}=1.1$	$\hat{\Theta}=70°$	.0222	$\hat{p}=1.0$	$\hat{\Theta}=30°$
	63	99.388	$\hat{p}=1.1$	$\hat{\Theta}=60°$	.0246	$\hat{p}=1.0$	$\hat{\Theta}=60°$
Greece (ports)	50	1216.4	$\hat{p}=2.0$	$\hat{\Theta}=60°$	.3483	$\hat{p}=2.0$	$\hat{\Theta}=30°$
	50	1218.9	$\hat{p}=2.0$	$\hat{\Theta}=30°$	.3489	$\hat{p}=2.0$	$\hat{\Theta}=40°$
	50	1234.6	$\hat{p}=1.8$	$\hat{\Theta}=30°$	.3489	$\hat{p}=2.0$	$\hat{\Theta}=50°$

Table 10.3. Estimates of p and Θ; refined scanning.

Country	degrees of freedom	min χ^2	$\hat{p}$	$\hat{\Theta}$	K/S	$\hat{p}$	$\hat{\Theta}$
Belgium	28	49.014	p=1.25	Θ=80°	.0107	p=1.28	Θ=80°
		49.427	p=1.24	Θ=80°	.0107	p=1.27	Θ=80°
		49.894	p=1.28	Θ=60°	.0124	p=1.25	Θ=80°
The Netherlands	31	<u>36.607</u>	p=1.03	Θ=70°	.0186	p=1.00	Θ=60°
		<u>38.490</u>	p=1.03	Θ=60°	.0231	p=1.00	Θ=40°
		<u>43.197</u>	p=1.00	Θ=60°	.0242	p=1.00	Θ=50°
FRG	51	<u>52.195</u>	p=1.00	Θ=30°	.0287	p=1.00	Θ= 0°
	51	<u>53.161</u>	p=1.06	Θ=60°	.0287	p=1.00	Θ=80°
	51	<u>56.203</u>	p=1.03	Θ=30°	.0330	p=1.00	Θ=50°
Spain	64	<u>85.630</u>	p=1.03	Θ= 0°	.0360	p=1.00	Θ=20°
	64	97.958	p=1.00	Θ=80°	.0370	p=1.00	Θ= 0°
	64	100.43	p=1.03	Θ=50°	.0388	p=1.00	Θ=30°
France	91	<u>99.564</u>	p=1.12	Θ=50°	.0104	p=1.10	Θ=20°
		<u>104.48</u>	p=1.00	Θ=30°	.0128	p=1.10	Θ=60°
		<u>104.81</u>	p=1.28	Θ=80°	.0129	p=1.10	Θ=50°
GDR (rail)	30	<u>32.054</u>	p=1.00	Θ= 0°	.0217	p=1.00	Θ= 0°
	30	<u>32.345</u>	p=1.06	Θ= 0°	.0337	p=1.00	Θ=80°
	33	<u>32.365</u>	p=1.00	Θ=80°	.0361	p=1.00	Θ=70°
GDR (road)	33	<u>23.617</u>	p=1.09	Θ=70°	.01587	p=1.00	Θ=70°
	33	<u>31.765</u>	p=1.15	Θ=60°	.01651	p=1.00	Θ=20°
	30	<u>31.924</u>	p=1.00	Θ= 0°	.01809	p=1.00	Θ=20°

Ireland	40	1336.3	$\hat{p}$=1.00	$\hat{\Theta}$=70°	.0949	$\hat{p}$=1.00	$\hat{\Theta}$= 0°
	40	1406.7	$\hat{p}$=1.00	$\hat{\Theta}$= 0°	.1099	$\hat{p}$=1.00	$\hat{\Theta}$=10°
	40	1425.8	$\hat{p}$=1.06	$\hat{\Theta}$= 0°	.1118	$\hat{p}$=1.00	$\hat{\Theta}$=20°
Czecho-Slovakia	37	42.071	$\hat{p}$=1.09	$\hat{\Theta}$= 0°	.0489	$\hat{p}$=1.00	$\hat{\Theta}$=40°
	38	42.271	$\hat{p}$=1.18	$\hat{\Theta}$=20°	.0508	$\hat{p}$=1.00	$\hat{\Theta}$=50°
	39	45.963	$\hat{p}$=1.06	$\hat{\Theta}$=30°	.0519	$\hat{p}$=1.00	$\hat{\Theta}$=30°
Great Britain	63	80.770	$\hat{p}$=1.00	$\hat{\Theta}$=70°	.0194	$\hat{p}$=1.00	$\hat{\Theta}$=70°
	63	83.266	$\hat{p}$=1.06	$\hat{\Theta}$= 0°	.0222	$\hat{p}$=1.00	$\hat{\Theta}$=30°
	63	85.492	$\hat{p}$=1.09	$\hat{\Theta}$=80°	.0246	$\hat{p}$=1.00	$\hat{\Theta}$=60°
Greece	61	173.85	$\hat{p}$=1.00	$\hat{\Theta}$=30°	.0865	$\hat{p}$=1.00	$\hat{\Theta}$= 0°
	61	196.68	$\hat{p}$=1.00	$\hat{\Theta}$=70°	.0930	$\hat{p}$=1.00	$\hat{\Theta}$=20°
	61	196.99	$\hat{p}$=1.00	$\hat{\Theta}$=80°	.0938	$\hat{p}$=1.00	$\hat{\Theta}$=80°
Switzerland	38	31.484	$\hat{p}$=1.00	$\hat{\Theta}$=10°	.0229	$\hat{p}$=1.00	$\hat{\Theta}$=70°
	38	44.799	$\hat{p}$=1.03	$\hat{\Theta}$= 0°	.0242	$\hat{p}$=1.00	$\hat{\Theta}$=60°
	38	45.208	$\hat{p}$=1.00	$\hat{\Theta}$=30°	.0269	$\hat{p}$=1.00	$\hat{\Theta}$=80°

10.5. Discussion

In this chapter a number of road networks of European countries was compared with different distance metrics, in order to derive distance predicting functions. In location problems the objective function often reflects a desire to minimise the total costs of operating a system; the value of the system is a.o. determined by the distances in it. Mostly the two common ones, the Euclidean and the Manhattan distances will be applied in the models (Wesolowsky, 1972). The estimated distance functions represent actual distances between a set of points (cities) on a map. A number of applications mentioned in Love and Morris (1979) concern, vehicle travel times (Kolesar, Walker and Hausner, 1975), characterisation of road networks, verifying distances in road networks (Ginsburgh and Hansen, 1974) and facilities location models (Wesolowski, 1972). One can also mention, big routing problems (Berendse, 1976), migration models (Verster, 1979).

In this chapter contact frequency distributions are compared; comparing distributions instead of separate distances between each pair of points diminishes the number of computations, and when the number of classes is sufficiently large, gives useful results. Using the minimum distance method the calculated distance frequency distribution can be selected, as closely as possible to the observed one. The observed frequency distribution can be regarded as a sample of a theoretical contact distribution $f(p,\Theta)$, p and Θ being unknown parameters; both distributions are defined on the same set of points. Since the mathematical form of $f(p,\Theta)$ is not derived here, a number of p,Θ combinations is selected in order to calculate the related contact frequency distribution, comparable to the observed one. As a measure for the distance between both distributions the χ^2 value and the supremum of the vertical distance between the cumulative distributions were chosen as goodness-of-fit criteria.

Love and Morris (1972 and 1979) studied both urban and rural road distances; they fitted a number of different mathematical forms to urban and rural road distance data, for example the most general form in their 1972 paper:

$$d(q,r,k,p,s) = k\Big[\sum_{i=1}^{2}\big|q_i - r_i\big|^p\Big]^{\frac{1}{s}},$$

where k, p, and s are parameters and $q=(q_1,q_2)$ and $r=(r_1,r_2)$ are points in the plane.

The value of s appeared to be not markedly different from p when the function was fitted to intercity road distances. In 1979 they modelled other different distance functions and also investigated whether different functions apply to the urban or rural case.

In this chapter only one distance funtion with two parameters p and Θ is used:

$$d(q,r) = \Big[\sum_{i=1}^{2}\big|q_i(\Theta) - r_i(\Theta)\big|^p\Big]^{\frac{1}{p}},$$

where $q_1(\Theta) = q_1\cos\Theta + q_2\sin\Theta$ $\qquad r_1(\Theta) = r_1\cos\Theta + r_2\sin\Theta$

$\qquad\qquad\ q_2(\Theta) = -q_1\sin\Theta + q_2\cos\Theta$ $\qquad r_2(\Theta) = -r_1\sin\Theta + r_2\cos\Theta$

First 99 comparisons between distributions were made; a survey of possible outcomes of the χ^2 values and the "vertical distance" values is shown in table 10.1 for three countries; both minimum distance criteria appear to point reasonable in the same direction looking for the optimal parameter values; the χ^2 criterion shows relatively more small values, looking at the "column totals" distribution.

Estimates of p and Θ are presented in table 10.2 and 10.3; table 10.2 shows the results of a global scanning (p=1.0, 1.1, 1.2, ..., 2.0 and Θ=0°, 10°, 20°, ..., 80°). Both criteria show low estimates for p, a second scanning was done in table 10.3 for p=1.0, 1.03, 1.06, ..., 1.3 and Θ=0°, 10°, 20°, ..., 80°.

The distance between both distributions shows, espectially when the "vertical distance" is measured, low significant p-values; the χ^2 value criterium shows less significant results, although in the second scanning 22 of 36 values are significant or 8 out of 12 countries. In general the distance between both distributions became smaller in the second scanning; the p-values related to the χ^2 criterium increased somewhat. The estimates of Θ do not show (both in table 10.2 and 10.3) a very stable picture.

In order to test the sensitivity of the outcomes, for each country three estimates, related to each criterion, were computed, the best, second-best and third-best; those estimates differ, in general, not much and so do the distances between both distributions. A stable picture can be observed for each country when p estimates are considered; most values are very close to p=1.0; some examples; for Belgium we found p=1.25, p=1.24, and p=1.28; for France p=1.12, p=1.00, and p=1.28; for the Netherlands p=1.03, p=1.03, and p=1.00; for FRG p=1.00, p=1.06, and p=1.03.

11 General conclusion

To deal with spatial economic problems associated with activities in various places, it is necessary to get an accurate picture of the distance between those places. Much of the theoretical work on the notion of distance considers space as continuous, and concentrates on point to point distances. But practical work in spatial analysis and planning uses a discrete conception of space and concentrates on discrete spatial units. The relationship between these two approaches is a well-known problem in measurement of any kind; in the transition from continuous to the discrete approach in space in particular, many issues have arisen. In this study both approaches have been studied extensively for the distribution of distances in space and in several ways the results of both approaches are compared.

Distance between two places is certainly one of the most important specific structuring relations in spatial analysis (Huriot, Thisse, 1984). According to Beguin and Thisse (1979) a pregeographical space is defined as any set of at least two places, endowed with a length-metric and an area measure, i.e. a triplet of the form (S, α_L, μ_A), where S is a given set of places, α_L be a length-metric on S and μ_A an area of the corresponding subset. The existence of at least one place allows the introduction of an area-measure, and the existence of at least two places leads to the introduction of a length-distance.

Places are represented by integrable subsets of the plane so that the area of a set of places can be defined by the area of the corresponding subset of the place.

Only the relative position of places and area are necessary to define distributions of distances.

In this study three types of distributions have been defined:
(1) the distance distribution
(2) the road-area distribution
(3) the contact distribution.

Measuring distances between places requires the definition of distance measures; mostly Minkowski distance measures for $p=1$, $p=2$, and $p=\infty$ are used; both continuously and discretely distributed places are considered; the places are located in well-defined areas as there are squares, rectangles and circles (also in two squares).

Dealing with the distribution of distances in spatial analysis almost always contact distributions are meant, often only Euclidean distances are used and the places are continuously distributed in well-defined areas, mostly circles.

The characteristic differences between the three defined distributions are caused by the way of measuring the number of distances.

In this study all distributions on well-known areas are analytically derived; with the method used it is possible to derive distributions on any well-known shape. A special case is the distribution of distances on two separate squares. All distributions are extensively presented in a graphical way; one gets an impression of the influence of different parameter values on the shape of the distributions.

The distributions of distances in a pregeographical space are compared with distributions that can be observed on maps, showing observed distances between cities in European countries. These distributions differ in many ways from the analytically derived distributions. In chapter 7, 8, 9, and 10 the importance of these differences is investigated in detail.

Since only cities inside a country are considered the observed distribution has to be a contact distribution. The discrete points, representing the cities, are distributed in a random way and distances are measured over networks. Therefore the observed and analytically derived distributions can be compared in different ways.

The most global way (chapter 8) is, to compare the contact distribution on a rectangle, filled with continuously distributed points and using a well-defined distance measure (p=1, p=2) with an observed contact distribution representing the network distances between a random set of cities in a country. The null-hypothesis, stating that the observed distribution is a sample of the derived distribution, is not rejected in most countries. The most important problems concern the random shape of the countries and the network distances; in chapter 9 the shape of countries is estimated more accurately and in chapter 10 the network distances. In chapter 8 the areas of the estimated rectangles related to a contact distribution as close as possible to the observed distribution are compared with the real areas of the countries; both areas are but poorly related. In chapter 9 a contact distribution of a country is constructed in such a way that comparison with a derived contact distribution on a rectangle showed a much closer relation between the areas of the country and the rectangle (for p=1 and p=2); the main reason for this approvement was the sidestepping of both the randomness of the set of points and the network characteristics of the distances. Distance values between two points, except Euclidean distances, depend on the orientation of the axes; therefore when contact distributions on rectangles are estimated and compared with distributions on random shapes, the orientation of the axes is important. In deriving the best contact distribution on a rectangle, the best orientation has to be estimated too. This was done extensively for Belgium and promising results were found; the goodness-of-fit value (χ^2) appeared to be very sensitive for the orientation value.

Finally in chapter 10 another comparison was made. In order to estimate a distance measure of observed network distances in a country, the observed contact distribution was compared with a theoretical contact distribution; disturbing factors such as the use of only well-known distance measures p=1 and p=2, and the rectangular shape with continuously distributed points were sidestepped. The theoretical distribution was derived by considering a set of points (almost) equal to the observed set and distances were measured using the general expression for Minkowski distances with two parameters p and Θ (the orientation of the axes); p and Θ were estimated in such a way that the related distribution was as close as possible to the observed one (using the minimum distance criterium). The estimated value of p appeared to be close to p=1.0 and the orientation of the axes was not very stable in most countries. In order to check the results it could be useful to investigate more different distance functions (as Love and Morris, 1972 and 1979, did), or to use a more dense grid in order to approximate the real locations more closely.

Further extensions: in this study distributions of distances are derived in pregeographical space; this is an abstract space in which coordinates, distances and densities are dominating concepts. The described method of deriving analytically different types of distributions is applicable to each well-defined shape; only the rectangle, square and circle are explicitly mentioned here. Both continuously and discretely distributed points are considered; especially the discrete point patterns could be investigated further (only one regular point pattern was considered here), in order to examine the relation between the structure of the point pattern and the distribution of distances.

Differentiated space is a representation of real-world spatial phenomena; this space posseses less regular and ideal structures; in this space distributions of distances can be observed or simulated. Much attention should be paid to the comparison of theoretical and observed distributions. Having observed an empirical distribution it is interesting to see whether any standard theoretical distribution has a similar distribution and can be taken into consideration as a possible theoretical model; much experimental work will be needed, before conclusions can be reached; one has to develop test hypotheses of the "goodness-of-fit" type, and much attention should be paid to the sampling of correct distances.

In this study the comparison of distributions concerns two subjects: a) the shape analysis,
   b) the network analysis.
The real shape of regions is very complex and difficult to measure; in literature a lot of different shape parameters are defined. The work should be focussed more on selecting (depending on the problem) a small set of relevant parameters. The theoretical models, that describe observed patterns in a meaningful way, should not be too complicated, but still be as useful as possible; finding the right balance will require a lot of effort. In this study a theoretical distribution of distances derived on a rectangle was used as a model for simulated contact distributions in European countries. In a number of cases this, relative simple, model appeared to be fairly good, but it can be insufficient to describe complex territories; in that case a solution could be to use another model or one may divide the territory in different regions.

Theoretical distributions are derived for a few special distance measures (the Manhattan and the Euclidean distance measure); in a differentiated space mostly network distances are observed. In many problems in distribution management an accurate picture of the distribution of distances is needed, so estimates of the real distance measure should be made; this was done here for a number of European countries. The estimation method could be refined by using more different theoretical distance models, by collecting more distances inside the area, or by distinguishing between urban and rural zones; also good statistical tests should be developed.

In general the relation between distances within a spatial structure and the spatial interaction phenomena should be considered; as an example one could focus on distances inside cities and draw conclusions about the shape of the city in relation to the observed distance distribution. Maybe it is possible to derive good theoretical models of distributions and classify cities according to this models.

References

Bachi, R. and Samuel-Cahn, E., Applications of parameters of shape to statistical distributions, Regional Science and Urban Economics, pp. 205-27., 1976.

Barton, D.E., David, F.N., Fix, E., Random points in a circle and the analysis of chromosome patterns, Biometrika, 50, 1 and 2, pp. 23-29, 1963.

Beguin, J. and Thisse, J., An aximatic approach to geographical space, Geographical Analysis, vol. 11, no. 4, 1979.

Berendse, J. Waar moet dat heen, hoe zal dat gaan, een groot routerings-probleem, masters thesis, Technische Hogeschool Delft, 1976.

Blair, D.J. and Biss, T.H., The measurement of shape in geography: an appraisal of methods and techniques, Nottingham University, Bulletin of quantitative data for geographers, no. 11, 1967.

Broeder, G. den, Between Newton and Cauchy: the diagonal variable metric method, Theory and testresults, Journal of Applied and Computational Mathematics, vol. 6, no.4, pp. 267-73, 1980.

Brooks, C.E.P. and Carruthers, N., Handbook of Statistical methods in meteorology, London, H.M.S.O., 1953.

Bunge, W., Theoretical Geography, Sund Studies in Geography, Sund, 1966.

Cramer, H., Mathematical methods of statistics, Princeton University Press, 1946.

Craxton, F.E. and Cowden, D.J., Applied general Statistics, New York, 1948.

Christofides, N., et al., Distribution Management, Griffin London, 1971.

David, F.N. and Fix Evelyn, Intersections of random chords of a circle, Biometrika, 51, 3 and 4, pp. 373-79, 1964.

Evans, I.S., The selection of class intervals, Transactions of the Institute of British Geographers, New Series, 2, 98-124, 1977.

Fairthorne, D., The distance between random points in two concentric circles, Biometrika, 51, pp. 275-77, 1964.

Falk, T.R. and Abler, R., Intercommunications, distance and geographical theory, Geografiska Annaler, Series B, 62, pp. 59-67, 1980.

Gardiner, V. and Gardiner, G., Analysis of frequency distributions, CATMOG 19 (Concepts and techniques in modern geography), 1979.

Ginsburgh, V. and Hansen, P., Procedures for the reduction of errors in road network data, Operational Research Quarterly, vol. 25, no. 2, pp. 321-22, 1974.

Gilbert, E.N., Estimators for distances, Journal of Applied Probability, 14, pp. 260-71, 1977.

Green, J.R. and Margerison, B.Sc., Statistical treatment of experimental data, Elsevier Scientifid Publishing Company, Amsterdam-Oxford-New York, 1978.

Haggett, P. and Chorley, R.J., Network Analysis in Geography, Edward Arnold, London, 1969.

Hammersley, J.M., The distribution of distance in a hypersphere, the Annals of Mathematical Statistics, 21, pp. 447-52, 1950.

Halmos, P.R., Measure Theory, Springer Verlag, New York-Heidelberg-Berlin, 1979.

Horrowitz, M., Probability of random paths across elementary geometrical shapes, Journal of Applied Probability, 2, pp. 169-77, 1965.

Huntsberger, D.V., Elements of Statistical Inference, Boston, 1961.

Huriot, J.-M., and Thisse, J., Distance in spatial analysis, Institut de Mathématiques Economiques, LATEC L.A. (CNRS no. 342) Université de Dijon - CNRS, 1984.

Kendall, M.G., The advanced theory of statistics, Volume II, third edition, Charles Griffin and Company Limited, London, 1951..

Kuiper, J.H., and Paelinck, J.H.P., Frequency Distributions of Distances and Related Concepts, Geographical Analysis, vol. 14, no. 3, pp. 253-59, 1982.

Lipschutz, S., General Topology, Theory and problems of Schaum's Outline Series, Mc.Graw-Hill Book Company, 1965.

Lord, R.D., The distribution of distance in a hypersphere, The Annals of Mathematical Statistics, 25, pp. 794-98, 1954.

Love, R.F. and Morris, J.G., Modelling Inter-city road distances by mathematical functions, Operations Research Quarterly, vol.23, no.1, 1972.

Love, R.F., and Morris, J.G., Mathematical models of road travel distances, Management Science, vol.25, no. 2, 1979.

Matusita, Kameo, A distance and related statistics in multivariate analysis, from: Multivariate Analysis, Proceeding of and International Symposium held in Dayton, Ohio, june 14-19, 1965, Ed. by Paruchuri, R. Krishnaiah Academic Press, 1966.

Mood, A.M., Graybill, F.A. and Boes, D.C., Introduction to the theory of statistics, third edition, Mc.Graw-Hill, Kogakusha, Ltd. 1974.

Muller, J-C., Non-Euclidean Geographic Spaces, Mapping functional distances, Geographical Analysis, vol. 14, no. 3, pp. 189-203, 1982.

Norcliffe, G.B., Interfential Statistics for Geographers, London, 1977.

Nordbeck, S., Computing distances in road nets, Regional Association Papers, 12, pp. 207-20, 1965.

Paelinck, J.H.P., with J.-P. Ancot and J.H. Kuiper, Formal Spatial Economic Analysis, Gower Publishing Company Limited, 1983.

Paelinck, J.H.P. and Nijkamp, P., Operational Theory and Method in Spatial Economics, Laxon House and Lexington, Farnborough and Masachussets, 1975.

Perreur, J., Contribution à la théorie de la localosation de l'entreprise, thèse Université de Dijon, Faculté de Science économique et de gestion, 1974.

Raa, T. ten, Distance distributions, Geographical Analysis, vol. 15, no. 2, 1983.

Rodriguez-Bachiller, A., Errors in the measurement of spatial distances between discrete regions, Environment and Planning A, vol. 15, pp. 781-991, 1983.

Rogers, A., Statistical Analysis of spatial dispersion, the quadrat method, Pion Limited, London, 1974

Ross Mackay, J., Chi-square as a tool for regional studies, Annals, Association of American Geographers, vol. 48, p. 164, 1958.

Ross Mackay, J., Comments on the use of chi-square, Annals, Association of American Geographers, vol. 49, p. 89, 1959.

Smith, M.J. de, Distance distributions and trip behaviour in defined regions, Geographical Analysis, vol IX, pp. 332-45, 1977.

Taylor, P.J., Distances with shapes: an introduction to a family of finite frequency distributions, Geografiska Annaler 53 B. pp. 40-53, 1971.

Thanh, L.M., Distribution théoriques des distances entre deux points répartis uniformément sur une surface, from: Sutter, J., ed., Les déplacements humains, aspects methodologiques de leur mesure, Editions, Science Humains, Diffusions Hachette, pp. 172-84, 1962.

Thanh, L.M., Contribution a l'étude de la répartition des distances sé-
        parant les domicles de épaux dans un département français. In-
        fluence de la consanguinité, 196..

Tinbers, J.A., Route factors in road networks, Traffic, Engineering and
        Control, 9, pp. 392-94, 401, 1967.

Unwin, D., Introductory Spatial Analysis, Methuen, London and New York,
        1981.

Wesolowsky, G.O., Location in Continuous Space, Geographical Analysis,
        vol. 5, no. 2, 1972.

Wolfowitz, J., The minimum distance method, Annals of Mathematical Sta-
        tistics, vol. 28 (1), pp 75-88, 1957.

Wonnacott, T.H. and Wonnacott, R.J., Introductory Statistics for busi-
        ness, John Wiley and Sons, Inc. New York, London, Sidney,
        Toronto, 1972.

Zobler, L., Decision making in regional construction, Annals, Associ-
        ation of American Geographers, vol. 48, pp. 140-48, 1958.

Zobler, L., The distinction between relative and absolute frequencies in
        using chi-square for regional analysis, Annals, Association of
        American Geographers, vol. 48. pp. 456-47, 1958.